AGONY?
DON'T GET ME STARTED...

DENISE ROBERTSON

AGONY?
DON'T GET ME STARTED...

First published in the United Kingdom in 2006 by Max,
an imprint of Little Books Ltd,
48 Catherine Place, London SW1E 6HL

10 9 8 7 6 5 4 3 2 1

A CIP catalogue record for this book is available from
the British Library.

ISBN-10 1 904435 64 5
ISBN-13 978 1 904435 64 8

Every attempt has been made to trace any copyright holders. The author and
publisher will be grateful for any information that will assist them in keeping future
editions up to date. Although all reasonable care has been taken in the preparation
of this book, neither the publisher, editors nor the author can accept any liability
for any consequences arising from the use thereof, or the information contained
therein.

Printed and bound by William Clowes Ltd, Beccles, Suffolk

For John

CONTENTS

Introduction		9
Chapter 1	Childhood	12
Chapter 2	War	30
Chapter 3	Victory	49
Chapter 4	Peace	60
Chapter 5	The Fifties	71
Chapter 6	Nest-building	85
Chapter 7	Coming Ashore	98
Chapter 8	Poltergeist	110
Chapter 9	A Sting in the Tail	121
Chapter 10	Verdict	132
Chapter 11	Farewell	139
Chapter 12	Going Home	151
Chapter 13	New Beginnings	162
Chapter 14	Ghosts	172

Chapter 15   Hardship   184

Chapter 16   Downfall   194

Chapter 17   Starting Again   205

Chapter 18   Two for the Price of One   214

Chapter 19   Threatened   221

Chapter 20   The Stocking Game   227

Chapter 21   Miracles   236

Chapter 22   Homesickness   247

Chapter 23   The Shadow of Aids   258

Chapter 24   This Morning   267

Chapter 25   The Stars Burn On   273

Chapter 26   The Viewers   281

Chapter 27   The Bubble   288

Chapter 28   A Return to Sadness   295

Chapter 29   Alone Again   304

Chapter 30   An Unexpected Song   310

Chapter 31   Diana   319

Chapter 32   All Human Life   329

Chapter 33   Fate   343

Epilogue   349

INTRODUCTION

I N MAY 1998, I flew to Chicago to spend a week shadowing Jerry Springer and to make make five short films about the man. The week was filled with laughter, and Jerry was friendly and interesting – much more thoughtful than he appeared on screen. The shows were something else. One of them was so explicit that it could not be aired in America, although you might have seen clips from it featuring the 'man who married his horse'. Another centred on sexual orientation, and featured a pre-op trans-sexual called Stephanie. She had the face of a Madonna and a bust Katie Price (aka Jordan) might have envied; but during the recording her hands plucked nervously at her dress, and when I interviewed her later her eyes, fringed with thick false eyelashes, were infinitely sad.

I had seen eyes like that before – but it wasn't until I was in the plane on my way home that I remembered where, and when.

It had probably been in the first year of the war. I was a small child, holding my mother's hand as we walked through town. Children pick up vibes, so I soon realised that my mother was becoming agitated. Around us on the pavement, people were stopping in mid-sentence, heads were turning, and my mother was tugging at me, desperate to bundle me into the doorway of Saxon's toy shop. 'Come away,' she insisted, making me all the more determined to see what was going on.

I pulled away from her and darted back. A tall man in a navy raincoat was mincing along on high-heeled shoes, his silk-stockinged ankles disappearing into turned-up trouser legs. There was a floral cravat at his throat, a handbag swung from his crooked arm, and his mouth was lipsticked under a thin moustache. His eyes were fixed on some far-off horizon, oblivious of the crowded pavement and the consternation he was causing. I had seen people dress up before, but then everyone had laughed. Now, no one was amused, and the man with the handbag wasn't laughing, either.

My mother was fond of taking me to see Jesus as he hung on the cross in the garden of St Cecilia's Roman Catholic church. Jesus had not only died for us, she told me; he had also suffered, which was worse. Born a Catholic but now lapsed, my mother had retained her Catholic conscience. Suffering, she told me, was good for your soul, but much to be pitied; and crucifixion was the worst suffering of all. I grasped that it wasn't a picnic because St Cecilia's Jesus had the saddest eyes I'd ever seen. Until now. The man in the navy mac and the lady's shoes looked sadder than Jesus. I felt a surge of compassion for him. Before I could translate pity into action, however, my mother had me by the collar, and two policemen were moving in on the man in the mac. As they hustled him away, I saw that his eyes were bright with unshed tears.

Flying high over America on my homeward flight, I realised I had looked into those eyes again. I understood now why all my requests for an explanation of that scene in the street more than half a century earlier had met with an embarrassed silence. You could be arrested for transvestism in those unenlightened days. Transsexuality was not even considered to exist – certainly not by a child in a house intimately acquainted with St Cecilia's.

The world had moved on since then, and Stephanie was in no danger of arrest. But the suffering seemed to be the same. I lay back in my seat – upgraded because I was a 'face' – and remembered.

1
CHAPTER

CHILDHOOD

I WAS BORN in Sunderland, in a house already repossessed by order of the mortgagee. Kindly bailiffs allowed my heavily pregnant mother to keep a favourite chair, and she clung to it like a spar from a shipwreck for the rest of her life. I know that because she told me. My mother could wring your withers with a sad story like no one else I ever knew. The chair went with her as we journeyed to a rented house in another neighbourhood; and, a reminder of her wonderful stories, it stands in my home today.

If my family had a mantra it was 'If daddy hadn't lost his money'. It was repeated several times a day; and in my early years I continually scanned the pavement in the hope of finding the missing millions. To a small child, there is only one way you lose things: you drop them. The truth was very different. The money was certainly lost, but in a business venture that went sadly wrong. My father worked for the Rose Line, a shipping company operating out of the Port of Sunderland. Eventually, Thomas Rose, the owner of the Rose Line, persuaded him to open up a subsidiary company in Newcastle, named Rose Broderick. My father's money would establish it; Thomas Rose's money would come later.

That money was never forthcoming. My father sold all the shares he possessed to keep the business afloat; he mortgaged his home; but all in vain. A QC's opinion on whether or not my father should sue Thomas Rose refers to my father as 'naive'. I prefer the word 'trusting'. He expected a colleague to keep his word, and he was let down. So the mortgaged house was repossessed; the bailiffs took most of the furniture; the housekeeper, the washerwoman and the nurserymaid were bade farewell. My father never recovered from the disgrace, but the hurt to my mother was even deeper. She had 'married up'. Her lifestyle had been the envy of her friends. Now she was, or felt she was, an object of pity.

Her father was a tubby Irishman called Francis Cahill, who had risen to be company secretary of the North Eastern Marine, but never really changed his humble lifestyle. Her mother was of Swedish/English stock, and had died young of tuberculosis – or so I was told. It was only at the end of her life that my mother confessed to me that the problem had had as much to do with drink as with TB. My mother had grown up in a tiny terraced house until her friend's boss, my father, fell in love with her. It was a 'good' marriage, blessed with a beautiful daughter and marred only by the birth of a stillborn boy. My mother and father went on European holidays; she could indulge her passion for clothes and hats; there were even jewels, presented when she christened two of the Rose Line ships. Suddenly, when my sister Joyce was nine, it was all gone – and then, to add to the disaster, she discovered that she was pregnant with me. My father's widowed mother immediately disowned him. Losing his money was a misfortune, but bringing a baby into the world without the wherewithal to rear it was unforgivable.

My grandmother was what Liverpudlians would describe as 'a

piece of work'. Born in Ceylon to British parents who were tea planters, she and her sister were shipped back to England as children when their parents died, presumably of some disease that killed them both. She was adopted by a wealthy, childless uncle, who treated her as a daughter. But when he died, his widow remarried, and under the laws of that time her fortune became the property of her new husband. What should have been my grandmother's inheritance now belonged to him. Asked to forgive her adoptive mother on her deathbed, my grandmother refused; and although she had a comfortable lifestyle she was forever embittered by what she saw as having been cheated of her due.

She married John Young Broderick of Belle Vue Park, whose father was a citizen of note and co-founded the YMCA and the Volunteer Life Brigade in Sunderland. They had three children, two sons and a daughter. The daughter, Violet, ran off to marry a man of whom my grandmother disapproved; her elder son, my Uncle Blake, was crippled by asthma, the disease that killed his father. My father, called Herbert (his mother's maiden name), who had been her white hope, was now destitute. She refused to speak to him, or to see me when I was born. As far as she was concerned, I did not exist.

In this she reckoned without Nurse Booth. Nurse Booth was an expensive lying-in nurse who attended wealthy ladies during and after their confinement. She had been at the birth of my sister and brother, and she saw me into the world at a reduced fee, borrowed I think from Uncle Blake, who kept in secret touch with his banished brother. Her final payment was made with the last sovereign my father had in his sovereign case – all the money they possessed.

Nurse Booth was a redoubtable character. Ladies, she believed, were lucky to have her, not she to have employment. When, paying a visit to check on me at five or six months, she discovered my grandmother had never laid eyes on me, she put me in my pram and wheeled me to my grandmother's door. It was a clash of the Titans, and the nurse won.

Not only was I accepted, but I became the apple of my grandmother's eye. My visits to her always produced a half-crown, so when we had nothing to eat I was hastily dressed and taken to see Granny. I soon cottoned on to the purpose of these visits. Not only would I get two shillings and sixpence, and be gratefully embraced afterwards by my mother, but if I tap-danced in the bay window Uncle Blake would tip up another shilling. Riches! I became a performer almost as soon as I could walk.

Uncle Blake was an invalid, a shrunken figure who lived for books. He had worked at one time, and had money. Now he was almost housebound, and always buried in a book. These were kept behind glass, and one day he caught me trying to open the bookcase doors. Patiently he explained that books were for people who could read. When I could read, he said, he would open the bookcase for me. I could start with Kipling's *Jungle Book* and the *Just So Stories*. He showed them to me: slim blue volumes with line-drawings as illustrations. From that moment on, I had only one ambition – to learn to read. I used labels on sauce bottles, adverts, anything bearing the printed word. Asking, studying, recognising . . . bit by bit it began to make sense, and it was intoxicating, an end to boredom.

I was then about three, and hungry for reading matter. There was a make of toilet roll – Izal, I think – that included little mottoes in its rolls. As you pulled off so many sheets, a tiny printed slip would flutter to the floor. One day I sat on the lavatory and undid a whole roll, reading each motto as it fell. My mother was horrified. Toilet rolls could be ill afforded. She patiently rolled it all up again – and changed brands.

Thwarted, I took to newspapers – hard work at first, but ultimately rewarding. The day came when I could read from the front page, the bookcase was unlocked, and the Kipling books were handed over. I have them still. Allowed to roam the bookcase, I was able only to finger them at this stage, and to understand a sentence or two, but I was conscious that books were treasures more precious than gold. And my mother would exhibit me and my reading prowess to all her friends, which must have been as sickening for them as it was embarrassing for me.

One night my father didn't come home. At breakfast time he came through the front door, and I heard him say, 'He's gone.' Uncle Blake had died of heart failure, brought on by years of asthma. A half-century or so later I would make him the hero of my novel *Beloved People*, calling him Philip Blakeston Broderick, and giving him the love life he never had in reality. I like to think he would have approved of that book, and would even have kept it in his bookcase.

By now my father had obtained a job as Relieving Officer for Public Assistance (the Social Security of the day), and we lived in a council house in the district, Grangetown, for which he was supposed to care. Public Assistance was a grim affair, and the Means Test was only part of it. My father never spoke about his work, but in later years my mother told me that he sometimes cried over the inhumanity of the system he had to operate. If an elderly person had no means of support, he or she would be taken into Highfield, which was, in effect, a workhouse. But before this could be done, my father had to seek out their children and ask them to formally reject their parent. In most cases, they themselves had little or nothing, so they were forced to say they refused to help. Once this formal disavowal was made, Daddy had to go back and tell the parents that their child had rejected them, and that therefore they could enter Highfield. Can you think of a crueller charade? The rates of relief were pitiful, but accommodation was the worst problem.

One day a woman appeared at our door, asking for my father. She was distressed, so I, ever curious, clung to his side. She needed somewhere to stay, and she kept repeating, 'My waters have broken. For God's sake, my waters have broken.' He turned her away, but I could see he was shaken. So was my mother, who kept asking him why he couldn't help. I demanded to know what was going on, and she sat down on the stairs and drew me close. The lady was having a baby, she said, and had nowhere to go to have it.

Our visits to St Cecilia's had included many a story of Bethlehem, so the issue, as far as I was concerned, was plain. This was a case of no room at the inn, and we had space. She could have the baby here, and, with a bit of luck, the Star in the East might hover above our house.

There was a sad shaking of heads, and the matter was never referred to again. But I have always wondered whether that baby came safely into the world. My guess is that she had probably left an abusive husband, and would have been driven back to him by my father's refusal to give her shelter.

My mother was at once the most lovable person and the most impossible. I soon learned not to admire any of her birthday or Christmas presents: if she thought you liked them, she would insist that you have them. She would have given away the shoes off her feet; and once she did give my shoes away. I remember being brought home sitting on the side of a neighbour's pram because she had taken off my sandals in the park and given them to a child without shoes.

But it is the episode of the doll that lingers in my memory. I was not overwhelmed with toys in childhood, because money was scarce, but one year I was given a doll made by Czechoslovakian refugees. It was the most wonderful doll ever, with a grown-up face and wonderful wavy hair. My sister had a rush of generosity and knitted clothes for it – clothes that took off! I loved it with all my heart. And then the plant woman came round. She called every few months, carrying a huge wicker basket filled with plants that she would sell or exchange for old clothes or bric-à-brac. This day she and my mother had a whispered conversation, and then my mother took me aside. The plant woman's husband had died, and her little girl was grieving. She needed something to take her mind off her loss, and it had to be something good. Old toys wouldn't do.

I knew what my mother was thinking. I climbed the stairs to fetch the doll, and I can still remember how strange my legs felt, bogged down in reluctance. The doll was handed over, and I tried to feel brave and benevolent. I couldn't. I felt gutted and it still hurts, sixty years on.

But if I lost that doll, there were others. Each summer we would go to Saxon's toy shop to choose one. Thereafter my mother would put down sixpence a week, so that by Christmas the doll was paid for. (I always knew what I was getting for Christmas because my mother was incapable of keeping a secret. I would wake in the dark, and feel for the pillowcase, hoping against hope there would be just one surprise.) During the ritual of choosing the doll, we would walk up and down the rows of dolls, black and white. 'Look at the eyes,' she would say. 'Look at the eyes.' And so we chose – sometimes black, sometimes white: the eyes were what mattered. I'm sure it wasn't intentional, but she was teaching me a valuable lesson. Colour of skin is unimportant; only the eyes matter. I have been judging people in this way ever since, and it has seldom failed me.

As I grew, I became aware of my surroundings. My sister Joyce was ten years older than me, and there were studio portraits of her all around the house – arising out of lilies, curtseying in fancy dress, always beautiful and smiling. I had been born after my father's business crashed. There were no photographs of me because photographs were a luxury they could no longer afford. But to my child's mind there was only one reason for my non-appearance: that Joyce was worth photographing while I was not. For years I would lower my head in front of a camera. I was in my fifties when Terry O'Neill, the eminent photographer, took me to task for not lifting my chin. Now I face a lens boldly.

The house was not only filled with Joyce's image, it revolved around her welfare. When I was three or four, she almost died of pneumonia. She was saved by something called M & B 693, and from then on my parents wrapped her in cotton wool. We went to a cottage in Corbridge so she could convalesce, and I remember a gramophone there and two records, 'South of the Border' and 'Deep Purple'. She played them over and over, and I cannot hear them now without remembering the musty smell of that rented house, and the joy when Daddy came on the bus to take us home.

Joyce being so much older than I, I was, to all intents, an only child. On one side was a group of adults, sharing, whispering, making decisions. And then there was me, rebellious, unsettled, and determined to penetrate their charmed circle. I would refuse to go to bed and would huddle on the stairs, listening to them laughing and talking down below. I would follow my sister everywhere, desperate to get her attention, craving her approval.

One day I caught measles, and was confined to bed. After a week there was a whispered consultation between my mother and the doctor, and then my sister arrived and began to dress me with a rare tenderness – not the usual tugging of vest and liberty bodice over my protesting head. Suddenly I knew what the whispering had been about. I was dying! With only hours or days left, she was being nice to me. It was years before I found out that the doctor had suspected a heart murmur. When this failed to materialise, the new tenderness didn't last long.

It wasn't Joyce's fault. Looking back, I can see that I must have been an impossible child. I had also come into her life at the moment when the good times vanished. She lost her lifestyle, her private school. Who could blame her for thinking that the advent of the baby was somehow linked to this?

Money, or the lack of it, overshadowed our lives. My father's wage was about £3 a week, but this didn't stop him and my mother engaging a maid. Peggy was paid ten shillings a week. Our washing was taken once a week by her mother, Mrs English, and was returned immaculate for 2s 6d. I once asked my mother why they had done something as foolish as pay for help in the house when they were so hard up, and she explained. Her mother-in-law had warned her never to peel potatoes: it stained the fingers.

This didn't seem logical to me, but I rejoice that Peggy was part of my life. We loved her. On her day off she would take me to her house in Spelterworks Road. It was small and dark and built, it seemed, of cement, but it was a child's paradise. Her father was a sea-going man, there were foreign dolls in the bedroom, and a burst of budgies in the back yard. Furthermore, they had money, actual cash, something I seldom saw at home. Mrs English would take coins down from the mantelpiece, and Peggy would take me to Jones's shop to buy a palm leaf, a delicious palm-shaped sandwich of puff pastry filled with cream and garnished with icing sugar. Mr Jones, small, dapper and overalled, would tell me what a clever girl I was, and if I was in a good mood I would tap dance for him on the lino.

These visits were wonderful, and were even better when Mr English was home from sea, and would regale me with tales of seafaring. Once he brought me back a piece of sugarcane, a strange, exotic thing I showed to anyone I could buttonhole.

One day Peggy delivered me safely home, and then vanished because my grandmother was paying a visit. Granny always dressed in black, her hats had plumage on them, and she wore a veil that came down and was secured around her neck with a velvet ribbon. This day the veil was lifted and there was a row going on. It was the one and only time I ever saw my mother stand up to her mother-in-law. Granny had decreed that it was unsuitable for me to visit the maid's home. My mother thought otherwise. The Englishes were not only worthy, they were friends. Granny departed in a huff, muttering about speaking to my father. Fortunately for me, my mother spoke to him first. The visits continued.

My grandmother was a snob, but life had not been kind to her. She had nursed a sick husband; had seen one son become an invalid and die young; her daughter had eloped; my father had failed. But nothing could excuse the venom she sometimes displayed. Her sister-in-law, Aunt Rosie, came to live with her. She was a gentle woman who wanted nothing but to read the paper through a magnifying glass. Granny tormented her ceaselessly, mocking her clothes, her reticence, even the drop on the end of her nose. When Aunt Rosie died, I was about five, but I was well aware, even at that age, that she had had a welcome escape.

Granny was quite dumpy, rather like Queen Victoria, but she had a certain elegance. She never wore spectacles, but instead used a lorgnette, to great effect. Her hair was silver-grey and perfectly waved. I admired it enormously until the day I saw it on its stand on her dressing table. Or, rather, I saw the spare wig, for one was usually at the hairdresser's being groomed, while the other was on her head. She always peeled fruit with a silver fruit knife, and her maid would bring in tea on a railed tray. Most exciting of all, she would seal letters with red sealing-wax, and then press a little seal into the still warm blob. This, she told me, was to prevent tampering.

One day she took me to the Wellington chest, a set of mahogany drawers with a lock that came over from the side. Inside were white garments: a cap embroidered with the satin roses she could make by sticking a darning needle into cloth and then winding satin ribbon round it, and a nightdress similarly ornamented. 'They're my laying-out clothes,' she said. I looked puzzled, so she explained. 'When I die, they'll put them on me before I go into my coffin.' It was a macabre thing to tell a child not yet at school, but that didn't stop her. On Sundays she sat in a pew in St George's which bore her name. She had no intention of being improperly dressed on her final visit.

My memories of childhood are filled with love, but also with stress. My parents adored each other. My father always came home for lunch, and when it was time for him to go back to the office they would cling to one another in the hall, reluctant to part, while Joyce and I jeered and shouted, 'Hollywood!' On Sundays my father would take me by the hand and, if he had the money, walk down to the allotments to buy my mother a bunch of marguerites, her favourite flower. They called one another 'darling', and sometimes my father would call my mother 'honey'.

The only time they used each other's Christian names was when they were rowing about money, which was the only thing they fought over. Each of them had a list of who was owed money each month. My father wanted to pay those people with whom he came in contact; my mother wanted to pay her people. The two lists never tallied. There is no poverty like the poverty of people who once had money and don't know how to manage without it. Later I would join in the covering-up of needs, the pain of seeing treasures sacrificed one by one in order to survive, the endless struggle to keep up standards. And all under my grandmother's grim disapproval of any spending she considered inessential!

Once, in a burst of early Communism, I decided to take money from my granny's full purse and put it into my mother's empty one. This seemed simple justice. But, devout as she was, my mother didn't believe in miracles. She soon worked out where the money came from and told me gently that it had to stop.

When things were really tough, Mam would play the piano and sing, 'Even though the darkest clouds are in the sky, You mustn't sigh and you mustn't cry, Spread a little happiness as you go by.' And spread a little happiness she did. After she died, I lost count of the people, mostly strangers, who stopped me in the street to tell me how she had comforted them in times of stress.

Was she a snob? I think not. She simply longed for the life she had briefly enjoyed and lost. Although the house where I was born was terraced, it had had a drawing-room, a dining-room and a morning-room. Now she had only one room to be living-, withdrawing- and dining-room combined, and this was a crucifixion to her. She was always afraid the vicar would call and find it in disarray. It has rubbed off on me. I keep one room immaculate in an otherwise untidy house, just in case.

But however tough things got, my mother's faith never wavered. By now a Presbyterian, she found solace in church and in Jesus. On New Year's Day, I would groan at the thought that the next holiday would be Good Friday. On that day the curtains would be drawn, candles lit on the mantelpiece, and no music allowed. To this day I can't eat or cook meat on Good Friday. When one of my sons argued that this was illogical I told him quite truthfully that, although he could do what he liked, I would have to stick to fish, because if I did anything else my hand would drop off. Indoctrination? No. My mother tried very hard to indoctrinate me in other ways and failed. I honour her memory on Good Friday for no other reason than love.

As well as the cross of that single room, she had to cope with cooking. It wasn't her forte, and if she mastered something she cooked it again and again. She was also hampered by the fact that food of any quality was in short supply. Once she made barley kernel pudding, which was cheap and nutritious, and we all enjoyed it. So we got it every day for a month or more, until my father summoned up the courage to suggest a change. But if food was sparse, the table was always beautifully set. Indeed, polishing the silver was a ritual – the one bit of housework my mother didn't mind. There was wonderful cutlery, and little cut-glass rests for carving knife and fork – only the joint to carve was missing. But my mother's mince and dumplings was wonderful!

You always imagine your mother to be beautiful, but I think perhaps my mother was. She was blond, from her Swedish forebears, and her eyes were turquoise blue to the end of her life. She often wore Granny's cast-off black, but when there was a windfall and an outfit could be afforded she loved to dress up. And for special occasions my father would buy her Parma violets to pin on her lapel. He had given them to her early on in their relationship, so they had a special significance.

We never went on holiday until the last days of the war, when we spent a week in a cottage in North Yorkshire. This visit, which it was hoped would provide unrationed luxuries of bacon and butter, was ruined by the matter of the visitors' book. The cottage turned out to be more downmarket than my mother had hoped, and she avoided signing the landlady's visitors' book, which had to be kept in wartime, because she didn't want subsequent visitors to see we had stayed there. Every day became a battle between the landlady, who had one leg, and my mother. The landlady won – though I saw my mother hesitate before she wrote, wondering whether or not she could get away with an alias.

But magic days before the war were spent on the beach a quarter of a mile from our house (although my mother always made me wear a vest under my bathing costume); and even better ones on top of Tunstall Hill. It lay to the west of Sunderland and within walking distance of our house. Sitting up there, my father would tell me I had been born in the biggest shipbuilding town in the world. He didn't mention that there were shipbuilding cities, so I conceived the idea that Sunderland was the hub of the universe. I have never changed my mind. From the hill you could see the sea, a forest of cranes in the river, and too many church spires to count. When I was very small he carried me down the hill on his shoulders, and I felt like a queen. And one memorable Easter we rolled our paste eggs down the slope.

On winter evenings, watching from the window, I remember the lamplighter moving to pull the chains that lit the gas lamps, and feeling joy because this meant that Daddy would soon be home. I remember, too, the herring man, and the muffin man, and Walls ice-cream from a bicycle. And the French onion man. My mother could never resist his Gallic charm – whatever we went short of, it wasn't onions. In fact, my mother was a sucker for anyone who came to the door, believing that they must be starving to do it. They never went away without money or food, no matter how little there was to share. And she was a sucker for gypsies, believing every word they said and treating their scratty pieces of heather with a reverence that would have befitted orchids.

Occasionally someone in my father's family would leave him a legacy. Then there would be jubilation and spending. When Aunty Rosie died, I got a pink fluffy dressing-gown. When money came, I would think our troubles were over, but they never were. Sooner or later the money would be gone, and it would all begin again. But those interludes of affluence were magic. We would have tea at Blackett's restaurant, where there were waitresses in black dresses and starched aprons and caps – or the Havelock café, which had flock wallpaper. And there would be new clothes.

New clothes had a special smell and feel, and the thrill of this has left me with a love of fabric and patterns. I remember dresses Joyce had with fabric belts and intricate patterns. I remember my mother's one good evening dress, black with slit sleeves that fell back to reveal a turquoise lining. And I remember Mrs Jefferson's patches. Mrs Jefferson was our next-door neighbour. She had long white hair that she would dry in the garden on summer days, and she loved her church. Once, to raise money for it, she got a huge number of patches from a dressmaker, made them up into bundles, and sold them for threepence a time. If I could lay my hands on threepence, she would take me into her back bedroom, pull the huge box from under the bed and let me choose. I would carry a bundle home and unwrap it. Bits of velvet, lace, cloque, muslin, stripes, florals, satins... I can touch and smell them still. Magic!

My clothes were usually bought by Granny. Red-haired little girls should wear brown, she decreed. So I wore brown velvet dresses with Peter Pan collars and half-belts, and I dreamed of muslin and purple-and-yellow marocain. One glorious day Granny made me a party dress. Or rather, she took a pale-blue taffeta dress and ornamented it with her handmade roses and little sprigs of forget-me-nots, all covered with blue net. It was, quite simply, a dress for a princess. I would have worn it every day, everywhere, but I soon outgrew it. There was never another one.

Our hopes were pinned on Mammy's songs. She not only played, she composed. 'All in a Moment', 'Mr Sandman' – they tumbled out, transcribed on to paper by Mr Hooker, the church organist. She sent them away, always convinced that the ship would come in. Once, Hutch, a famous singer, toyed with the idea of recording one, but it never happened. The songs stayed in the music stool, and the ship stayed far out to sea.

I'm not quite sure why, but I was a very fearful child. I hid it well, but it was there. That's why I remember so clearly the kindness of strangers, the feeling when you realised that this person would not hurt you. One day I had a blister on my heel. We were in Heslop's grocery shop, and I was crying with the pain of it. A woman came in, and lifted me on to the counter. She took something from her bag and pressed it on my heel. I can remember the feel of her cool fingers and the relief as the blister was covered. When she went away the shopkeeper told my mother the lady was Dr Helen Blackley, the medical officer of health. I have never forgotten her. Such memories are the reason why I cannot see a child without wanting to reassure it.

Periodically my father would be ill, and have to lie in a darkened room, all visible parts of him covered in cloths soaked in calamine lotion. This was 'Daddy's illness'. Years later the family doctor told me it was urticaria, and that Daddy had been lucky to get that instead of the family asthma. All I knew in childhood, though, was that there was deathly fear that sickness would lose him his job. Many times he struggled up and went to work when he should have stayed in bed.

But life was not at all grim. There was a lot of laughter and always something interesting on which to eavesdrop – quite often gems about 'Mrs Simpson', who became the Duchess of Windsor and was the Devil incarnate as far as my mother was concerned. Each winter Sunderland staged illuminations on the seafront, and I can remember being carried there by my father, seeing a fairyland of lights. Another year we went on the tramcar, rattling through the magic place, eyes wide.

And then one day we went to the pictures to see Anna Neagle – a double bill, *Queen Victoria* and *Sixty Glorious Years*. I knew something was up at home, but I didn't know what. I sat between Joyce and my mother, wriggling because I was heartily sick of Anna Neagle, and was wondering what was going on. I wondered and I worried. On the bus going home, they were excited. Would it be there? What would it be like? 'What is it?' I asked. 'Shhh!' they said – until, at the fourth or fifth time of asking, Joyce said, 'We're getting a wireless. Granny's worried about a war starting, so she's given Daddy the money for a wireless.' I wondered if it would get Radio Luxembourg and the Ovaltineys or the Marguerite Cream programme, like Aunty Eve had on her wireless, but I didn't mention it. A state of war presently existed between my mother and her sister Eve. This was a not infrequent state of affairs and it was better not to refer to it.

When we got home, there it was, huge and brown, with flowers cut into the wood, the gaps filled with fabric. We stood and gazed in awe as Daddy tuned it in. There was no mention of Ovaltineys or Marguerite Cream, just a very solemn voice droning on. From that moment on it became the hub of the house. A few weeks later, on a Sunday morning, I was playing with a ball in the garden when my mother appeared in the doorway. 'Come inside,' she said. 'War's been declared.'

2
CHAPTER

WAR

To my childish eyes it seemed that the world changed overnight. In fact, preparations for war had been going on for months, but the first I knew of it was when the shrubbery at the end of our street was cut down and a huge water-tank installed. This, I was told, was for putting out fires. No further information was forthcoming. At the same time my father uprooted the flowers in the garden and began to 'Dig for Victory'. If he didn't, he told me, grimly forking the ground, we would all starve to death when the U-boats got busy. I asked what U-boats were, and got the usual reply when he wasn't sure how much I should be told: 'Ask your mother.' I was sure the LDV would protect us. All the men seemed to be enlisting in the Local Defence Volunteers, popularly known as Look, Duck and Vanish, which I thought positively rude even if it did make everyone laugh.

The wireless became the focus of my father's attention. I couldn't understand the news broadcasts but I soon learned the buzz words. Any mention of Churchill was good and would make my father bite his moustache in approval. The Prime Minister had also brought back Anthony Eden, which made my mother almost swoon with satisfaction. She thought my father resembled Eden, and was forever on at him to buy a Homburg hat like the one Eden wore.

We now had a stirrup-pump in the bottom of the pantry and a long-handled shovel which was to deal with incendiaries. 'Fire-bombs,' my father translated. It wasn't till my mother ran shrieking into the garden when a plane went overhead that Joyce told me that the Germans would soon rain down fire from the sky, which explained the water-tank in the shrubbery.

Joyce now had a mock-crocodile case to hold her gas mask. She was inordinately fond of this new accessory and carried it everywhere. My gas mask came in an ordinary cardboard box with a strong shoulder-strap, but I never carried it. After once trying it on, feeling the rubber sweaty against my cheeks and inhaling the musty odour of the filter, I had resolved that when the gas attack came I would inhale as much gas as I could and die quickly, rather than suffocate inside the mask.

I had other problems more pressing than gas or fire-bombs. I now attended Mrs McLaren's School, which was held in her semi-detached house. Granny was paying the fees, and I was given to understand that I was unbelievably privileged to be going to a private school. That was not how I saw it. I hated Mrs McLaren's with a rare passion. The class was composed of mixed ages, and we younger children spent a lot of time rolling up newspaper to make paper sticks for Mrs McLaren's fire. This I considered to be a waste of good reading matter.

When we weren't rolling we were reading aloud from books called – predictably – readers. I was the only one of the younger children who could read. While the others chanted each word after Mrs McLaren, moving their fingers along the line, I would skim down the page and turn over to see what came next. This was not allowed. At first Mrs McLaren told me not to do it. When I was unable to resist, she took to creeping up behind me. As I lifted the corner of the page, down would come her hand with a resounding slap. But the desire to turn the page rapidly became a compulsion, and the duel between her will and mine led to many a slapped hand.

This was not my only problem. Mrs McLaren was formidable. Her daughter, Christine, was terrifying. She took us for art, and once a week we were told to bring our paints because Miss Christine would be coming. The trouble was that I didn't have any paints, but pride kept me from revealing this. Nor did I mention it at home, where it would only cause more worry. Instead I lied and said I had forgotten them. For this failure I was made to watch while others painted or cut shapes into potatoes, dipped them in paint and pressed them on to paper.

The fourth or fifth time I 'forgot' I was sent to stand out in the hall for the duration of the lesson. Mrs McLaren was cooking in the kitchen, and I watched through the crack in the door, all the time wondering whether or not this boredom was worth Granny's precious money. Eventually Miss Christine hauled me to the front of the class and named me as a feckless individual who would not prosper and did not deserve to be a Mrs McLaren pupil. With this I heartily agreed.

But if school was hell, the threat of evacuation was worse. Children were being sent away to be safe from bombing. I didn't want to be safe, I wanted to stay home. We had an Anderson shelter now, sunk into the ground in the garden of the Jeffersons next door. Daddy cut a hole in the fence so we had access to it, and the Jeffersons and the Brodericks shared. There would be room, for the Jeffersons' grown-up children were off to war, and Mr Jefferson and my father would be on duty in the ARP and not in the shelter at all. So why did I need to go away 'to the country', which began to assume the proportions of the African jungle?

There were two wide-eyed little girls at Mrs McLaren's now who spoke no English and cried a lot. My mother explained that they were Jewish, and had been sent out of Germany to save their lives. They had been adopted by Jewish families, and would now be happy and well cared for, she said. I was unconvinced, but time proved her correct. They were cared for and loved by their adoptive hosts. I felt deeply for them over the parting from their parents, but it reinforced my own fear of being sent away.

Peggy went off to work in a factory producing war material. There were tears when she went, but Mammy said we must be proud of her for helping to win the war. She promised to keep in touch but, like thousands of others, the war carried her out of our lives and into a new life of her own. All over the country, girls who had worked as domestics were off to do war work, and 'cleaners', mostly married women, took their place. Domestic help was now at a premium, and cleaners could pick and choose where they offered their services. Granny's maid went with the rest, and my mother was elected to find her a cleaner. This was easy enough – at first! They generally stayed in the stone-flagged kitchen for a week, two at the most, before coming to tell my mother that they would sooner stick pins in their eyes than work for the remnant of eighteenth-century slave-owner that was her mother-in-law.

In the absence of a cleaner, my mother was forced to step in. Domesticity to my granny's exacting standards was beyond her. Each time she found a new cleaner, she whooped with joy. And I took to sitting in the window after forty-eight hours, so that I could announce gleefully that yet another ex-cleaner was approaching our door. Heaven forgive me, I enjoyed the ensuing howl of anguish and the begging and pleading that would go on before my mother accepted that 'never again' meant just that.

We had a cleaner and we loved her. She was Mrs Iley, and, being a good Catholic, she had a large family. I remember her as a rosy-cheeked woman who was always kind to me and would tell me about her children. One day my mother told me that Mrs Iley had given birth to twins. We went to visit her, lying in bed with a baby on each arm, the picture of perfect happiness. I couldn't wait to tell Granny. Her sniff of disapproval could have been heard at sea. 'More children? Disgusting.'

I couldn't let this pass. 'Babies are lovely,' I said. Her reply was withering. 'No, they're not. If you have none to make you laugh, you'll have none to make you cry.' It was forty years before I understood the heartbreak that lay behind that remark, but it gave me the title for my fifth novel, *None To Make You Cry*.

Peggy was not the only one who went to war. My mother was sad to lose Mr Newton, the fishmonger, who had to close his shop because he'd been called up. She promised to patronise him as soon as Hitler was defeated and he opened up again. And our paper boy had laid aside his hessian shoulder-bag and was now riding round on a motor-bike as a despatch rider for the ARP.

I missed Mr Newton very much because I was secretly in love with him. He was tall and dark and unmarried. In retrospect, I wonder whether his filleting prowess caused a little flutter in my mother's bosom, although no impropriety ever took place.

When the first air raid came, we were already used to the wailing of the siren and the steady blast of the All Clear, for there had been plenty of false alarms and trial runs. My mother insisted on taking

Pete the canary with her, but the rush down the garden sent the poor bird into such paroxysms of fright that it raced around the cage, beating its wings, for the duration of the raid. This went on until my father decreed that Pete should take his chances in the house. My mother was terrified – of possible bombs, certainly, but more because my father was out there somewhere, unprotected. So the mother/daughter roles were reversed. I patted her hand and told her it would all be over soon. Perhaps the agony aunt was born there, in the must and damp of a shelter sunk six feet below ground.

But if Hitler did nothing else, he perked my father up no end. Failure had almost broken his spirit. Now he had a purpose: to do his bit for the war effort. He was issued with a tin hat and a navy battle-dress jacket with 'ARP' on the shoulder. His role was to be a Rest Centre Officer. When houses were destroyed by bombs, he would take those occupants who survived into a 'rest centre' in a school or church hall, and ultimately arrange their re-housing, probably in a commandeered house. This post was a cut above that of the ordinary warden, and was a source of much satisfaction to my mother. She didn't care for Mr Davey, the warden for our street, who took his duties, in my mother's opinion, a trifle officiously.

Eventually Daddy was issued with a superior tin hat with a leather band inside, and they spent a happy half-hour in front of the mirror deciding the right angle at which it should be worn. Arduous though his duties would be as the raids grew more frequent and destructive, my father was having a good war. But this did not dim his burning anger at the loss of his business, and the way many of their friends had melted away with the money.

One day an invitation to a silver-wedding party arrived. It was from a couple called Sherratt who had once been close friends. The two couples had attended each other's weddings and socialised together, in palmy days. When my parents could no longer afford to entertain, or go out to dine or dance, they had vanished. The invitation delighted my mother. A night out! My father had other ideas. He would, he told her, sooner cut off his arm than see the Sherratts. 'Have you forgotten?' he said. I only half understood what it was all about, but I understood his determination. 'It was a long time ago,' my mother said, her eyes filling with tears. 'Not to me,' was the bitter answer. 'Not to me.' The invitation went in the waste-paper basket and was never mentioned again.

But there were other friends who stayed the course – the Dennises and the Herdmans, whose friendship lasted through thick and thin, and in the case of the Herdmans endures to this day. Aunty Edith Dennis always bought me a Christmas present, and this was usually the one surprise in my stocking, as long as I could prevent my mother telling me what it was. One year it was a jigsaw of 'Rock-a-bye Baby'. Gorgeous!

Even if that silver-wedding invitation had been accepted, there would have been complications. My grandmother's grip on the family was even tighter now. She seldom went out, and had become gloomier. Daddy had to go every night to help her to bed, and nothing could interfere with this ritual. Had they accepted the silver-wedding invitation, they could not have gone until Granny was safely locked in her bedroom. I went with him on summer nights. She would be waiting in her living-room, and I would sit with her while my father prepared a black vacuum flask. This had a peculiar smell and was called 'Granny's medicine'. Years later, when someone was drinking rum, I recognised the smell. Whatever else was in Granny's flask, it was well laced with Navy rum.

My father would help her upstairs while I carried the flask. She would go into her room, he would kiss her finally on the cheek and place the flask on the bedside table, and then we would hear the door being bolted before we left the house. At the time I saw that house as perfectly normal. Now I realise it was a time-capsule: flocked wallpaper, gas mantles, heavy oil paintings, a stone-flagged kitchen, half-drawn curtains, and, until it vanished with the war, always mimosa in a glass épergne in the drawing-room. When the war effort demanded that her wrought-iron railings be cut down to be melted, and the cast-iron urns that were usually filled with geraniums should go too, it seemed as though she lost the will to emerge from her front door. She grew increasingly bitter.

One day I was there when she opened an envelope that had come with the post. It contained photographs of two soldiers, one in a forage cap, one in a broad-brimmed hat. She looked at them for a moment, then threw them into the fire. I couldn't bear this, and fished them out with the poker, charred at the edges. 'Why did you do that?' I asked.

'Because I didn't want them. They're nothing to do with me.' She left the room then, but I carried the photos home and showed them to my father. He shook his head sadly. They were his nephews, the sons of his sister who had run off years before. The strange thing is that even as a child I sensed that the photographs had meant something to her, but that pride wouldn't let her acknowledge it. All her children had disappointed her. She just couldn't accept that what had happened was inevitable because it was life. And, dependent on her financially as we were, my father could not stand up to her. She knew and exploited that.

The situation was no easier on my mother's side of the family. She had one sister, my Aunt Eve, who was secretary to the Chief Constable and unmarried. It soon dawned on me that my aunt did not care for my mother. More than once, when we visited my grandfather, there would be a blazing row, I would be bundled into my coat, and we would make a swift exit. Aunt Eve also lost no opportunity, when we were alone, to point out to me my mother's failings. 'The trouble with your mother', she said one day, 'is that she has come down in the world and won't admit it.'

Soon after that I saw my grandfather sitting in his chair, crying quietly. 'What's the matter with Grandpa?' I asked. The reply was half-whispered: 'He's upset about the IRA.' I had heard of the IRA, who planted bombs in pillar-boxes over some mysterious argument I didn't understand. My grandfather understood it only too well. His native Ireland, or part of it, was at loggerheads with his adopted country, a country he had come to love.

He was also receiving some kind of treatment for a condition of his throat that he had convinced himself was cancer. No protestations to the contrary from the doctors treating him would change his mind. Grandpa Cahill had always supported his sister-in-law, Aunt Sue, who had been left to him, so my mother said, as her mother's legacy. Aunt Sue would often take me out, especially to the cinema where Aunt Eve had free seats by virtue of her police connections.

Aunt Sue had an easy method for keeping me quiet. 'You haven't got a ticket,' she would say as we rode in the bus or sat in the cinema. 'You must be very quiet because if they find out you'll go to prison.' In vain I protested that I did not want to go on these expeditions, 'Aunt Sue loves you,' Mother would say, and brook no argument. I'm quite sure Aunt Sue did love me, but she wanted an easy life and terrorising me achieved it. If she had known it would cause me to become a lifelong compulsive ticket-checker whenever I travel or go to the theatre, she might have found a more humane way of keeping control. As it was, the trips out with Aunt Sue came to an end as soon as air raids became an almost daily occurrence. She was terrified of being bombed or, worse, strafed from the air, because Germans machine-gunned everything that moved – so she told me.

Whether it was fear of air raids or my grandpa's distress over the IRA, huge changes were afoot. Suddenly Grandpa went into a mental hospital, 'for a rest'. He never emerged from it, and died a few years later. Aunt Sue went off to a church-run home in the Yorkshire Dales, and Aunt Eve sold the tiny terraced house and bought a smart semi-detached. There was an almighty row over this, with Aunt Eve insisting the new house was hers, although it was bought in part with the proceeds of the family home. According to my mother, Aunt Eve had smuggled a document into the mental hospital and got my grandfather to sign it. My mother felt robbed of her future inheritance; Aunt Eve felt that she was guardian of the two old people and should protect their interests. It led to an estrangement between my aunt and my mother which lasted for years, but Aunt Eve was triumphant. If my mother had come down in the world, she, the spinster sister, was going up.

Despite all these tensions, our life at home was happy. My mother played and sang, we laughed a lot, and always there was the spectacle of two people deeply in love. But I still had to endure the privations of Mrs McLaren's. I had a friend by then, a child called Lilian, who lived in our street. If she was not at school she would come to wait for me at Mrs McLaren's gate. Mrs McLaren didn't like this. Lilian's crime was that she went to a state school. She also wore a pixie hood. Mrs McLaren didn't approve of pixie hoods. Lilian was not to be encouraged.

It came as a huge relief to me when Mrs McLaren fell ill, and I was pitched into the hurly-burly of the local state school. Here paints were provided, and the fact that I was a fluent reader was cause for praise. What they did not provide, however, was the Evans exam book.

I had always understood that our money worries were not for public consumption. I also understood that to ask for something which required coin of the realm was to add to my parents' distress. The Evans exam book was a crammer designed to get you through the 11-plus, and it cost, I believe, one shilling and sixpence. Like the paints, I said I had forgotten it whenever I was required to produce it.

The teacher, Miss Rogers, was a disciplinarian. In time she would grow fond of me, make me copy my compositions into her special Honour book, and tell me I was destined to be a famous writer. Now, faced with a child half-way through term, coming from a private school and therefore bound to be uppity, she was not going to brook disobedience. Spittle appeared at the corners of her mouth as she chastised me, even threatening me with the cane.

I had never heard of canes until I encountered Miss Rogers. Now, almost every day, she would cane someone, usually a dark-haired boy called Gordon Bell or a giant of a boy called John Reed. She swore she could see their misdeeds reflected in her glasses when she was facing the board with the class behind her. So Gordon and John got six of the best on their palms, and returned to their desks with their sore hands tucked in the opposite armpit. The canings seemed to affect them hardly at all. I felt sick at the sound of cane on flesh, and I burned with the injustice of it. They were being punished for little or nothing, and that did not seem fair.

That we spent many nights in the air-raid shelter did not, as far as I remember, affect our school work, nor even bother us too much. Sometimes there was shrapnel to be found in the street, or the sight of planes overhead. Once we even saw a dog-fight in the sky between British fighters and Germans planes. All in all, children seemed to thrive in wartime.

The threat of evacuation receded, as far as I was concerned, when Geoffrey Crawford, an adored only child, went down when the Germans torpedoed the *City of Benares*, a ship loaded with evacuees on their way to safety. Eighty-seven children perished, along with scores of adults. The Crawfords lived in our street and my mother's anguish for them was dreadful to see. 'Their only child,' she kept saying. She put Geoffrey's photo on our mantelpiece, and wrote a poem about him which was published in the *Sunderland Echo*. It likened him to Jack Crawford, the fourteen-year-old cabin boy, born in Sunderland, who rescued the British flag at the Battle of Camperdown and nailed it to the mast. Whenever we went to the park to see Jack Crawford's statue we said a prayer for Geoffrey, and speculated about what a wonderful man he would have been if he had lived.

But if my mother had decided my place was at her side, her fear of air raids had intensified. They came thick and fast. One winter night we were showered with incendiary bombs. There was snow on the ground, and as the fire-bombs landed in snow there was a sizzling sound. It reminded me of the time someone had dropped a two-pound bag of sugar in Heslop's grocery shop; when it burst it had made that same shushing sound. I rather enjoyed counting the sizzles. It didn't occur to me that they weren't all landing in our vegetable garden until, when the All Clear sounded, we had to welcome our friends, the Harts, into our house because fire had temporarily destroyed their own.

I don't believe there has been enough praise for the people who dealt with war damage. Half-destroyed houses were magically restored or, if that was impossible, demolished for safety, becoming empty spaces where rose-bay willow herb ran riot. If houses had not been restored so quickly there would have been a serious housing shortage, for the temporary rest centres were not equipped to hold people for more than a night or two.

To protect us we had the smoke-screen men. Most nights, big trucks would trundle along the main road and park. Somehow they gave off smoke that rose and formed a protective cloud across the town. Nearby householders would send the men tea and whatever biscuits they could find, and one night I was allowed to take these offerings. Joyce had just tonged my hair for me, and I felt fabulous. The two soldiers climbed down from their cab and accepted the tea. 'You're a pretty little girl,' the older one said. 'Yes,' said the young one, 'just like Alice Faye.' Alice Faye was a dazzling blond American star. I didn't walk back home, I floated.

Eventually our avenue was hit by a big bomb. It fell in the middle of the road, demolishing the houses on both sides, although the householders mostly escaped unharmed, safe in their Anderson shelters at the far end of their gardens. The crater left by the bombs was huge and water-filled. We ventured near the edge and lobbed in pebbles, which seemed to be falling forever. But before long the crater was filled, the road repaired, and normality returned to the street.

I was enjoying the war. Even then I had an eye for the dramatic, and there was drama aplenty. Much of this drama centred on the wireless and the King's speeches. His hesitant diction, punctuated by long pauses as he struggled to get out a word, would have my mother, eyes closed, feverishly praying under her breath. 'That poor man,' she would say, and tell me that the Queen sat beside him when he made a speech and held his hand for comfort. 'Better than that other woman.' I knew whom she meant: the Duchess of Windsor was not the hand-holding type, and we had been lucky to get the Queen instead of her.

But the main act was undoubtedly Churchill. I loved his speeches for the simple reason that my father would glow with pride and my mother, not one of nature's great cooks, would vanish into the kitchen at the oration's end and produce some culinary delight just to celebrate.

I didn't see anything wrong with our rations, but my mother grumbled constantly. We ate delicacies like black-pudding sandwiches and baked-bean pie, which was as dry as dust and hard to swallow. Leek-and-cheese pie was nice, and dried-egg omelettes were mouth-watering, even though you could have soled your shoes with them. Occasionally we got black-market bacon from Mr Curle, who lived opposite and had some connection with the docks; and Aunt Sally, my mother's cousin, would bring us an occasional egg from the country. We never tasted sugar. We swapped our sugar and jam with the Jeffersons next door for their tea, the one commodity my mother couldn't do without.

We listened nightly to wireless accounts of the Battle of Britain. In the first ten days of the battle, the Air Ministry reckoned that a thousand German planes were being sent over Britain each day; and tales of tiny British Spitfires and Hurricanes fighting them off went from mouth to mouth. There was a real effort to keep up each other's morale, an effort made necessary by the sniping of Lord Haw-Haw, a Briton who now broadcast for the Germans and poured scorn on every part of the Allied war-effort.

My mother also gloried in the story of Dunkirk, where tiny boats, some of them hardly sea-worthy, crossed the Channel to save our forces. According to her, every last man had been saved; but it was still a defeat. I knew this from the fact that my father simply looked sad instead of gnawing his moustache as he did to denote an excess of pride and emotion. He perked up considerably as war in the air was successful, and took to digging the garden with renewed vigour. We had potatoes, broad beans, carrots, even celery, which had to be 'earthed up' and 'blanched', which meant putting old buckets over it as it grew. But his pride and joy were his marrows, which he grew in a cold frame and fed with a thin strip of blanket, one end in water and the other laid beside the marrow, presumably to keep it moist.

I have no doubt whatsoever that my mother was a virgin when she married, and remained true to my father till her death, but she was susceptible to a handsome man. Sunderland suddenly seemed full of foreign troops. Poles, small and smart with maroon berets and sometimes gold teeth gleaming when they smiled; Czechs and Dutch and French and, after Pearl Harbor, Americans – although my mother declared US troops 'loud', and showed them no favour. Poles were different, for some reason. When there were Poles on the bus as we travelled into town, she would pretend not to notice them, but I knew they had made an impression by the way she hitched up her fox fur or straightened her hat. My mother always wore hats. They were as indispensable to her as the earrings she donned each day as soon as she was awake.

Each Sunday night, when the wireless played the national anthem of every Allied country, she stood to attention in the sitting-room out of respect for each of the occupied countries. She had always stood for the British anthem; now she accorded the same respect to our Allies. As one country after another fell to the German onslaught, I was glad we could take in their refugees, but I did occasionally wonder whether our island would sink under the weight of so many newcomers.

As the war progressed, I became aware of a new worry. Since Joyce's brush with death and M & B 693 she had never worked. Now, though, the Government was calling up unmarried women and sending them to work in the armed services or in munitions factories. To lose their child to war would be anathema to my parents, therefore a registered occupation had to be found. If you worked in one of these you were exempt from call-up. With a fair amount of string-pulling, such a job was found. Joyce would work as a clerk at the newly built Emergency Hospital for wounded soldiers in the grounds of Cherry Knowle, the local asylum. Amazingly, after so long away from school and nine-to-five working, she took to it, amid great relief all round.

It was at about this time that *Gone With The Wind* came to the Regent Cinema. Films did not open simultaneously around the country then, as they do now. There were fewer copies, and towns and cities far from London had to wait their turn. Our turn came, and my mother went, alone as usual, as Daddy was putting Granny to bed. She came back, eyes shining. This was the greatest love story ever told, she announced; better even than Greta Garbo's Marguerite dying of consumption. I must see it.

The snag was that there wasn't enough money for two more tickets. At the next matinée, she stood outside the cinema, clutching me by the hand, until she saw a woman in a hat, a sure sign of respectability. She asked the woman if she would take me in with her, and, a little bemused, the woman accepted my ticket money and agreed. I sat through a bewildering feast of colour and sound and passion, comprehending hardly a word and wishing it would soon be over. It lasted three hours or more. My mother was waiting when we came out. It was a winter evening, and her hand clutched her coat together at the neck. 'There now,' she said, 'wasn't it wonderful?' It hadn't been wonderful at all, but I knew it was desperately important to her that it should have been. 'It was marvellous,' I said firmly. 'The best film ever, Mammy.' We walked home together under a starry winter sky, me wrapped in incomprehension, she in a blissful fug of Civil War love and lust, happy as two people could be.

And then came Pearl Harbor and the entry of America into the war. This, I gathered, was a great event, something that would shorten the war and flatten Hitler and Mussolini. It didn't stop air raids or shortages, but the Yanks arrived to brighten our lives. They occupied a field not far from our house, and dispensed candy bars over the wall to any passing child.

Nothing, I gathered, created friendship quite like a Hershey bar, unless it was the mysterious 'nylons' that Joyce and her friend talked about non-stop. I knew stockings were in short supply, for Joyce and her friends now used streaky leg tan and drew seams up the back of their calves with eyebrow pencils. My mother obtained the occasional pair of silk stockings because the stocking-buyer at the town's department store was a friend from church. These stockings came in boxes and were wrapped in tissue paper from which they emerged, twin tubes of tan. Nylons, according to Joyce, were thinner than cellophane and utterly, utterly gorgeous. Some girls, she told me, hung around Americans just to get a pair; and certainly girls were congregated around the camp whenever we passed on the bus. Whether or not nylons were the attraction, there was something going on.

Everyone talked as though the whole nation was behaving well, but spivs abounded, and there was looting, too. One night Binn's department stores, which stood either side of the main street, were bombed. The resultant blaze could be seen for miles, and my father watched in awe as soon as the All Clear sounded. It was a mile from our house, but we could see it clearly. Joyce declined to get out of bed, much to Daddy's disgust. 'The fire of a lifetime,' he declared, 'and that girl won't get out of her bed.' The following morning a trail of abandoned loot stretched all the way out of town. People had taken whatever they could find, and dropped it when their arms tired. We found a huge cardboard wheel of furnishing braid in our garden. To me, this was all exciting, but my father was disgusted, so I decided to be disapproving too.

This failure on Joyce's part to get out of bed was a regular occurrence. She hated getting up in the mornings, and Daddy would get rattier and rattier as she ignored his calls. He would cry, 'Have you left work?' but sarcasm was wasted on her. Eventually she found the perfect way of getting an extra five minutes. 'I'm saying my prayers,' she would call out, and my mother would decree that she must be left to her devotions. Then Joyce would turn over for a blissful snooze that had nothing prayerful about it.

It was about this time that the row over the black coat began. As many of her friends went into uniform, they seemed suddenly more grown up. She felt this, too, and decided she wanted a black coat. 'No,' said my parents in unison. Girls of her age – 'nice' girls – didn't wear black. Joyce persisted, and eventually got her way. Black wool with an astrakhan collar: she felt the height of fashion.

Air raids intensified in 1943. There were also landmines, large bombs that apparently floated down in parachutes and did even more damage than ordinary bombs. It was a landmine that fell on Granny's house, or rather in the next street. She was in her Morrison shelter, and they pulled her from the ruins of her home, a morass of mangled pictures and broken china. She was allotted a commandeered house in Cuba Street, half a mile away; the remains of her possessions were put on a lorry, and then she was hauled into the cab. She exited her home like Boadicea, riding a chariot which, though petrol-driven, was no less formidable. Not even Hitler, I thought, could down my Gran.

Five months later, however, she was moved to our house, and died there. 'Never knew a heart like it. She'd've lived forever if it hadn't been for Hitler,' the doctor decreed. I was given her watch, and the little kidney table that had held her night-time rum ration. The rest of the salvaged furniture went to Joyce, for she had fallen in love and that, to my mother's daughter, could mean only one thing. Marriage!

3
CHAPTER

VICTORY

The tide of the war began to turn with the Germans' humiliating defeat at Stalingrad in January 1943. Ironically, that was the year when Sunderland suffered its worst air raids. I have a vivid memory of passing the beautiful St George's Square, its Georgian houses razed to the ground. A child's rag book was trapped in the rubble and fluttering in the breeze. I recreated that scene in the second volume of *The Beloved People* and it is still imprinted on my mind.

Looking back, I realise that I was never afraid. Half of me knew that a child had died there, but it didn't occur to me that I might die, too. And I had unwavering belief in victory. Only once had news of a further German advance worried me enough to ask my father if all would be well. He turned and reached for a black book, H. G. Wells's *A Short History of the World*. 'When you're old enough to read this, you'll see that right always triumphs in the end.' I have that book still, and it comforts me because I know my father's theory to be true. It's just that sometimes an awful lot of people have to suffer before the just end.

In April of that year, Churchill announced that church bells, kept silent until now so they could be used to warn of invasion, could be rung again. My mother's jubilation knew no bounds. Our church didn't have bells, but she travelled far and wide hoping to catch a peal from a church that did. But June brought the terrible news that Leslie Howard, her favourite film star, who had played the weak but irresistible Ashley in *Gone With The Wind*, had been shot down in the Bay of Biscay on his way home from persuading Spain, a neutral country, to show British war films. We mourned him as a family member, even though none of us shared Mammy's warm feelings.

By the time the Italians surrendered in September, our interest in the war had given way to a fever of preparations for Joyce's wedding to Douglas Davidson, a farmer's son working with the War Agricultural Committee. My mother rued the fact that he had red hair, but otherwise he was considered most acceptable. They would marry in our church, St George's, in December, and I would be one of the bridesmaids. As this meant a rare new dress, I was overjoyed; and, if I'm honest, I was a little bit excited at the thought of getting rid of Joyce. I loved her, but she was too far ahead of me for there to be a real rapport between us. With her gone, I might become queen of the heap.

In between bouts of wedding fever, Joyce and my mother were gripped by Miniver mania. Greer Garson, star of the film *Mrs Miniver*, was English. Furthermore, I was told, *Mrs Miniver* was going to win the war because, when the Americans saw how brave we were being, Lend Lease would increase and the war would be over double-quick. Even at my tender age, I doubted that one film could overcome the might of the Axis powers, but I nodded enthusiastically. When it came out that Greer Garson was having an affair with Richard Ney, who played her son in the film, there was more nodding. Who could resist Mrs Miniver?

The run-up to the wedding was unbelievably exciting for me. The bell seemed to ring every five minutes as one neighbour after another knocked to offer a clothing coupon towards the trousseau, or sugar or eggs for the cake. The trousseau was to include cami-knickers made from parachute silk, which would have butterflies embroidered on them. I was to have a blue dress of the same material as the bride's dress, and Joyce's two friends, Jean and Elaine, would wear tan.

The week before the wedding, Jean went down with diphtheria. She was whisked into hospital, and we all sat around waiting to see whether anyone else was infected. Mercifully we were all clear, and the wedding, slightly unbalanced by the loss of a tan bridesmaid, went ahead.

But there was no feeling of elation, no sensation of getting rid. Suddenly and sharply I wanted Joyce to stay, to be there in the bedroom next to mine, there if Mammy and Daddy had a row over money. As a small child, I had climbed into her bed and been told it would 'all be all right in the morning', and it always had been. I hadn't needed to make that moonlit trip across the cold lino for years, but it had still been a comfort to know she was there. And now she wouldn't be, and I felt bereft.

The wedding, financed by Daddy's inheritance from Granny, was a great success, and my new permed curls a focus of admiration. Which made it almost worth the torture of having been wired up to the Eugene machine in Connie Love's hairdressing salon.

Once the wedding was over and Joyce had gone to live in Granny's now repaired house, the progress of the war returned to centre stage. And there was the furore over Bevin boys, the young men of military age whom Ernie Bevin, the Minister for Labour, was forcing down the pit to produce more coal for the war effort. Personally, I thought it would be safer to go down a mine than brave U-boats on the sea or Heinkels in the air. As for fighting in Burma or Italy, hewing coal had to be easier than dodging bullets. But the young men chosen by ballot to be miners were, for the most part, less than grateful. I knew that I lived in the Durham coalfield, and that men were toiling somewhere beneath my feet, but all that seemed a million miles away from our suburban street. I could not have known then how great an impact mining and miners would have on my life.

The war was going well. At times Daddy's moustache was almost chewed off in an ecstasy of pleasure. Night after night, RAF bombers were attacking Germany's strategically important cities; the whole of Sicily was in Allied hands; and Italy had not only surrendered but declared war on her former ally, Germany. Which was the cause of much hilarity because, as someone put it, the Eyeties couldn't knock the skin off a rice pudding.

We had a new hero, too: a Texas-born West Point graduate called Dwight D. Eisenhower, who was to be Supreme Commander of Allied Forces with Air Chief Marshal Arthur Tedder and General Montgomery as deputies. My father and I discussed these details solemnly. My mother played martial songs on the piano or sometimes 'Lili Marlene', which was a German song about a soldier's love for his sweetheart. Germans, my mother said, were not bad people, just easily led. Once Hitler was gone, they would all behave nicely again. This last caused my father's eyes to roll skywards and sent him out to the garden to attack his leek beds.

At night we clustered round the wireless to hear the familiar tones of Alvar Liddell: 'Tonight RAF planes attacked the marshalling yards at Hamburg.' Or Bremen or Stuttgart. I never wondered what marshalling yards were: that RAF bombers were at work was what mattered. Forty years later, on my way to London by train late at night, I looked from the train window and saw railway lines running parallel to the track I was on, dozens of them, some empty, others with trains on them, waiting to be sent to other places. And suddenly I knew what marshalling yards were.

The wireless did not always broadcast war news. There was *ITMA* … Ivy the char, 'Can I do you now, sir?', and Funf, the spoof German spy. My father loved Funf and would lapse into Funf-speak, causing my mother to get flirtatious and call him her little Führer. There was a lightening of the atmosphere all round – until you heard that a boy from the next street had died at Monte Cassino or in Burma.

In early 1944, Welsh miners came out on strike. It seemed disloyal of miners to strike in the middle of hostilities, but my father told me that miners had been shabbily treated before the war. 'They're beginning to recognise their strength,' he said. 'They shouldn't strike when there's a war on, but this may be their only chance to get a hearing.' If he didn't totally disapprove of their strike action, then neither did I. My father was the best and wisest man in the world, as far as I was concerned.

And then suddenly it was D-Day. 'Allied naval forces, supported by strong air forces, began landing Allied armies this morning on the northern coast of France.' The announcement was delivered as calmly as though it were the weather forecast, but its effect was electric. Throughout the day we were glued to the wireless, appreciating the drama of it and yet fearful for the men we knew, children of neighbours and friends, who might even now be wading ashore with bullets whizzing past their ears. I kept reminding myself of the black-bound H. G. Wells in the bookcase. 'Right always triumphs,' Daddy had said.

My mother prayed a lot. She had taken to lighting candles on the mantelpiece at times of stress, an action that irritated my father no end, as candle wax dribbled down his special brass candlesticks. He was inordinately fond of the mantelpiece, which held two of his mother's vases that had survived the bombing. They had to be at the absolutely right angle, both patterns aligned, and not a millimetre out of place. This caused problems as he, Mammy and Joyce, all smokers, were constantly combing the mantelpiece for forgotten fag ends when cigarettes were in short supply. Once found, all three would lay claim to the stub and words would ensue. But my father never said anything about the candle-burning, and Mammy wouldn't have been deterred if he had. She prayed for the Allied forces and occasionally for the Germans, who would be beaten into the ground before long. Later that month, when the Germans began to lob flying bombs at London and the south coast, she prayed for St Paul's Cathedral, a place she revered.

Only now was I appreciating the intensity of my mother's religion. She might have escaped a Catholic upbringing, but she resembled the most fervent Catholic in her belief in God. Prayer, she believed, could achieve anything. Child though I was, I couldn't help noting that prayer hadn't stopped us losing our fortune and having to live hand-to-mouth. I didn't despise prayer but I had more faith in honest toil, and in keeping your eyes peeled for opportunity.

If my mother was religious and morally upright, she was never narrow or mean-spirited. Unlike my father, she forgave easily, and could be surprisingly tolerant at times. A scandal erupted in the

neighbourhood when a very elderly man married his young
housekeeper and promptly produced two sons. Disapproval ran
rampant, and the other women ostracised what they saw as a
fortune-hunter, but my mother went out of her way to offer
friendship to the woman, who had a hunted look. One day we
passed their garden and saw the four of them as a family, laughing
in the sunshine. 'See,' my mother said, 'they love each other.' I
couldn't understand what all the fuss was about, or why the other
women disapproved, but I was proud of my mother for sticking up
for anyone who was being shunned.

After D-Day the tide of success rolled on. Paris was liberated,
then Brussels, but the Germans still held Warsaw. The Poles in
Warsaw rose up and tried to take back their city, but were defeated
by lack of supplies and ammunition, something my father blamed
on the Russians who were, according to him, 'too tricky by half'.
This confused me. For as long as I could remember the Russians had
been Allies and could do no wrong. What had changed?

Just before Christmas that year, Glenn Miller was lost in a plane over
the Channel. His music had dominated the airwaves for the whole
duration of the war. 'Moonlight Serenade', 'In the Mood',
'Chattanooga Choo Choo' – my mother played them all with tears
in her eyes, and told me he would never be forgotten because his
music would live on forever.

I was more interested in the fact that we now had street lights
again, muted admittedly but still welcome. It would be almost
another year before lights were restored in full, but to have street
lights and lights in tramcars once again was a sign of better times
ahead. No more stumbling around in the dark with a torch whose
beam had been cut to a pinpoint by glued-on brown paper.

We had a gardener now, Mr Blackett, who was barely any taller than me but wielded a mean spade. When I look back with adult eyes at the way we employed staff on an income of almost nil, I can't believe it, but I know it happened. One day he came running down the garden yelling at the top of his voice. 'In-send-ee-airy. An insend-ee-airy!' It was indeed an incendiary bomb, presumably one that had fallen that snowy night in 1943. It was dark-grey and tubular, and seemed to be made of granite. One end was broken off and the other was a metal fin. My father was greatly taken with it. He made a wooden stand to hold it, and it stood on the piano for several years until a visiting policeman informed us that it was live, and it had to be taken away in a van.

It was now the spring of '45, and thoughts were turning to peacetime. In spite of the V1s and the even more destructive V2s that had followed them, we now knew we would win. It was only a matter of time. A plan for the rebuilding and future of London had been published, and the Government had revealed plans to build between three and four million houses to specifications that made my mother's eyes widen. 'Constant hot water!' she repeated over and over, as though she could hardly believe it.

Around this time, Grandpa Cahill died in the hospital from which he had never emerged, which resuscitated the drama of the smuggled will. According to my mother, Aunt Eve had coerced their father into signing a will that disinherited my mother and left everything to Eve. The will had been drawn up and witnessed by Aunt Phyllis Lawson, my mother's cousin and Aunty Eve's friend, who was Sunderland's first woman solicitor. The name Lawson came from the Swedish Larsen, a sea-captain who had fallen in love with a Sunderland girl, and from whom we were descended. So Aunt Phyllis was 'family', and the betrayal therefore more hurtful.

Was Aunty Eve right to do what she did? I don't know. She said she did it to protect Aunt Sue, but I think her animosity towards my mother played a large part in it. She resented my mother's happy marriage, and was fond of telling me how much more fortunate she herself was to have 'friends'. My mother, she implied, might have a husband, but this wasn't nearly as good as 'friends'. My father, she suggested, was not half the catch my mother had believed him to be.

To counter this, I had the vision of my parents wrapped in each other's arms. I also had my mother's injunctions to be kind to Aunty Eve because she didn't have a husband, and was therefore much to be pitied. No wonder I grew up somewhat confused! But I knew Aunty Eve enjoyed running down my parents, and with the fierce loyalty of children I resented it.

There was a period of hostility after the will incident, but it lasted no more than six months or so, and then my mother decreed that Aunty Eve had been driven to do what she did because she was alone and scared of the future. Anything less scared than my Aunt would have been hard to find; but it was a relief when the breach was healed.

The drama of the last days of the German Reich unfolded, and although I felt satisfaction at their downfall, I also felt a degree of pity for them – until details of the death camps began to emerge. There had been whispers, but nothing to prepare us for the truth. I sat in the cinema watching newsreels of British soldiers, masks across nose and mouth, using bulldozers to shovel up bodies in Buchenwald and Belsen and Auschwitz, and read details of torture, of human beings killed because warders wanted their tattooed skin for lamp shades, of shrunken heads, and children used as medical guinea pigs and operated on without anaesthetic. Above all there was the emaciation: people starved until only their eyes remained alive in shrunken faces. It was a sharp growing-up. Never again would my world be quite the place of love and trust it once had been.

And there was a fresh reason for mourning. Franklin Roosevelt, a hero of my father, died on the eve of victory. My mother immediately lit the candles and prayed, and then we walked up to the nearby American camp and told the subdued and half-tearful GIs at the gate how much we sympathised. But the shock of Roosevelt's death was as nothing compared to the shock result of the July 1945 general election. Churchill, who had almost single-handedly, or so it seemed, brought us to victory, was out, and quiet, moustached Clement Attlee was in.

Over and over, my parents discussed how it could have happened, and rumours abounded. My mother blamed Labour for dirty tricks, especially the *Mirror* newspaper which had suggested that Churchill would lead us into a further war. My father was more thoughtful, and seemed to believe that people had voted for a new way of life. Once, when my mother was pining for 'the good old days', he had answered 'Good for some.'

When I questioned him about that remark, he said that before the war life had been unfair for some people, and started to tell me of a ship-owner who had kept his mistress in splendour while his workers were paid a pittance. I was struggling to understand what a 'mistress' meant. I knew it was a *significant* word from my mother's sharp intake of breath, but she then put an end to the conversation by using his proper name. 'Now, Herbert, that's enough of that.' Another unexplained mystery. My life seemed to be full of them.

The following month the atom bomb vaporised Hiroshima. I listened as the radio told of birds shrivelling in the air, and the giant mushroom-cloud seemed to be pictured everywhere. There was no satisfaction in this new development. Instead there was a feeling of awe, and also fear of what had been unleashed upon the world. 'The Japs will never surrender,' my father said. 'They'd rather die.' Three days later, a second bomb on Nagasaki brought Japan to its knees. Old rules of chivalry and honour vanished in the mushroom cloud, and the Emperor surrendered unconditionally. Mr Attlee broadcast at midnight: 'The last of our enemies is laid low.'

My father woke me up to hear this moment of history, and my mother said a prayer for all the prisoners of the Japanese, for there were very real fears that Japanese soldiers might decide to kill their prisoners and commit *hara-kiri* themselves. The King spoke on the radio the following day, my mother holding her breath when he halted on the words, but he made it to the end, due no doubt to some splendid hand-holding by the Queen.

Two days of public holidays followed, with bonfires on every bomb-site or piece of waste ground. That first night, after a huge family debate, I was allowed out with a neighbour's daughter to see the celebrations, but I was told not to go further than the surrounding streets. Instead we took a tramcar to the town centre, which was packed with men and women in uniform, drinking, dancing, and embracing passing strangers.

After a while we drifted away from the main street, and I saw a soldier, his arms around a young girl, his head bent to hers. They moved away against the background of a flickering bonfire, and into a shop doorway. 'Come away,' my companion said. 'They're doing something rude.' It didn't look rude to me. To me, those two entwined figures represented the joy of peace. I turned away and caught the tram home, tired, but content that a whole new and wonderful world was awaiting me.

4
CHAPTER

PEACE

B IT BY BIT the trappings of war were dismantled. Air-raid shelters vanished from gardens or were converted to other use. Army camps, which had been dotted here and there, were scaled down or simply vanished. The blue uniforms of wounded soldiers were seen more often than khaki; and, on a great day, the barbed-wire barricades were rolled away and the beach was re-opened. I had expected a re-opening on VE Day, but it had taken much longer than that. There were rumours that land-mines had been hidden in the sand to deter invading Germans. Whether or not this was true I never discovered, but the moment when we could cross Corporation Road, walk down Spelterworks Road where Peggy lived, and then descend to the shore was a moment for jubilation.

The boys were fascinated with the trappings of war there – cement blocks and gun-emplacements still grim reminders. There was also a lot of litter, the detritus of military occupation; and, when we at last reached the sea, the shore line was not the glorious gold expanse of memory. There was the familiar black edge of coal dust that rimmed the seaboard of the Durham coalfield, but the water was cloudy, probably with effluent from the paper mill.

In spite of this, I was determined to assert our new freedom. I cast off my shoes and socks and waded in. Scum stuck to my legs but I didn't care, not even when I stumbled on a rock and gashed my ankle. A week later the gash was a suppurating sore, which was cured after weeks by some magic powder a friend of Aunt Eve brought from the hospital where she worked. It was, I was told, incredibly rare and precious, and had been invented to save the lives of soldiers wounded in the war. Its name was penicillin.

My father was enthusiastically restoring the garden to flowers – far too soon, as it turned out, for food would be in shorter and shorter supply as we struggled to feed the newly freed countries of Europe. Queues at food shops grew even longer. Each Saturday I stood in line at Firth's cake shop in the hope of getting a cake, and often the cakes ran out before the queue did.

One day news of a banana shipment to Chalk's the fruiterers ran through Grangetown like wildfire. I couldn't remember real bananas. The only bananas I knew were the small, dark-brown dried sort which sometimes came in food parcels from abroad. I was up at the crack of dawn, but still only made the middle of the queue. Would the bananas last until I reached the counter? My mother had told me I could eat one on the way home as a reward for my aching legs. I received our quota with trembling hands, and peeled one as I walked away. What a disappointment! It was bland and mushy, nothing like the exotic sweetmeat my mother had promised it would be. To this day I can take bananas or leave them alone.

There then occurred what I, a dedicated Sherlock Holmes fan, came to call The Case of the Russian Painter. My mother was a sucker for people who came to the door peddling their wares. When a tall, handsome, if emaciated, man appeared, wearing the red tie of a wounded soldier, she fell instantly under his spell. He was, he told her over tea and the last of our biscuit ration, a White Russian who had fled Communism only to be wounded defending Britain against Fascism. Once he had been a landscape painter of renown; now he was reduced to house-painting to keep body and soul together. Did we need any decorating done?

When my father came home that night, my mother persuaded him that we needed three rooms stippling. Stippling, the Russian painter had assured her, was the acme of interior decoration as practised in all the courts of Imperial Russia. My mother told my father that stippled walls were the one thing missing from her life. No matter where the money came from, we must support a war hero. Daddy spoke briefly with the Russian painter, and the deal was done.

The following day he arrived with two buckets of distemper, one yellow, one orange. First he painted the living-room yellow, and then went upstairs to do one bedroom orange, the other yellow. All the while my mother plied him with black-pudding sandwiches, tea, and the Chinese figs my father had kept locked in his bureau in case of famine. In between these feeding exercises, she played the piano, songs with an international flavour. Her Russian repertoire was scant, but the Russian painter professed himself keen on Paul Robeson, so 'Aye-ee-o-ko' from *Sanders of the River* figured prominently.

When the last bedroom was distempered, the stippling began. He soaked a large sponge in the orange paint and then threw it against the yellow walls of the living-room. It made a huge, pineapple-shaped orange mark on the yellow wall. He went on throwing until all four walls were covered in pineapples, resembling a Martian attack – for the stipples seemed to be flying straight at you.

My mother's piano-playing grew more subdued, and she ventured to suggest that perhaps one stippled room would do. But he had contracted for three, and three we were going to get. Upstairs he did orange on yellow and yellow on orange, producing the same air-bombardment effect. When he had finished, he relieved my mother of what seemed like a large wad of notes, wolfed the last of the black pudding, kissed my mother's hand, and departed. He would, he promised, remember us long after he had returned to his homeland and freed Russia from oppression.

My father came home to find my mother weeping in the kitchen, unable to stand being in the living-room a moment longer. He chewed his moustache for a while, and then set about distempering the living-room a fetching shade of green. Half-way through he asked for refreshment, and when he heard the painter had had the last of the black pudding he said something rude about Brummies. My mother said, 'Surely not!' My father said he knew a Birmingham accent when he heard one, and the nearest that painter had been to Russia was singing 'The Volga Boat Song' in the pub.

The green distemper almost obliterated the orange stipples, but they glowed through faintly for the next several years. In my bedroom they remained defiant for a long time, but after the first week or two of ducking as I entered I hardly noticed them at all

In Nuremberg, the Nazi leaders were being tried for war crimes. I believed passionately that William Joyce, Lord Haw-Haw, should not be executed. He had given his heart to Germany, which might make him a fool but didn't, in my book, make him a traitor. I didn't voice this view outside the home. Most people were baying for his blood, and I was having problems enough.

The lesser one was music lessons. My mother wanted me to play the piano and I was enrolled as a pupil of Miss Daisy Whittaker. I loved Miss Daisy, who was small and dark and was dressed from head to foot in black. So was her sister, another Miss Whittaker, who worked in the family fruit business and scared me witless. They were obviously still in mourning for their dead father, for their mother, whom I seldom saw, wore widow's weeds. Imagine my shock when, on the first day of spring, Miss Daisy changed into a white, flower-sprigged cotton dress. The black stockings and shoes remained, and looked odd, but the floral frock was a welcome change as far as I was concerned.

Miss Daisy took me through the scales and as far as 'The Bluebells of Scotland', and there I stuck. Why should I learn to play the piano badly when my mother played like a dream? Miss Daisy said I showed aptitude but no appreciation. I trudged to my lessons, Aunt Eve's old leather music-case banging against my legs, until the money for lessons dried up and I got a merciful release.

My other problem was bigger, and growing. I hated school. I had won a scholarship to the Church High School, thrilling my mother, who had put me in for it, as it was the school I would have gone to if Daddy hadn't lost his money. But sending me there, even on a scholarship, was expensive. The blue-and-grey uniform had taken the last of Granny's money, and the never-ending requests for extras were an increasing strain. I was also aware of my mother's unease at the fact that we lived in a council house with one living-room. 'Don't let them know where you live,' she told me; and when the parents of a class-mate insisted on giving me a lift home one day her eyes filled with tears at the thought.

I enjoyed the lessons and did well in everything but maths, but I was finding it increasingly difficult to go there each day. There were other strains at home, too. Joyce's first baby had been still-born, and she was inconsolable. She and my mother had drawn even closer, and, with hindsight, I think I was probably jealous and felt excluded.

At last I began to escape from school. I suppose it was truanting but it certainly bore no resemblance to joyful wrong-doing. I would slip out at the end of a lesson and make my way to the park. There I would sit and cry, or read a book, until it was time to go home and say what a wonderful day I'd had. I must have been severely stressed to behave like this, because I was always mortally afraid of being naughty. The High School's method of discipline was to put offenders 'on report'. Three 'reports' equalled one 'full report', and that meant trouble. What happened when you got a 'full report' I never found out, because in my three years as a pupil I received only one report – for talking in the cloakroom. For this I was sent to stand outside the Headmistress's door. Miss Horabin was quite formidable and went off eventually to be Head of Roedean. The system was that you had to stand there until the bell went, at which time you were free. If, however, Miss Horabin entered or left her room, you would receive a dressing-down.

I stood there, ears cocked for the sound of her footsteps or a door opening behind me, and I started to feel faint. Eventually she appeared, asked why I was there, and, when I told her, she told me quite kindly not to do it again. I should have felt relief, but instead I felt even fainter. It was the following day that I made my first escape. Was there a connection? I can't be sure.

Of course, my truanting came to light. My shocked parents listened to my tale of woe and decided a week off would be the answer. It was the worst thing they could have done. When I went back at the end of the week, I was worse. Going through the door felt like entering a tomb. Another pupil was recruited to shadow me, but by the third lesson her attention lapsed and I was off.

After another week or so, my mother took me to see our doctor – not our own kindly GP, but another who had a reputation for dealing with difficult cases. His suggestion was that I be given a good thrashing. My parents had enough sense to see that this would make things worse, and continued to take me to school, or give me 'days off to cheer up'. On one occasion they scraped together enough money for a treat: a trip to the Sunderland Empire. I sat in the stalls watching Noel Coward's *Bitter Sweet*, reflecting that the following morning I would be back in the tumbril – the bus to school – and on my way to the guillotine.

In all, I was away from school, or only half there, for nine months, attempting to educate myself with the aid of the Schools Programme on the radio. When the local authority began to get restive, my parents took fright. Joyce had worked for a young psychiatrist at the Emergency Hospital, and now he agreed to see me. My mother took me there, telling me on the way that this was another thing we would have to keep quiet about, because seeing a psychiatrist was something of a disgrace.

The psychiatrist was handsome and determined: he would see me alone, and would brook nothing else. We sat in his room and chatted. He sympathised, and encouraged me to talk about school and home and life in general. I saw him several times over a period of weeks. I never felt interrogated, nor that I was imposing on his time. I simply felt as though a burden was lifted from me each time we met. I don't know what he did, or whether or not it was a recognised psychiatric technique, but that it was effective there could be no doubt.

Eventually he laid his cards on the table. He had the power to free me from school forever. However, in his opinion I was clever. A return to school would allow me to exploit this intelligence and achieve things. He would suggest another school, a fresh start, but it would be up to me whether or not I took advantage of it. What I must do was realise that although I was still young it was my life, and my right to choose. I was to go home and think it over. He would implement the necessary arrangements, when I had decided.

A week later I told him I wanted to go back to school. He had shown me an open door, but had left me free to enter it or walk away. It was a technique I would later use for both myself and other people, to great effect. So I went back to school, but this time to Bede, the grammar school to which I would have gone when I passed the 11-plus if the High School scholarship had not intervened. I had lost a year's schooling, and I was almost a year younger than the other girls in my year. The headmistress, Miss Moul, suggested I drop back a year; but eventually I was allowed to take my place in the top stream.

Dior's New Look in the early post-war years fed the fantasies of women starved for too long of pretty clothes. In war-time skirts had to be short and straight to save material and precious coupons. Now skirts became fuller and longer, waists smaller, and heels higher. I was now dressed almost entirely in Joyce's hand-me-downs, and as there was a ten-year gap in age between us, they sometimes looked incongruous. I did have one new dress, pale-blue crepe with a dark-blue bow at the neck. Alas, it shrank when washed, and I spent a terrible night at a school dance trying to persuade it to cover my knees.

I suppose I should have learned dressmaking or saved up for outfits, but I had found something even more satisfying. Every spare moment and every spare penny was spent on trips to the cinema; and when I wasn't sitting in that dark cavern of delight I had my nose in a book. One day when I was in my bedroom, lost in some absorbing volume, my mother peeped in at the door. 'Oh dear,' she sighed, 'I wish you had friends like your sister.' But I did have friends – Kipling's Stalky, Scarlett O'Hara, Sherlock Holmes, and – shockingly – Amber St Clair in *Forever Amber*. This last, though supposed to be scandalous, was actually quite boring. Daringly, I entered it on my reading list, expecting fireworks, but my English mistress, the redoubtable Miss Waggott, never turned a hair – rather to my disappointment.

My trips to the pictures fed my desire for beautiful clothes. Technicolor Hollywood was at its height, and cinematic costumiers vied with one another to produce lavish creations. Denied the clothes themselves, I instead made lists of the clothes I would have one day, complete with accessories. I remember designing, on paper, a turquoise-blue linen sports dress, whose skirt would come off to reveal matching shorts. I had pink twin-sets with pearls, and grey pleated skirts, and, echoing Joyce again, a black bouclé coat with an astrakhan collar.

Shabby as I was, I was not short of boyfriends. I might not have been the best-dressed girl in the room, but if I got near enough to engage them in conversation I would get my man. Years later, on my first foray into television, I was teamed with an extremely beautiful woman who wore the most amazing clothes and jewellery. I didn't try to compete. I concentrated instead on making my mouth go, and it seemed to work.

And I now had a new diversion. Joyce had had a healthy baby girl, Catherine Barbara Gillian. I was in my element with a baby to fuss over. She meant the world to me then, and still does. She is closer to me and kinder than many a daughter.

It was the practice at Bede to take the compulsory maths or Latin a year in advance of O levels. I had six months to catch up, but I did it, and passed. I went on to get distinctions in history, English, biology, and religious knowledge, credits in French and art, and a pass in geography. I had always enjoyed exams and these were no exception. Besides they were the key to my ambition: to leave school and earn some money.

With successful results I looked forward to the world of work, but Miss Moul had other ideas. My mother was summoned and told that it would be a sin if I left now. I would undoubtedly get a place at university, and rise to great heights. It was up to my mother to make this happen. She came home and relayed this to me. 'We can manage it if you really want to go,' she said, and I knew she meant it. But I was adamant: I was getting a job, and that was that. She asked me once more to change my mind, but there was undoubtedly relief in her eyes when I refused. I revere university life and all it has to offer, but I have never regretted that decision. For me it was the right one – but no child should ever have to make such a decision on the basis of money alone.

On the day I walked through the school gates for the last time, I felt an overwhelming surge of relief. It was like coming out of prison.

Two weeks later, in the thick of job-hunting, I was not so sure. I was turned down by a jam-factory office because I was over-qualified, and by a drawing office because my handwriting was too untidy. My father's ambition was that I should work in a bank so I had several interviews in those, all of which I tried to fail. In spite of this I was offered a job, but when it was revealed that I would have to go away to a training school in the south my parents turned it down, much to my relief. Eventually I was taken on as a clerk at the

Royal Infirmary, to work in the Fracture Clinic. I intended to stay there just long enough to get a job I really wanted.

On the first day, I went to work in a brand-new tweed coat, flowing-skirted, double-breasted, and with a velvet collar. It felt as though all my birthdays had arrived at once.

5

CHAPTER

THE FIFTIES

THE 1950S WERE a strange decade. On one hand there was the looming menace of the Cold War and the uneasy feeling that Russia had spies everywhere. But there was a sense of gaiety, too, as one by one shortages disappeared. The plain white utility crockery of war-time was replaced by dazzling design and bizarre shapes. Nylon stockings, though still in short supply, became the finest present any woman between 17 and 70 could be given. The AA reported all-time record motoring at Bank Holiday weekends, as petrol rationing ended. We didn't have a car, but I had boyfriends with cars – most often belonging to their fathers, but tickets to adventure nevertheless. And we had a young Queen and a new Elizabethan Age.

I was thoroughly enjoying work. I had gone to the Infirmary as a stop-gap but increasingly I found myself absorbed in what I saw there. One day, when I had only been there for ten days or so, a sister told me to stand by a trolley while she found a doctor. I held the man's hand and tried to make sense of his murmurings. It was a while before I realised that his boot, on the end of the trolley, held his foot, amputated in a railway accident.

Another evening I was alone in the Fracture Clinic Waiting Room when an elderly man came in. There was a dead rabbit dangling from his pocket, and he held an empty milk bottle that he then smashed on the edge of the desk. Waving the jagged neck of the bottle, he told me he had come to 'get' the doctor who had seen him earlier. I looked around for help, but none was forthcoming, so I advanced from behind the desk and said, very firmly, 'Give that to me.' To my amazement he handed over the bottle without a word, just as Sister Smith came down the slope. Later she told me he had dementia, and came in regularly. His name was Henry, and he and I eventually became good friends.

I had been engaged as a clerk but soon I was promoted to medical secretary. It came about in a strange way. The Senior Consultant, David Brown, arrived in the office one evening as I was preparing to go home. I was the only clerk there and he looked disappointed when I told him this. He asked if I did shorthand. I didn't have any knowledge of shorthand whatsoever, but I said yes, relying on the fact that I could write fast. He asked if I would mind staying to help with something out of the ordinary. A patient with a rare spinal condition had died and his next of kin had given permission for some of his vertebrae to be removed and examined in the hope of helping others with the same complaint. He needed to do that now, and must have someone to take notes.

We sat in a darkened room off the theatre, a single huge light above us. I tried hard not to look at the mass of blood and bone as he dissected and explored. Instead I kept my eye fixed on the paper as the medical terminology flowed, all the while blessing the fact that biology had been my favourite subject. Back in the office, I transcribed squiggles and blurs of my writing, typing them out laboriously with one finger because I couldn't type either.

I must have done a reasonable job because before long I was set to work with a consultant surgeon, Charles Rob, in his daily clinics. He was an ex-Wing Commander and, in my eyes, a war-hero. He was shy, taciturn, irascible when roused, and one of the finest men I have ever known. At first he didn't want me there, preferring to write his own notes in his beautiful hand. So I would leave, and Sister Smith, the sister in charge of the clinics, would send me back, bow quivering under her chin in indignation. If I wrote the notes, his through-put of patients increased and she emptied her waiting-room faster. It was a battle of wills between senior nurse and doctor, and in those days sisters always won.

Eventually he tolerated my presence but gave me nothing to do. I boxed clever, anticipating his needs and presenting him with a knee-jerk hammer or an X-ray form before he could reach for them. Eventually, after much stone-walling on his part, we became a team and he regarded me as an ally. A bachelor, he had every intention of remaining so. On one occasion an attractive woman doctor came in at the end of his clinic to persuade him to come to her quarters where she had an excellent brandy. Her eyes flashed me a message: 'Get out.' I began to gather my papers, but when I tried to leave I found he had gripped the back of my white coat with his large hand and was anchoring me to my seat as he made his apologies. She never forgave me.

I was now making my first acquaintance with miners. All my life I had lived on top of the Durham coalfield. I knew vaguely that men toiled underground to get the coal we burned in our grate. Now I was seeing the real price of that coal. Every few minutes the doors of the Fracture Clinic would swing open and a miner would be admitted, occasionally dead on arrival. They were noble men, bearing their injuries with grace. They worked at pits often christened after the members of the coal-owning aristocracy – Dorothea, Lady Maureen, Londonderry D. There were men injured in the shipyards, too, but they came less often, and on the whole their injuries were less severe.

I enjoyed the men's cheerfulness, but my favourite days were Fridays, Children's Clinic. I soon found that I could stem tears with my Open Door policy. Many of the children had spent months, sometimes years as inpatients because TB of the bones was still rife and necessitated immobilisation on a frame. When they were brought back for follow-up checks they feared being kept in, and would cry in terror. 'All right,' I would say. 'You can go home now if you want to, but if you stay you can get examined, and then go home. It's up to you.' It always worked, but I then had to cross my fingers that X-rays wouldn't reveal that they'd suffered a relapse and would need to be re-admitted.

I loved the children, all of them. I remember them still: blond Yolande who wore a calliper; feisty Alexander who would use his crutch as a weapon if he had to; and a thousand others. Sometimes now, they come up to me in the street, middle-aged and with children of their own, and say, 'You used to dandle me on your knee.' Occasionally I would be overcome by some of the pain and difficulty they had to endure, but I learned to school my emotions after my boss pointed out that they already had enough to put up with without the added burden of my distress. In fact, she threatened to take me out of the clinic altogether, and the tears soon dried.

Occasionally, however, tears were useful. One little boy was suffering from a curable bone condition affecting his hip. He was in the process of being adopted by a loving couple, but one day the would-be-mother arrived at the office in tears. The adoption was to be stopped because he was considered less than perfect, and at that time the belief was that children with a disability should not be put up for adoption. She was howling with distress, and by the time I reached the Consultant's Office I was bawling like a baby, too. Mr Rob, the man of few words, looked up as I knocked and burst through the door. 'Before you ask,' he said, 'you can have anything you want.' He was joking, of course, but his letter to the adoption authorities was forthright and the adoption went ahead.

One baby who came to the clinic was in the Cottage Homes. He had bilateral talipes, which meant that both his feet turned inwards and had to be splinted in order to correct them. His name was Keith, and I fell in love with him. His mother had abandoned him, so he was in the care of the local authority. They were perfectly happy for me to take him out on Saturdays, and I brought him home and cared for him, parking the pram in the hall. My parents looked bemused but didn't argue, although this procedure went on for several years.

Eventually he was joined by another child, David, a beautiful baby whose mother was in a sanatorium. I pushed them home in a twin pram, accompanied sometimes by my best friend, Evelyn. I had a day of baby bliss, and pushed them back in the evening. Then Evelyn and I would go to the Seaburn Hall and dance to the famous bands that played there. Edmundo Ros, Harry Roy, Eric Delaney – these men were revered like the pop stars of today. A glittering ball spun round on the ceiling as we quick-stepped to Delaney or rumbaed to Ros.

Clothes were still a problem. We were desperately hard-up at home. Once you reach rock bottom, it is very hard to get back. My wage made a difference, but not much, and I could afford new clothes only occasionally. I decided to take up dressmaking, and acquired a sewing machine. The fabric buyer at Binn's, Sunderland's leading department store, would put material away for me until I could afford it, and I became a dab hand at using paper patterns.

My efforts were not always successful. One Saturday, the dress I was making was unfinished, but I had nothing else to wear. As the time to catch the bus to Seaburn Hall drew near, Evelyn helped me to sew on the buttons, which went from neck to hem. We didn't bother finishing off, simply taking the thread from one button to another. On the dance floor disaster struck. One button came loose and, as we whirled, the others followed one by one, until, clutching the dress together, I fled to the cloakroom for pins. It was not to be my last acquaintance with the cloakroom ladies and their pin-cushions.

The cloakroom had another attraction, perfume machines. You had a choice of various brands, but my favourite was the magic Christian Dior, he of the New Look. You put in sixpence, pressed a button, and got a squirt behind the ears or in your cleavage, depending on how far down you bent.

One thing I was careful about, though, was my feet. In the clinic I saw every form of foot deformity, and a lot of it could be put down to too-tight shoes. Stiletto heels were fashionable, and I loved them as much as the next girl, but I had no desire to wind up with ugly feet. I teetered on heels for special occasions, but whenever possible I went barefoot, and still do today.

Nowadays it is fashionable to regard the '50s as austere and dull, and to believe that real life began in the '60s. In fact, the '50s were a wonderful time to be young. When they began, the word teenager was unknown. When they ended, teenage culture ruled. Perhaps James Dean and Marlon Brando started it. If not they certainly embodied it, handsome, moody and disaffected. Britain had its teddy boys; coffee-bars dispensing the new frothy coffee sprang up on almost every corner; and skiffle became the music of the day. Every party came complete with washboard and tea-chest double bass, and it seemed that every boy owned a guitar. I say owned advisedly. They couldn't always play them.

Throughout the '50s, various boyfriends came and went in my life, even an engagement so unimportant that I can scarcely remember the name of the man whose ring I wore. In vain my mother chanted, 'Too many rings around Rosie, Rosie gets no ring at all.' I had a vague idea of what I wanted in a man, and sometimes, for a while, I would kid myself I had found it, but it never lasted.

And then a special man came into my life. Joyce had given birth to another stillborn baby when Gillian was four. Three years later she was pregnant again, and her obstetrician advised her to go into hospital for the rest of her pregnancy. The whole Orthopaedic and Fracture Department had moved from the Infirmary to a hospital on the Newcastle Road, which was near to where Joyce lived. While she awaited the birth, I raced round each lunch-time to feed Gillian and see her back to school. The incarceration worked. The baby, a boy, Paul, was delivered safe and sound, to much rejoicing.

But if there was a cause for rejoicing there was soon cause for hand-wringing. My mother had always been proud of her second cousin, my Aunt Phyllis Lawson. Six feet tall and silver-haired, she was Sunderland's first woman solicitor and a figure of some distinction in the town. Each day began with a visit to the hairdresser, a car trailing behind her. In the Lawson house hung the huge family painting on which the grandmother they shared was proudly pointed out to me.

Marie Lawson, Phyllis's aunt and my mother's cousin, was even more remarkable. She had trained as a solicitor, like her father, and then been barred from the profession because she was a woman. Furious at this she turned to engineering, became an expert, and was sent to America to oversee war-time Land Lease. She now lived in London, a millionairess, so Mammy said. While she had such family distinction to boast of, my mother felt in some part herself distinguished. Not even Aunt Phyllis helping Aunt Eve with the 'smuggled' will had made my mother waver.

So imagine her horror when the *Sunderland Echo* was emblazoned with the headline 'Woman solicitor accused of embezzlement'. It was true, and Phyllis went to jail, to my mother's chagrin and, I fear, my father's private amusement.

All this drama passed me by. I was besotted with the new baby. My every spare moment was spent with him and, thanks to the babies in the clinic, I was more adept at handling him than his mother, who was so amazed and delighted at his safe arrival that she seemed almost afraid to touch him. At weekends I took him in his pram and Gillian by the hand, and we walked down through Roker Park to the seafront.

Sunderland's coast line is second to none, its beaches a golden sweep. As I pushed the pram along the promenade, I dreamed of the day I would push my own child. Children. Six would be nice, I decided. It is a good thing we cannot see the future. If I had known all that lay ahead, I doubt I could have coped with it.

But at that time I was ready for romance. I wept for Princess Margaret when, pale and distraught, she decided not to marry Peter Townsend. I drooled over Grace Kelly's fairy-tale wedding to Prince Rainier; and, as always, I sat in the cinema and drank in screen romance. I cried so much over the original *Moulin Rouge*, the tale of the painter Toulouse-Lautrec and how he lost the love of his life, that I arrived home too distraught to get my key in the lock. My father answered my knock and immediately assumed I had been attacked, venturing out of the porch to see where the predator might be.

Each decade has its quota of events, but the '50s seemed more eventful than most. Churchill's resignation at eighty from the post of Prime Minister was the end of an era. Cast out at the end of the war, he had returned in triumph at the 1951 election. Henceforth he would be a mere back-bencher. Anthony Eden, my mother's idol, would take over and almost immediately fall from grace at Suez, all his bright promise fizzled out. In America, civil rights were still an issue, and I exulted in Rosa Parks's brave stand in keeping her seat on a bus when whites were supposed to take preference. There were race riots in London, and in other cities, too, towards the end of the decade, nipped in the bud by swingeing sentences.

But the most heart-wrenching event, for me, was the Hungarian uprising. For three days ordinary Hungarians fought Russian tanks and the hated Security Police. The voice of their premier, Imre Nagy, was broadcast by the BBC as he promised democracy. In Poland, young men and women took to the streets in support of the Hungarians, but both uprisings were doomed. It ended with a last, emotional broadcast by Nagy. 'Help Hungary . . . help . . . help . . .' And then silence. The Soviet Union used its iron fist, and the spark of freedom was snuffed out.

As refugees poured into Austria, a shop was opened in Sunderland to raise money by selling donated goods. It occupied the recently vacated premises of Meng's Café, the upmarket tea-rooms where you drank posh tea and listened to a musical trio. It had been a place beloved of my mother whenever the ship came in. Now that there were no more teas being served, what seemed like a thousand rats emerged from the basement at night, desperate for food. They swarmed over the second-hand goods and the 'Help Hungary' notices, providing a spectacle for people who stood, noses pressed against the shop window, unable to believe their eyes, and regretting every sandwich and pastry they had consumed in a Meng's that was now revealed to be rat-ridden.

By now I was earning a much better wage. Aunt Eve had an account with Parish's store in Newcastle, and, what's more, she got a hefty discount there. She decided she would allow me to get some clothes on her account, and I could pay her back in instalments. It was like being taken to an Aladdin's cave. I bought a camel coat, a navy suit, and, best of all, a pink corduroy coat with a hanging belt at the back. I thought I'd died and gone to heaven.

Until the following day. Aunt Eve phoned me at work and said she needed to see me urgently. I called on my way home, and met her, grim-faced. She had been talking to a friend who had suggested she was encouraging me to be extravagant. The clothes would have to go back to Parish's. From being humbly grateful I became defiant. Nothing was going back. I would pay as I promised. I kept my word but we never went to Parish's again.

Instead I opened an account at Books Fashions, the acme of style in Sunderland. It was sometimes a struggle to pay, but it was worth it. Soon it was Joyce who wanted to borrow my clothes, particularly a white coat with a fine charcoal stripe and a black velvet collar. Mammy told me hourly how much she coveted it, so in the end I gave it to her, knowing in my heart that it looked better on her slimmer figure than it did on mine.

I was going out now with a young doctor from the hospital, and he suggested we went to Edinburgh for the weekend. I had never been away from home before, and the entire family, Joyce included, waved me off from the front door. We went in his battered sports car. It was winter, but the sun shone as we motored over the border into Scotland. Edinburgh was a revelation. We walked up to Arthur's Seat, ate in a place called Wee Willie's, and studied the various clans in the tartan shop. I had borrowed my mother's fox fur, and felt the height of fashion with it slung round my neck.

But as we began the homeward journey, it began to snow. We got as far as Carter Bar, on the border, before the car got bogged down. We tried to push it out of the drift, slipping and sliding as we did so. Eventually we got going again, but as we got back into the car I felt a sudden discomfort around my chin. The wet fur had frozen. Each clump of hair was now a needle. As it thawed, the fur and I had one thing in common: we both looked like drowned rats.

My father's job had improved markedly with the advent of the Welfare State. He had moved to an office in town, and presided over a much more humane system; but he had been forced to retire when he reached 65. Immediately he went to work for a car firm, where he kept the books but worked long, long hours, sometimes till nine at night. Much to his chagrin, Aunt Phyllis had walked straight out of jail into a cushy job with the new towns corporation at Peterlee, thanks, no doubt, to her legal qualification. His bitterness was based on the fact that he had done his best all his life and, in his eyes, it had not paid off. Phyllis had broken the rules, and had not only survived but triumphed. It was hard to bear. In vain I pointed out that he had been the best father in the world. He felt a failure, and he hated the constant worry over money. But I had learned two valuable lessons from his example. The first was never to look back, and the second was not to let money, or the lack of it, spoil things.

I seldom went to the Seaburn Hall now. Bill Hayley had ushered in the era of rock and roll, and the big bands came less often, if at all. Besides, Joyce had acquired a television set, and I was fascinated by it. I went to the Seaburn Hall one night to please a friend, but I was bored. When a tall, very thin, blond man asked me to dance, I agreed because it seemed rude to say no. He was a lot older than me, and a merchant seaman.

We talked a little as we circled the floor, and his accent intrigued me. I was good with accents but this one I couldn't place. He told me he came from the Shetland Isles. He also asked for my phone number, and I gave him the hospital number. His ship was leaving port that night, he said, but he would be back. I smiled, and sought refuge in the cloakroom. I also forgot him.

I had a technique for dealing with men who rang me at work. Unless I wanted to see them again, I simply pretended to be someone else, sitting in for Denise who had been called away. I had a variety of voices I used, and if the caller rang again and again I would gently suggest that Denise wasn't really that nice, and they might do better elsewhere. This technique worked brilliantly, until the day one man agreed that, indeed, Denise wasn't that nice. 'You sound lovely,' he said. 'Would you like to see me tonight?' A hastily dreamed-up husband got me out of that scrape, but I became more cautious.

When Alex Robertson, the Merchant Navy man, rang, I accepted his invitation to go out for a meal, more out of curiosity than anything else. He carried himself very well, but he wasn't handsome. On the other hand, he was different. One evening could do no harm. He took me to Sunderland's new and first Chinese restaurant. I had never been there, and admired the way he negotiated the menu with ease. This was hardly surprising as he had been all over the world since he went to sea at fourteen, sleeping on a donkey's breakfast, a straw-filled bag you made up for yourself. He had worked and saved until he had enough money to pay his way through Marine School and obtain his Third Mate's certificate. After that, it had been back to sea until he could afford to sit the next exam, and so on.

Now he had a Master's Certificate, and was Second Mate on the *Netherlands Coast*, whose skipper, Eddy Fisher, was his hero. Eventually he would like to have his own ship. Till then, he said, he was happy where he was.

It was that happiness that attracted me. Alex did not try to impress. He spoke quietly, and seemed to like everyone he knew. It made a pleasant change from boys of my own age.

Each time his ship docked in Newcastle, we went out. I learned about his home in Shetland. His mother had died of cancer the year before, and he had taken six months off to nurse her. He had obviously adored her, and his sister, Annie, who had been unfailingly kind to him through his childhood. Our lives could not have been more different. I had seldom seen money in my home. His family kept their money in a bowl in the sideboard, the proceeds of sheep-rearing and his father's trips to sea. In Shetland, he told me, you either tilled the soil or became a seaman. He had done the latter because the soil did not appeal. 'Weren't you ever tempted to take money if it lay around like that?' I asked. 'No,' he said. 'I saw how hard they worked to make it.'

He was a voracious reader, and he loved music. I told him my favourite piece of music was Charles Trenet's 'La Mer'. The next time we met, he brought the record for me. I didn't tell him I didn't have a record-player. It was the thought that counted. Another time I admired some shoes in a shop window. The next day they were delivered to the hospital, one size too small (until I changed them). I was careful not to admire anything after that. I liked this man a lot, but I didn't want to get involved. Nice as he was, he wasn't the one.

The routine of meeting when his ship docked went on for four or five months, and then he rang me and said he particularly wanted to see me as he had something serious to tell me. 'He's going to propose,' I told my mother. She was less than overjoyed. She hadn't met him, but much as she wanted me to be married, she thought a man in his middle thirties was too old for me. I told her not to worry. I had my little speech of graceful non-acceptance all ready.

We dined in a posh restaurant in Newcastle with candles on the table, but he was obviously not enjoying his food. Eventually I decided to put Alex out of his misery. 'You said you had something important to say?' I prompted. Indeed he had! He didn't intend to see me again, because he was getting too fond of me. If this went on, he would want to marry me, and, as he had decided some time ago not to marry, he felt, in fairness to me, that we should end our friendship.

I tried not to smile because he was deadly serious. I told him it was fine. I valued him as a friend, but of course he was right. Neither of us wanted commitment. We parted at the end of the meal and went our separate ways.

6
CHAPTER

NEST-BUILDING

ALEX ROBERTSON AND I had made our farewells at the beginning of December. I had a good Christmas. Paul was three now, Gillian ten, and Christmas was built around them. I had a new boyfriend, too – not someone who made my heart flip, but what was different about that? And my work at the hospital was absorbing. I was no longer working for Charles Rob. I had been promoted, and was in charge of the department, but my heart was still in the clinic. I had loved watching patients being brought back from the edge, sometimes minus a limb or the use of it, but making their way, learning new skills, cracking jokes about their problems.

Not that every story had a happy ending. One day a young army officer was admitted after a motor-cycle accident. I saw him lying on a trolley, his face ashen behind quite an impressive moustache. I looked at the case notes, but they told only half the story. I learned from the military policeman who accompanied him that the soldier was based at a nearby military camp. Apparently he had been riding a new motor-cycle around inside the camp when a girl hanging around the gates had begged for a ride. Foolishly he agreed, they set off, and she was thrown from the pillion and killed. He escaped with minor injuries. A few days later a senior officer came to sign him out. 'What will happen to him?' I asked, and winced at the reply, hearing that he would be court-martialled and dismissed the service. 'He was promising, too,' the officer said. 'Would have gone far. And his wife has left him. Wouldn't even come up to see him. Pity.' I agreed. It was a terrible punishment for a moment's foolish showing off.

I had forgotten the soft-voiced Shetlander until he phoned me at work at the end of January. 'It's no good,' he said bluntly. 'I need to see you.' I wasn't much interested in his needs, but his cheek in coming back piqued me. I agreed to meet him for an early dinner – 'but I can't stay long. I'm going on somewhere else.'

We went to the Bamboo again, and, looking back, I can see that he played a very clever game. I was prickly, just looking for an opportunity to send him on his way. He didn't present me with one. So began a period of weeks in which we ate at the Bamboo as soon as I left the hospital, and then I went on to meet someone else. I enjoyed our conversations. Alex was older than the other men I'd known, more widely travelled and better read. There were three things to do on a ship other than going mad, he told me: drink, gamble or read. After seeing men come off a long voyage with all their pay owed in gambling debts, and a short spell during which he had tried the bottle, he opted for reading.

His tastes were wide-ranging, and he was interested in world events, a subject that almost obsessed me, as Castro swept to power in Cuba and protestors against desegregation had to be quelled with fire-hoses in Arkansas. I couldn't bear the thought that black children were being barred from state schools in defiance of a Federal order. The argument had rumbled on for two years or more, and it looked as though racism were winning. Alex sympathised with the way I felt. The other man in my life did not. Nor could we have a decent argument. His view was simple: they were they and we were we, and the twain would meet over his dead body.

One night as we circled a dance floor I had a sudden revelation. I didn't want to be here. I wanted to be back in the Bamboo, talking, laughing, feeling at ease. The dual dates were over from then on. I looked forward to Alex's phone calls telling me that he was on his way back to Newcastle, and the evenings at the Bamboo lengthened. I was in love, but not yet ready to admit it to someone who had gone off and left me once before.

He proposed in Philip's Fish Restaurant, a posh place in the heart of Newcastle. I turned him down. He repeated his proposal in the street as we left, and I walked away. I was on a traffic island in the middle of the street and he still on the pavement when he asked a third time. 'I can't get married,' I said. 'I'm not domesticated.' When Alex was angry or agitated his accent intensified and became the soft Shetland burr. 'It's a wife I want, not a housekeeper.' We both burst out laughing, and if the yes never got said it was certainly understood.

A week later we were engaged, the antique ring a sapphire surrounded by diamonds. That was nice, but the feeling of somehow coming home was infinitely more precious. For the first time in my life I had someone with whom I could be myself.

So began one of the happiest periods of my life. It was the era of big cinematic musicals. We went to see *Carousel* and *South Pacific* and *Call Me Madam*, among others and then a non-musical, *The Inn of the Sixth Happiness*. I watched Ingrid Bergman struggle to bring a hundred Chinese children over the mountains to safety, and cried my eyes out. He wasn't in the least embarrassed at having to steer me, swollen-eyed, from the cinema.

The *Netherlands Coast* ran to and from the Continent, usually returning to Newcastle. I would wait on the bridge and see its masthead light as it came up the river, and we could be together. He told me of other countries, other rivers. He loved the Rhine, where, at Christmas, every ship had a lighted Christmas tree at its masthead. He liked Germans, too, forgiving them for torpedoing and imprisoning him in the bowels of a German ship from which he was rescued by Norwegian dockers. He had friendships with German stevedores, which was incomprehensible to me even fifteen years after the war. With teeth gritted, I bought children's clothes at Marks & Spencer for him to give as gifts.

I admired his forgiving spirit but, as far as the Germans were concerned, I couldn't share it. I was convinced that the British and Americans were incapable of the collective cruelty the Germans had displayed, and nothing Alex could say would move me. I went on thinking that way until news came of the Mei Lei massacre, a Vietnamese village wiped out by ordinary GIs.

As an engagement present Alex bought me a car, a blue Ford Anglia. Now I had to learn to drive. My mother was very lukewarm about Alex, thinking him too old for me and not the son-in-law she had envisaged. Joyce loved him, and suggested that choosing him was the first sensible thing I'd done. My father was non-committal until the driving lessons began. I would return in tears each time, terrified of hill starts, unable to grasp the principle of three-point turns, reversing into confined spaces with my eyes shut and a prayer on my lips. The resultant stress caused more moustache-chewing and mutterings of 'that damn car' by my father. The driving débâcle was an omen, according to my mother. The union was doomed.

I persevered, but it was hard work. The first time I took my test a pram with a baby in it suddenly careered into my path. I made an impressive emergency stop, and the examiner retrieved the pram and restored it to its hysterical owner, but after that I was finished. I failed on over-caution. But I passed the second time and became, if not an enthusiastic driver, at least a safe one.

I suppose 'that damn car' was my father's way of saying, 'that damn man', but he was mollified when Alex asked him to help us choose a house. Daddy wanted me close to home, so he vetoed every house we looked at until we viewed a semi-detached in the next street to ours. 'Perfectly sound,' he decreed, and the deal was done. Everyone was happy except my nephew, Paul. I had lavished a lot of attention on him. Now the three-year-old sensed a rival. Alex arrived home one day with a present for me, a watch. I had never before owned a brand-new watch. The one I wore had been Granny's. I oohed and aahed over the gift, and when I turned my back it vanished. We found it in the lavatory bowl, where Paul was busily trying to flush it away.

We planned to be married in St George's, where I had been christened and gone to Sunday school. The wedding preparations were a blur of dress fittings, hymn- and menu-choosing, and the thousand other arrangements that must be made. I was to carry roses and stephanotis, and my mother demanded a bouquet twice the size of mine. It was, she reminded me, really the bride's mother's day. So she chose pink carnations to match the pink lace inset in her grey dress, and everyone was happy. I was realising now how much I loved my parents. The thought of leaving them was almost unbearable, until Alex pointed out that I would be in the next street and could go home whenever I chose. He had a way of calming my fears, and never, ever suggesting that I was being stupid or unreasonable.

I drove up to Aberdeen to collect Alex's father and his niece, Irene, from the Shetland boat. Irene was to be my bridesmaid, along with Gillian and two friends, Eileen Hart, whose family had come to us when they were bombed out, and Alma Erskine, who worked with me at the hospital. And there were presents from many Shetlanders, people whom I had never met but who wished us well. Best of all was a huge, fluffy eiderdown made by his sister Annie herself. It was a labour of love, and doubly precious for that.

We were giving the bridesmaids silver bracelets. I knew my mother admired them so we bought an extra one and I left it with my father to give her at bedtime on the wedding day, together with a note telling her just how much I loved her and always would. Our relationship was sometimes stormy, but I knew how much she loved me. Alex had helped me to understand that.

We honeymooned in Paris. I had hardly ever been away from home, apart from a few days in London and that weekend in Edinburgh. Now I was flying to a foreign country, to a hotel on the Rue Montmartre, almost in the shadow of the Sacré Coeur. I was overwhelmed with homesickness. The streets below the shuttered windows looked alien, the people uncaring and strange. 'I want to go home,' I said. It was eleven o'clock at night. 'All right,' Alex said. 'I'll fix it in the morning.' But in the morning the blossom was out on the trees along the springtime boulevards, the sun was shining, and my new white court shoes printed with roses drew admiring glances from the Parisian women. I decided I liked Paris after all.

Soon after we returned to England we went to Shetland to meet Annie, John her husband, and Donnie, Irene's brother. I liked Annie on sight, blond like her brother, with a face made rosy by exposure to wind and sun. I saw her toiling to cut peat, or tending her lambs, chickens running in and out of the kitchen. She shared with Alex a quality of serenity. She sat in the evening churning wonderful salty butter, or knitting in the way that Shetland women have, never looking down as the needles fly in and out of a dozen colours, weaving the Fair Isle for which they are famous. She made me brunnies, a cross between a biscuit and a scone, made with sour milk, and delicious; and at night we looked out on the voe below, a silver sliver of water cutting into the black land. There were no street lamps to dilute darkness, and it was the first time I had ever seen the earth as nature intended. When I was aghast at Irene's walking home alone in that dark, they all laughed me to scorn. Shetland was the safest place on earth.

Alex had lived with his father. Now it was agreed that his father would come to live with us. A former seafarer, he was keen to get back to the life he had once known, and Sunderland was a sea-port.

We came home to our house in Sunderland. It had three bedrooms and a garden filled with blossom, laburnum and rambler roses. French windows opened on to the lawn and a trellis that seemed permanently filled with songbirds. Hitherto I had never given a fig for decoration. The stippling still ornamented my bedroom wall at home, and it hadn't bothered me. Now I indulged in an orgy of colour charts, carpet samples and furniture catalogues. The front room was white with a pale green carpet my father said would last no more than six months. My bedroom had a royal-blue carpet, white walls and curtains, and a bedcover in white linen printed with anemones. I made the curtains myself on my battered sewing-machine, working like a slave until it was done. And, for the first time in my life, I had a television set and a radio. The house was complete.

When everything was finished, I looked around and realised I had nothing to do. I had given up work because it would have been foolish to be working when Alex came ashore. Now I was bored, and not even the television could console me. When he came home it was heaven, but after the first few hours I would be watching the clock, conscious of the minutes ticking away to the time he must leave again. One day this tension led to a row and I walked out. By the time I reached my parents' house I was crying. My father opened the door and I said, 'I've come home, Daddy.' He was firm. 'You haven't come home,' he said. 'Your home is with Alex.' I turned on my heel, feeling rejected. Now I realise how wise he was. I went home, and within minutes all was well.

I spent as much time as I could with Joyce or at home with my parents. Joyce was obsessed with Jacqueline Kennedy, the wife of America's new President. She admired her clothes, her looks, her soft voice. I thought Mrs Kennedy was OK, but JFK seemed to me to be hope for the future. Africa was in turmoil, the Cold War rumbled on, but when JFK spoke he had the Churchill effect. You could see the possibility of things coming right.

When Alex's father came to stay I was less lonely, but I desperately wanted to be pregnant. Each month when I realised I was not, it was a disappointment. After four or five months I visited the doctor, who laughed at my eagerness. 'Come back after a year, and if nothing has happened I'll worry too.'

At the end of the first year I was getting ready to seek advice about infertility when something happened that drove the idea of a baby out of my mind. It was five days after my wedding anniversary, and we'd all been at Joyce's house for the evening. Alex had gone back to sea the day before, and as I dropped my parents off my father, who had taken to cooking since he retired, promised to make me a cake the next day to cheer me up. I joked that he was spoiling me and kissed him goodnight.

The next morning a neighbour of my mother's knocked on my door: would I go home as soon as possible, as my father was ill? I knew from the man's anguished face that it was more than that. I found my father dead in his chair, his morning cup of tea beside him. He looked calm and peaceful, and I kissed his cold cheek. We had always been close, and the bottom had dropped out of my world. My mother was broken-hearted, but buoyed up by her faith, a faith I could not understand but marvelled at.

Alex came home on compassionate leave, and sustained me through the funeral. The next day my mother told me she was giving up her house and coming to live with me. When Alex was away, she reasoned, I needed company – that was why she was coming to me and not to Joyce. In fact, Joyce would not have agreed to her moving in and told me not to do it, but I could see no way out. Alex was agreeable. We had given his father a bed-sitting room upstairs. Now we emptied the new front room and installed my mother's furniture. 'There,' I said, when it was done, 'your own home.' I expected gratitude, I was met with the accusation that I was trying to shut her away. She never used her room and simply lived in ours.

I was glad that she was trying to make a life without Daddy, something I would once have thought impossible. It was the first time that I realised my mother was brave. My father had cherished her for forty years, but she had found the courage to stand alone.

Three months after my father's death, to my great surprise, I found I was pregnant. Thoughts of a baby had disappeared while I mourned. Now one was on the way, but at my first visit to the obstetrician he warned me it was not going to be an easy pregnancy. Hypertension, which had caused Joyce's two stillbirths, was possible. I must go on a strict salt-free diet, go to bed every afternoon, and avoid stress. I was so delighted to be pregnant I would have lived down a well if it meant a live baby. Mammy went into town each day to get me salt-free bread, I tried to sleep through the afternoons, and I counted the days until I would have a baby of my own.

One day we heard a commotion in the street. Someone had been knocked down by a passing car. I went out to see if there was anything I could do. The figure lying in the road was familiar to me – Henry, my friend from the Fracture Clinic, the man who had once threatened me with the broken bottle. I could see he had died instantly, and I tried to console the distraught driver. 'He just walked in front of me,' he said. I nodded and tried to explain. 'You couldn't help it,' I said. I don't think we used the term Alzheimer's then, but I tried to explain senile dementia. 'And he's at peace now.' It was true. He wore a half smile, as though all those things that had perplexed him had been swept away.

All was not well with Alex's father. He had been anxious to visit his old haunts and pursue the life he had known as a seaman, but what he had forgotten was that a lot of time had passed, and this time he had no shipmates to share his leisure. He would sit in his room talking to himself, or go out in search of somewhere to make friends. Eventually he went off his food. Alarmed, I took him to the doctor, who referred him to a geriatrician. She was firm with me, saying we had been very wrong to bring him away from Shetland. His only hope was to go back there. Neither Alex nor I wanted this, but eventually he did go back, and lived for several more years.

It was an icy winter, and I yearned for the summer. I could picture the pram in the garden among the blossom, snow-white nappies on the line. Annie sent me a traditional Shetland baby shawl, which had to be fine enough to be pulled through a wedding ring, and some delightful matinée jackets with pink and blue Fair Isle borders. The layette was complete.

The due date came; no baby. Two bottles of castor oil later, taken at the obstetrician's command, and I hadn't felt a pang. My mother suggested walking up a steep bank in the park. We toiled up, our feet crunching in the snow, and slid down. Toiled up again, slid down. We did this until we were both exhausted, but to no avail. The obstetrician shook his head. 'Can't leave it any longer. Come in tomorrow and we'll induce you.'

Alex was panicking, and ruing the fact that I was pregnant at all. He had never been as enthusiastic about a baby as I had been, but, as it was something I wanted, he had gone along with it. Now he had regrets. That night, as we got ready for bed, my waters broke with what felt like the twang of a snapping violin string. I went into labour in the taxi and stayed like that for twelve hours, until the baby's heart started to falter. 'It will have to be a Caesarean,' the doctor apologised. 'Just get on with it,' I said, and then they were wheeling me to theatre.

When I came round there was no baby in the crib next to the bed. Now it was my turn to panic. The staff nurse was tall and beautiful, but stern. 'You mustn't get upset. Your baby is fine, we're just keeping an eye on him.' Him! I had wanted a girl, had embroidered roses on the Viyella nighties. But, more important, why did they need to keep an eye on him? I began to cry, tears of weakness and terror, until she relented. 'You can see him for a moment, but that's all.' As she bent to put him into my arms, I noticed her name badge. 'Staff Nurse Thubron.' 'I used to know a boy called Thubron,' I said, remembering a tall, black-haired boy I had known in my teens. She smiled. 'Yes. I married him last year.'

The baby was breathtaking, so beautiful I could hardly believe it. Alex might have been lukewarm during my pregnancy, but now he was like a man inspired. It was, he told me, the most marvellous baby ever born. I was the cleverest woman in the world. As he left to rejoin his ship, happiness radiated from him. He would be away for ten days and then at home for two weeks. The next day I received a letter, posted before he sailed. It told me how much he loved me and how much he would love our son. 'I'm coming back to take care of you both,' he finished.

Ten days later, Joyce came to take me home. Alex would be back that night and she would stay with me until then. I felt shaky on my feet after spending most of two weeks in bed, but very capable of caring for the baby. We had no sooner hit the house than a row developed over the washer, and Joyce left. I was alone with my baby. I sat with the unpacked case at my feet wondering whether or not to cry – and then I remembered I was now a mother, and got on with it.

The next few weeks were heaven. By day we worshipped at the baby's feet. By night we looked at him asleep in his cot and pinched ourselves to make sure it was true. My mother was pleased with the baby, but she was not a hands-on grandmother. As for baby-sitting, I was not to count on her, she said, but occasionally would be OK. As I had no intention of ever leaving the baby's side, this was immaterial.

I have never understood the modern passion for giving birth by C-section. I spent the first few weeks worrying that I would split open, and envying those friends of mine who had leapt around like gazelles the day after delivery. But whatever the discomfort or the

Above: My parents, relaxed and happy in the balmy days before I was born.

Below: Big sister Joyce and myself as a baby.

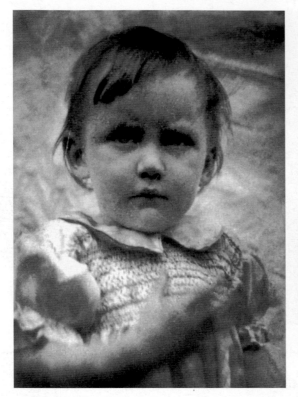

Above: I'm frowning even at two.

Above right: Proud of my new coat.

Right: The beauty of this picture of Joyce haunted me as a child.

Above: A sunny day by the river on a Bede school trip to Chester.

Below: Some of the staff of the Orthopaedic and Fracture Clinic. Don't we look a cheerful lot?.

Above: Polyphotos were all the rage at the time Bryan and I got engaged.

Right: Alex and I on a very, very happy day.

Below: Bryan at the time I first knew him. I thought he was gorgeous . . . I still do.

Above: Early days on This Morning with the Liver Birds in the background.

Left: I'd just heard my first TV play had won an award. No wonder I look happy.

Above: Broadcasting at Metro Radio was usually serious stuff but here I'm smiling.

Below: Jack and I with the boys on our wedding day.

unsightliness of the Caesarean scar, Mark Alexander, as we had decided to call him, was worth it. I carried him proudly to the hospital to show Charles Rob. As he peered into the blanketed bundle, the baby let out a yell. 'Ah,' he said cheerfully, "placid, just like his mother." Mr Rob and I would correspond until the end of his life. I could always pick out his letters because of his beautiful handwriting. One day, thirty or more years later, a letter came written in a different hand, on his behalf. A few weeks later I heard that he had died.

Alex was proving a dab hand at nappy-changing, winding and bottle-feeding. In fact, we almost fought over whose turn it was next. When the day came for him to return to sea, he was, for the first time, reluctant to go. I drove to a vantage point at the mouth of the Tyne and held the baby in my arms as his ship moved out to sea.

This became a ritual; but as the weeks passed and the baby became more responsive, Alex's unwillingness to leave us grew. Eventually I came to a decision. There was only one thing for it: he must come ashore.

My determination to make this happen was reinforced by one event. Alex had been at home for a few days, and I was to drive him back to his ship in the early hours of the morning. When we got up there had been a blizzard in the night. I got him to the ship in Middlesbrough, but he was terrified of what would happen on the drive home, especially as the baby was asleep in his carrycot on the back seat. It was a frightening return journey, with the car skidding off the road twice. Once a man in a van told me to abandon the car and come with him, but when he saw the baby he heaved me back on to the road; and eventually I reached home. That night the television announced that the road through Castle Eden had been closed all day. 'No, it wasn't,' I said aloud in the empty room. 'I got through.'

7
CHAPTER

COMING ASHORE

I HAD TO work hard to convince Alex that we could survive if he came ashore. All he had ever known was the sea. He was a navigating officer, not an engineer. Sea-going engineers can work in any engineering environment; but a knowledge of how to steer ships equips you for little else. I decided the answer was a post office. I would run the post-office side, Alex the general dealer's. Reluctantly, Alex agreed to my making tentative enquiries. We went from one corner shop to another, and his face grew whiter with each viewing. The snag was that, although you bought the shop and post office as a going concern, there was no guarantee that the GPO would transfer the licence to you. You were buying a pig in a poke.

I then thought of a boarding house by the sea. I was as far as thinking blue and pink bedrooms when Alex, the Shetland accent becoming thicker by the moment, put his foot down. He was not taking on a post office or boarding house, and that was the end of it. I was working out how to get round him when I saw the advert: 'Assistant Harbour Master wanted for small, north-east tidal harbour.' Here was a job he could do well, and it was at Seaham, only five miles up the coast.

Alex came back from the interview shaking his head. The job was his, but he couldn't take it. The wage was some £13 a week, less than I presently received from him for housekeeping. There was no way we could live on it. My reply was firm: not only could we live on it, we could thrive on it. As long as we were together, we could manage anything. Well, almost anything.

Alex had never learned to drive because he was almost always at sea. If he came ashore he would need to learn. He agreed to taking some preliminary drives with me as instructor. The third time we almost ended up under a lorry it was mutually agreed that I would remain the driver. He could steer a ship across an ocean. Traffic was a different matter.

There was another snag to the Seaham job. The Harbour Master, Captain Hudson, took all weekends off. As Assistant Harbour Master, Alex would get one day off a week, Thursday. And the harbour was tidal. It had huge gates which had to be closed at just the moment when the tide equalised. The gates would hold in the water, keeping the ships afloat as the tide receded outside. They were reopened when the tide came in and the pressure of the sea outside equalled the pressure within.

That meant he would be out of his bed most nights, as the tide came and went twice a day, altering by only a few minutes each day. So he would work one day at 11 a.m. and 11 p.m., the next day 11.15 a.m. and p.m., the next 11.25, and so on. It was a crazy regime, with a pitiful wage, but it did mean there would be no more tearful goodbyes, no further need to leave his precious son. He took the job, and we set about house-hunting.

For years the local council had banned private house-building. Seaham had vast council estates, for which we would not be eligible, but houses for sale were scarce as hen's teeth. In vain we scoured the evening papers. Houses sold mostly by word of mouth, and we were not there to hear. The winter that year was harsh; there were no bus services at night, and so there was nothing for it but to put the carrycot in the car at dead of night and drive Alex to work. Most nights I put a coat over my nightie, until one night, on the coast road, the car slipped on ice on the homeward run and slid into a snowdrift. As I dug out the wheels, pink silk flapping wetly around my ankles, I resolved to dress more sensibly in future.

But the spring came, as it always does, and the days lengthened, until I was driving home in the dawn, the baby asleep on the seat behind me, and with the comforting knowledge that Alex would be home before long. No further need to listen to the shipping forecast, wondering if he was in an area of Force 10 gale. Now he was near to me. It was a lovely thought. I think there are times in life when you can know perfect happiness. These times do not last, but while you have them they are unbelievably precious, making memories to hold in your heart forever.

It was at that time that I saw something on television which had a profound effect on me. Pope John XXIII was visiting hardened prisoners in a Rome jail. He was looking at them with a degree of love I would have reserved for those dearest to me. It made me resolve to be less judgemental of people and, looking back, I have been the happier for it.

My mother did not approve of our move to Seaham. Everything she cared about was in Sunderland. When a house came up in Seaham, a terraced house in a colliery street leading down to a railway line, she looked and shuddered. Nevertheless she elected to go there with us. Why, when she was so much closer to Joyce, she did not move in with her, I do not know. There was a brief episode when she took herself off in the huff and moved in with Joyce; it lasted a week, and they parted by mutual consent.

The house purchase had gone through, and we were packing up to leave our white house with its rose-filled garden, when Alex went off to work one evening. I was holding the baby in my arms when whatever was on the radio was interrupted by an announcement. President John F. Kennedy had been shot dead in Dallas, his pretty wife sitting beside him in the car. Again, I felt that sense of guilt – that feeling that I could have, should have, somehow prevented this happening – which I had felt when Marilyn Monroe died. If only I had been able to speak to her, I felt sure I could have helped her. Now I felt the same thing about Kennedy. Later on I would learn that this is almost universal: we all feel implicated in an unnecessary death, even of people with whom we have had no contact.

I needed to speak to someone, and the one person I wanted to speak to was Alex. He had told me never to ring him at work, as Captain Hudson wouldn't approve, but I was desperate to share this news. To my horror it was Hudson who answered. I stammered out a request to speak to my husband. When Alex came on, I blurted out the news. He didn't reply. Instead he turned away from the phone and I heard him say 'Kennedy is dead.' There was a moment's silence and then a hubbub of horrified voices. It is an aural memory that will live with me forever.

And so we left Sunderland behind and moved to Seaham. It was a mining town of some 25,000 people, created by the Londonderry family as a place from which to ship the coal that poured out from their mines. Street after street of terraced houses, built for the miners, led down to the harbour, with a fringe of better housing to the west, the domain of colliery managers and the like. We had a house in one of those narrow streets, but it was warm and spacious, with a staircase leading out of the living-room and a narrow back yard.

If my mother had worried about my bringing people back to a council house, she was paranoid about this house, mourning my back garden and bird-filled trellis as though she had permanently dwelled outdoors. But she liked our neighbours, welcomed the toddlers who came to play with Mark, and, once she had fathomed the bus service, went merrily into Sunderland every day to meet her friends.

Seaham was still recovering from a disaster the previous year, when the lifeboat had gone to the rescue of a fishing cobble, and both boats had gone down with loss of life. Some of the lifeboat men had worked at the harbour, and Alex came home distressed by the stories he had been told by men unable to save colleagues who were drowning before their eyes.

But the town was used to the death of young men. There were three pits in Seaham: Dawdon, Vane Tempest, and Seaham Pit, commonly known as The Knack. That first year I was keen to see the march to the famous Durham Gala, which would pass right by our windows. I heard the far-off thump of the colliery band, and then the marching feet – but when the magnificent banner came into view it was draped in black to denote deaths in the pit that year. Eventually the pretty young wife next door to me would be widowed by a mud slide, and I would see the light fade from her face.

But there was much about mining life that I loved. The tramp of feet as men went to the pit at crazy hours, tub-loading, back-shift, fore-shift, day-shift; their humour and comradeship; the little girls clacking up and down the street in their mothers' high-heeled shoes; the snow-white washing stretched across the back street, so that I had to wait until the wind blew the sheets high before I could drive along it. Each month, lorries delivered the concessionary coal to each miner's doorstep, and it had to be patiently shovelled into the coal house. Often there would be a spare bucket of the black and gleaming stuff for me, for those who didn't merit this black gold were much pitied.

This was a generous town, which loved to gossip, and above all loved the fact that nationalisation meant that they were the masters now, and not the hated coal-owners. Not that everyone was glad to be rid of the Londonderrys. Many a tale I was told of Lady Londonderry visiting in her long white gloves. Some people yearned for a return of the almost feudal system they had lived under; others exulted in its downfall. So the political divide was sharp, and entirely based in the past. As I would later write: 'Some of them vote for remembered pain, some for remembered glory, and very few at all for the needs of the day.'

The strain, and the long and irregular hours, were telling on Alex, but on Thursdays we got in the car and escaped to the Cleveland Hills, thirty miles away and a place of endless vistas and perfect peace. I bought a little primus stove, and we cooked sausages at a place we christened Look-Out Point, with the sea in the far distance to the east and the Pennines far off to the west. We were utterly, utterly happy. Money was tight, but we managed. I didn't buy clothes or make-up. Hairdressers were out, and I learned instead to home perm. I cut my old A-line dresses into the new straight shape, and made dungarees for Mark to protect the few nice outfits I could afford for him. And his Aunt Annie sent him the most intricate Fair Isle jumpers from Shetland, knitted with all the love and expertise she could muster.

When the local television station appealed for essays on north-east life, I poured out all my enthusiasm for this new place. To my amazement, the article was accepted. But when it was being filmed, the response in Seaham was muted. The little girls in high heels were scooped indoors by mothers fearful it would appear that their children were not properly shod. When I knocked on a neighbour's door to ask if we could photograph their pigeons, I was told they'd been sold. The pigeons could be heard cooing in the back yard as she spoke. I later learned she feared I was reporting her to the Health Inspector. Even the seagulls had deserted the harbour when we tried to capture them on film. But the experience woke in me a desire to write. First, however, I needed to experience the pit.

After much badgering, the National Coal Board agreed to let me go down the biggest of the three – Dawdon Pit, which was deep, and went far out under the sea. I knew I would go down a huge distance in the cage, but I was not prepared for how flimsy the cage was. I went down with one man as a guide. The descent was scary, as it seemed to go on forever. When we reached the bottom, it looked like a tube station, with plenty of width and height, and white paint everywhere; but as we moved on the way narrowed. My feet were sinking into inches of coal dust, the battery which powered my headlamp hung from my waist weighing me down, and the heat became oppressive.

We came upon a man, half-naked, squatting at the side of the tunnel. 'Is that a woman?' he said. 'Hold on while I warn the lads to watch their language.' He scuttled away to put his mates on their best behaviour. 'Put some clays on, marra. There's a lass coming in bye. And watch what you say.' Such was the courtesy of pitmen.

When I reached the coalface, I saw the cutting machine, like giant flower-heads, whirring and cutting great swathes of coal. As the coal fell away, other men rushed forward with props to secure the roof. There was the sound of trickling water, and the constant thunder of machinery. Everything was moving, walls, floor, roof; nothing you touched was still. Altogether, it was a descent into hell.

But it was impossible to miss the camaraderie, the jokes as the men shared their snap, huddled in nooks and crannies at the side of tunnels. They told me how the smell of a peeled orange would spread throughout the pit, showed me the cockroaches – blacklocks as they called them – who tried to get at their snap tins, and threatened me with the mice that they said were everywhere. We went back up in the cage with the men coming off shift, and I was again aware of the space falling away beneath me. 'This is the only bit I don't like,' I said. From behind me came a weary voice. 'Eeh, missus, it's the only bit I *do* like.'

The visit to the pit inspired me – but where did I begin? I decided to write a potted history of the Londonderry family who had owned the pits and all the land around, before nationalisation. I worked long and hard, researching in the library and reading every book on the subject I could find. Eventually I had written 10,000 words, and I posted it to the *Sunderland Echo,* which sometimes published historical articles. Within a week I was summoned to see the editor. He liked it, he would use it, but only if I could cut it to 2,500 words. Could I do that? I assured him I could.

It wasn't until I was back in the street that I realised that meant axing three words out of every four. It seemed like an impossible task until I remembered Miss Waggott, my English teacher. She had once given me ninety-eight per cent in an exam, and then written on the paper, 'Your writing is atrocious.' I had had trouble with précis, and she had taken me by both arms and pushed me bodily between the rows of desks. 'Stand back, girl. Stand back and look at it!' So I stood back from the article; cut it; it was published; and I received £5, £2.50 of which went on a photograph of the former Lady Londonderry, to accompany the piece.

My next assignment was the poet Byron, who had married a Seaham heiress. I continued to write for the *Echo* until I came across a radio programme called *Northern Drift*. It used new writing, short pieces on any subject under the sun. I sent in a short piece of prose entitled 'Treadmill', and received a glowing letter from the then editor, an unknown called Alan Plater. The director was another unknown; his name was Alan Ayckbourn.

With their encouragement, and the help of a later editor, Bill Price Turner, I went on to write short stories for the BBC, and eventually a short play for the ultra-highbrow Third Programme. It shared a bill with a play by Harold Pinter; and a broadsheet review of my play said: 'Like Pinter, she is a master at communicating non-communication.' I wasn't entirely sure what that meant, but I thought it was very posh. I can't remember what I was paid – a few pounds.

We were still hard up, and any money was welcome. Plater and Ayckbourn went on to become the great writers and household names that they are today. An invitation came, then, to write a school reader for the publishers, Macmillan. I wrote about a family in a pit village getting a bath installed, something that was happening all around me as colliery houses were brought up to date. It was thrilling to hold it in my hand – my first book, and I carried it to my mother. 'Very nice, dear,' she said. 'Don't let it go to your head.'

That year Churchill died. To the child who had seen his speeches as blessings because they lightened the atmosphere in her home, his passing was a blow. I cried as his coffin was borne down the Thames, and the cranes dipped in salute. Remembered fragments of his speeches came and went in my mind: 'Never before in the field of human conflict ...' 'We shall not fail or falter, we shall not weaken or tire ...' 'What is our aim?' I answer in one word: victory. Come ... let us go forward together.' It seemed that England held its breath as the sad pageant unfolded. It was the end of an era.

Afterwards I made black-pudding sandwiches, which my mother had made each time Churchill cheered her up. But they lacked the lusciousness of those remembered treats. Perhaps I did not have my mother's knack, or perhaps our palates were jaded by the plenty of peacetime.

I was entering into the life of Seaham now, delivering Meals on Wheels and becoming Vice-Chairman of the Physically Handicapped Association. And we moved to a new house, a solid three-bedroomed terrace house on a main road. My mother was pleased, as it was near a bus stop. I was aghast at the problem of moving house in a town where the removal van did not come complete with removal men. 'People move themselves,' the van owner told me. It was Guy Fawkes night when, helped by Tom, Dick and Harry, our possessions were installed higgledy-piggledy in the new house. As rockets soared outside, I poured myself a stiff drink and sat down to read the evening paper. It was full of the latest on the Moors Murders, a terrible tale of children murdered by Ian Bradley and Myra Hindley, and buried on a place called Saddleworth Moor. Little did I know then that Saddleworth Moor would one day become as familiar to me as my own back yard.

The yard at Princess Road was bigger than at our first Seaham home, but it was still a back yard, and I yearned for the blossom and roses of our first house. So I painted the walls white, and when Mark's birthday came round and his friends came to his party, I gave each of them a tiny pot of different coloured paints. 'This is a game,'

I said. 'You can each paint a brick, but only one brick.' They set to, here a yellow brick, there a red one, green, pink, blue. . . when they went home I painted some bricks higher up, and then stood back. If you narrowed your eyes, especially when you looked out through the window, the white wall looked as though it had climbing blossoms on it. Not exactly Eden, but better than nothing.

My writing was flourishing. One broadcast story followed another, and I was invited to a BBC reception in Leeds. The host was a young newsreader named Michael Aspel, unbelievably glamorous in a white jacket. When he said my work had been 'widely anthologised' by the BBC, I was immensely gratified. My stories were read on air by struggling young actors anxious to earn a fee. One was called Ben Kingsley, another Robert Powell. And I made my first broadcast on *Woman's Hour*. I can't remember the subject but I do remember that the producer asked me to change 'toilet' to 'WC'. 'Otherwise we'll get dozens of letters saying "toilet" is common.' I went home wondering just who had time to write to the BBC about anything, even toilets.

But as that summer of 1966 finally slipped away, the country was stunned by the horror of Aberfan, where a coal tip, a huge mountain of slag, had slid into a village and killed 116 children and 28 adults. Nowhere was the misery more heavily felt than in coal-mining areas. Seaham grieved for the Aberfan parents, and clutched their own children closer. We had our slag heaps, too, although much of the waste from the pits was dumped on the Blast, the cliff face that led to the North Sea. No one knew who to blame – the NCB, the Government, the coal-owners who had started the pit heaps in the first place?

I grieved with the parents both in Aberfan and Seaham. I was becoming more and more involved in Seaham life, and at last someone suggested I should stand for the local council. At present it was composed of 31 councillors, all Labour. Many of my own principles were Socialist, but I didn't like the idea of a one-party council. Eventually six of us stood as Independents. I went out canvassing, but the town was solid for Labour. Knocking on doors, I would be told politely that they always voted Labour; I would thank them and set off down the path; and then a call would come. 'Are you the lass that worked at the hospital?' Almost every house had a miner in it who had passed through the Accident Hospital during my time there. One woman said, 'You gave me a cuddle when he broke his back and I was gutted. You said he'd be all right, and he was. I'll give you a vote. Only don't let him know.'

On the night of the count I was crying when I got home. 'Don't be silly,' my mother said. 'You knew you wouldn't get in.' I shook my head. 'You don't understand,' I said. 'I did get in.'

But as I struggled to come to terms with my new responsibilities, there was another early-morning knock at the door. Like my father, Joyce had sat up in bed that morning and died of a coronary thrombosis. I'd had no chance to tell her that I loved her, or to say goodbye.

8
CHAPTER

POLTERGEIST

THE MORNING PASSED in a blur. A woman doctor arrived to co-sign the cremation certificate, and I took her into the room where Joyce was lying. She looked beautiful, a tiny smile on her lips. I had always envied her her pretty mouth. Now, looking at it, I felt my heart would break. We had never been close as sisters, but I loved her and I knew she loved me. As I answered the doctor's questions, mechanically because they seemed inconsequential, I was remembering all the times she had begged me to wear 'nice Peter Pan collars' instead of clothes she thought too daring. Of how excitement or pleasure made her hunch up her shoulders in ecstasy, like a little girl. How I had crawled into her bed when my parents fought, and been told it would all be all right in the morning. We had had so many rows; but lately, both happy wives and mothers, there had been an easing between us. We might have grown closer with time – except that it was now too late.

I did my best to care for her husband Douglas and the children. Gillian was unbelievably brave, but adamant that no one should cry. That was her way of getting through: show no emotion. Paul played with a train set on the floor in the front room, seeming not to

110

comprehend that his world had just rocked on its axis. The one time I felt anger was when the vicar told me, 'This whole thing is shot through with faith.' No, it wasn't: it was shot through with utter misery for everyone. I feared for my mother, losing her perfect daughter, but she was buoyed up by her belief in an afterlife when they would be reunited. I had no such comfort.

At the crematorium, as I stood in front of a sea of flowers, I heard someone sobbing behind me. It was Peggy, the maid we used to lock in the pantry and make faces at through the window. Across all the years she had remembered. We hugged and cried together, and then it was time to get into the car and go back to the house where a funeral tea awaited, prepared by Joyce's sisters-in-law. Someone had made meringues. I knew they were kindly meant, but they seemed bizarre on such an occasion – so inappropriate that I had to let myself out of the house and walk off my indignation. When someone you love dies, anger comes easily. It is mostly irrational, but it's comforting because, while you are angry, you do not need to mourn.

As the weeks went on it was as though Joyce haunted me. She had loved a song by Procol Harum, 'A Whiter Shade of Pale'. Now it seemed to be played everywhere – each time I turned on the radio, in shops, whenever I sat down to watch television. People even whistled it in the street. One line re-echoed in my head: 'your face, no longer ghostly, turns a whiter shade of pale.' She had always been pale, even as a girl. So had I – so pale that Mammy had dabbed us both as children with her Bourjois rouge, cautioning us not to let anybody know.

I marvelled at the way my mother handled her loss, seeming to draw strength from it, and helped by the fact that everyone conspired to make things as easy as they could for Paul. I was having a hard time, too, losing Mark to school. I walked him there every morning, collected him at lunch-time, walked him back, collected him at 3.30. In between trips, I watched the clock until I could see him again. I desperately wanted another baby, but Alex was unwilling. Mark's birth had been traumatic for him, and not the natural birth we had expected. Now he saw Joyce's death as somehow linked with her difficulties in pregnancy. Another baby for me might lead to the same end, and he wasn't prepared to risk it. In vain I argued and pleaded. The best I could get out of him was, 'We'll talk about it next year.'

My mother had grown very close to Alex. His patience had so worn down her initial disapproval that I would now joke that, if I left him, she would stay with him and not go with me. She took his side over the baby issue. There was plenty of time, she said. She loved her grandchildren, but she was not a besotted grandmother. Baby-sitting had to be negotiated in advance, and she set the parameters of time. But if she never pushed the pram, she told the most wonderful stories, and encouraged Mark's imagination just as she had encouraged mine.

Joyce's death had a profound effect on me. Much as you may love them, losing an older generation seems somehow natural. The loss of a sibling or a friend of your own age is somehow shocking. And it taught me not to put off important things. We could have become closer, had probably both intended to do so. Now the chance was lost.

I tried to concentrate on my council work to assuage my grief but I found the council chamber an ordeal. I would feel faint, and then my right arm would ache and go numb. I knew what this was –

evidence of heart trouble. I would drop dead just as Joyce had. Eventually I took my fears to the doctor. He knew about my sister's death. After examining me, he sat back in his chair. 'You're scared,' he said. 'You're grieving and you're scared.' 'But I have this pain in my arm,' I said. 'I'm not imagining it.' He leaned forward and poked my upper arm. It was as tense as a steel girder. 'You're walking around like that,' he said, 'wound up like wire. No wonder it aches.'

He was right. As long as I remembered to relax, my arm ceased to ache, and gradually my fears subsided. It was a good job they did, as life as a councillor was proving eventful.

Most of my fellow councillors were miners or ex-miners, and, almost without exception, they were fine men. One, Joe Dawson, a wizard at figures, would try to explain the intricacies of finance to me. Another, Jim Mortimer, would regale me with tales of the pit, telling a dreadful one about a little trapper boy found dead, impaled on a spike sticking out from the leather trap. The traps closed the entrance to tunnels, in an effort to stop dust. Trapper boys had to raise them whenever a putter came by with a pony and tub full of coal. This one never made it back to daylight.

The councillors were all friendly and helpful, but would vote against anything and everything I proposed. I was not within the Labour Group, and therefore, when it came down to it, I must be defeated. They would then sidle up to me at the end of the meeting and whisper, 'I really agreed with you, but I had to side with the group.' And I was learning that labels didn't necessarily mean what they said.

I was due at a council meeting one night when details of a speech by Enoch Powell about immigration came over the radio. He was speaking of rivers of blood, and generally painting such a distorted picture of society that I was driven to tears. I arrived, flustered, at the council chamber to find a Labour councillor entering. 'What's the matter?' he asked, looking at my red eyes. 'I'm upset over what Enoch Powell's saying,' I replied. He shrugged. 'Why? He's only saying what we are all ·thinking.' I sat in the chamber that night, marvelling at how the label 'Labour' could accommodate someone who certainly didn't have socialist beliefs.

I was still writing, too, and it was natural that I would write about being a councillor. *Woman's Hour* decided to do a joint interview with me and a woman called Connie Lewcock, a Labour veteran in Newcastle and a power in the party. I warmed to her on sight, a small, indomitable woman with twinkling eyes and none of the hostility that politics can sometimes engender. It was an instant friendship.

It was about now that I entered the realm of the paranormal. A family came to my door to request a move to another council house because their house was haunted. They hadn't yet seen a ghost, but every night there were ghostly rappings. Their children couldn't sleep, and they, husband and wife, were terrified. They looked it, too, so that night I put Mark to bed and went down to their house. A dozen neighbours were gathered in the sitting-room, all tense. I took my place by the door, and the noises began – here a rumble, there a bang, and everywhere the sound of in-drawn breath.

The next day I went to see the housing manager. 'You've got to be joking,' he said, when I requested a transfer for them. I was firm. 'I don't believe in ghosts either,' I said, 'but they can't live like this. You'll have to move them.' He bit his lips as an acceptable alternative to felling me to the floor. 'If I move them on account of a ghost,' he said, between gritted teeth, 'we'll have mass migration in this town because every bugger will have a ghost.'

I knew it was true. Almost every tenant wanted to live

somewhere else, preferably on a new estate. 'All right,' I conceded. 'But what do we do?'

That night, the housing manager accompanied me to the house, carrying a torch of gargantuan proportions. He listened for a while, flashed the torch around in the upstairs rooms, where the children were sleeping, and which were devoid of bulbs in the light sockets, and then declared it must be hooligans. The following night we came back accompanied by two policemen. Their helpful suggestion was that electricity might be escaping into the walls. By now the local paper was sniffing around, and the housing manager was desperate.

So was Alex, since his wife vanished every evening, leaving him to baby-sit. Eventually he said he was coming, too, to 'put a stop to this nonsense'. His Shetland accent intensified. 'Utter nonsense,' he said, and persuaded my mother to look after Mark. She told us God would protect us, and we should hurry back.

We walked down to the house, Alex pooh-poohing all my suggestions that something must be up. His scepticism didn't last long. By now the crowd in the small front room was doubled, and fear hung in the air. I saw the colour drain from Alex's face. 'Look at the dog,' he whispered. The family's small terrier was crouched by the fire, the hair erect on its back, its limbs quivering in terror. That was enough for my staunch man of the sea. The dog couldn't be fooled, ergo the ghost was real. I thought the dog was picking up on the terror emanating from the humans, but I didn't say so.

By now I was convinced we were being duped, but I couldn't see how. The next night the housing manager rounded up a posse, and we went down there, accompanied by another councillor, a fellow Independent, Arthur Brown. By this time my mother believed we were dealing with an unhappy spirit and was all for exorcism. 'If it's there, you'll feel a cold wind,' she told Arthur. He thought this was a huge joke, until we got into the inky blackness of the unlit bedrooms. Suddenly I saw the whites of his eyes in the darkness. 'Can you feel it,' he said. 'There's a cold wind on the back of my neck.' The next moment he was gone, ostensibly to check downstairs.

The children had been kept downstairs, because the housing manager wanted the upstairs, where the noises came from, to be empty and under surveillance. But tonight, cold wind or not, there were no noises, and we began to perk up. No children upstairs, no noises. Until suddenly there was a loud clack from the living-room, and then another. I looked at the children, all staring at their parents, all with hands folded in front of them. There was another clack. I moved nearer to the eldest child and, as another noise reverberated, I saw what she was doing. She had on heavy school shoes, laces unfastened. When attention was elsewhere, she would lift her foot and let the shoe half-fall from her foot so that the heel thudded on the bare floor. We had our poltergeist!

Tearful at being found out, she led us upstairs. There was a false ceiling on the stairs which she had pushed until it rippled and reverberated. An old cylinder vacuum in a cupboard would be lifted head-high and then dropped with a thud. She had a whole range of these implements. Did her parents know what she was doing? Was she put up to it in order to get a move? I never knew.

So I continued, with domestic disputes, threats of murder, smelly drains, and all the small wars that make up community living. I even began to enjoy them – until the council voted to evict three families who had rent arrears. One was a man whose wife had run off, and who had given up his job to care for his children and got into debt. Another family had spent the rent money on visiting a sick child in hospital; and the third family simply didn't believe in paying anything. Among them, the families had ten children. I couldn't believe we were going to put these families on the street – or, as was pointed out to me, into a hostel for the women and children, leaving the fathers to fend for themselves. In vain I lobbied various councillors. Joe Dawson was on my side, but powerless to help. Others were sympathetic, but unwilling to go against the Labour whip. Still others felt the families deserved it.

In desperation I rang Connie Lewcock. 'What am I going to do?' I wailed. She was forthright. 'Pull yourself together for a start. If you're going to win this – and you must – you won't do it with tears.' On her advice, I rang the MP, using her name as she had told me to. 'Ask him what this is going to look like,' she said. 'A Labour council evicting children.' The MP promised to look into it and ring me back. He never did, but the evictions were rescinded at the next meeting.

Mark was now beginning to dislike school, and I recognised the symptoms. When Alex would have let him stay at home, I insisted on getting him there. I knew from experience that one day off would be fatal. Fortunately, with the help of an understanding headmaster, Jim Robinson, he got through his bout of school refusal, but not before I had realised that I had communicated my own fears about school to him. Not in words but in anxiety. Children pick up vibes. I had never liked or felt safe at school and he had sensed that.

Once we got over this hiccup, three years had passed in a flash, and I was now up for re-election, which did not suit the Labour Group. 'You're a nice girl, but you're trouble,' one of them told me bluntly. They toured my ward with a loudspeaker, telling the voters that electing me as an Independent would mean a steep rise in rents.

'I want to vote for you, pet,' one old lady told me, 'but I can't afford it.' I was beaten by a few votes, and the first thing the councillors did when they got back in was to raise the rents. Such is politics.

I felt a measure of disappointment, but also huge relief. It had become obvious to me that as an Independent you could achieve little or nothing, and there was no political party to which I wanted to be affiliated. Besides, I had other worries. My mother was ill, having strange bouts of sickness and being unlike her energetic self. She went to the doctor and was referred to a surgeon. 'My gall bladder's got to come out,' she announced, almost gleefully. I was horrified, and suggested fat-free diets, anything but surgery. She was adamant. She wasn't going to have her life impeded by diets or sickness or anything else. Get it over and done with. She had her hair permed to look her best on the ward, purloined my newest nightdress, and went into hospital.

The day after the operation she was sitting up in bed, blooming, and telling me to tell the Oxfam shop she'd be back as a volunteer within the week. Two days later, when I went in to see her, she wasn't in the bed. There was another woman there, small and yellow and half-conscious. I went in search of the sister, who said my mother was 'in her bed – we haven't moved her.' I went back. My mother had changed beyond recognition. In twenty-four hours something had gone drastically wrong. I rang Alex, who came at once. He, too, was horrified at the change in her. 'We have to do something.'

It's very hard to make a fuss in hospital. Every fibre of your being is telling you not to make waves. Nevertheless, I could see my mother slipping away before my eyes. I made a fuss. The sister explained that at my mother's age this collapse was not surprising. I made more fuss, until a doctor came, a geriatrician. He questioned me about my mother, and how she had been before the operation.

He questioned and he listened. An hour later we were in an ambulance speeding to the renal dialysis unit in Newcastle.

The traffic parted like the Red Sea as the ambulance's siren blared, and I felt a surge of comfort. My mother was close to death, but the world did care, after all. It was making way for her. For two weeks she was given dialysis. I heard various diagnoses from various doctors, but the upshot was that the operation to remove her gall bladder had been botched. Something had gone sadly wrong, and had been overlooked. 'We're trying to bring her back, but we can't promise.'

I spent the next few days at the hospital as she drifted in and out of consciousness. I wanted my sister there beside me, but she too was gone. Occasionally I went outside for air. There was a fruit-machine arcade across the way, where I played a game. If I could get three cherries up, she would live. But there were only apples and pears. And I thought of all the times we had rowed … because she had pinched my winter boots, or spent her last penny on a posh hat, or just been maddeningly adolescent and not like a mother at all. Except when life had hurt me, when she had been the best and staunchest mother in the world.

When Alex was there at the bedside, his was the hand she wanted to hold. He comforted her like the son she had never had, showing no trace of resentment at the hard time she had once given him. In one lucid moment she asked me how much pension she would have accumulated by the time she came out, and her eyes gleamed when I told her it would be a lot. This woman who had lost everything in life, even her favourite daughter, never lost her zest for life. Just before the operation, when I was helping her into bed one night, she had said, 'You know, I have never gone to bed one night in my life without thinking something lovely would happen tomorrow.' At the time I had thought this yet another sign of her unwillingness to grow up. Now I realised it was the only way to live.

Eventually they had to feed her through a tube directly into her stomach. They went on pouring jugs of mush into it even after they had told me she would die at nine o'clock that night. After her death I felt strange. I had protected her from my earliest days, so why did I now feel unprotected, as though the lid had been taken off the family? 'She never grew up, you know,' I told the vicar. 'We sometimes called her Peter Pan.' He smiled. 'That's what the saying "Only the good die young" means. They may be old in years but they have stayed young in spirit.' I found that comforting, but I still felt bereft. In those far-off, golden, pre-war days we had been a family of four. Now there was only me.

9
CHAPTER

A STING IN THE TAIL

I MISSED MY mother terribly, ruing every cross word we had ever had – and they were many. She had been at once the most infuriating and the most loving mother in the world. Again and again I asked Alex the same question: 'Did she know I loved her?' And again and again he told me she did. That was the wonderful thing about him – he never lost patience with me.

On only one point could I not move him. No more children, for the time being, at least. Not till he was sure it would all be plain sailing. I tried to devise ways of fooling him, but it was futile. He had always taken responsibility for contraception, and he wouldn't relinquish it now. I raised the question of adoption in an attempt to frighten him. It didn't faze him. Yes, we could consider adopting – in a while, when things had settled down. I knew I could love another baby wherever it came from. And so could Alex, who had been known to take over neighbours' prams if he met them out walking. So it was a possibility. But not yet.

Our Thursdays in the Cleveland Hills were out, now that Mark was at school. But sometimes, on Saturdays, the tide was right, and we could get away for a few hours to cook on the little stove and feel as free as air. I would come back from these expeditions and fall upon pen and paper in my urge to write. The short stories poured out of me.

I even began a radio play, inspired by something I heard in the butcher's. In those days, soda water came in siphons, elaborate affairs with metal fittings. The deposit on a siphon was 2s 6d, refundable when you returned it empty. The butcher told me of a woman who regularly bought a siphon on tick at the corner shop, squirted the soda water down the sink, and then took the siphon back to another shop to get the 2s 6d deposit. This was to enable her to go to Bingo, where she was sure she would make her family's fortune.

I began it as a radio play, and showed it to Alan Ayckbourn. 'This isn't radio,' he said. 'The characters are doing more than they're saying. It's television.' I took the play home and put it in a drawer. Radio I could deal with; television plays were beyond me. And I was worried about Alex. He had developed a cough, and one wintry night, when he didn't come home, I went in search of him, and found him collapsed in the snow. Thereafter I went down to the harbour in the car and brought him safely back.

I had come to know a writer called C. P. Taylor, a Glaswegian who had settled in the north-east. He was enthusiastic in his support of new writers, and asked to see some of my work. In a hurry as usual, I picked up a pile of manuscripts and handed them over. The next time I saw him, he had picked out the play, *The Soda-Water Fountain*. 'This is good,' he said. 'Too good to leave in the drawer.'

All through my life I have sometimes been conscious of the wheels of fate whirring. That night I drove home to put the play away, but the television was on in the living-room and a man called Kenneth Allsop was announcing a search for writers new to television. The judges would be Keith Dewhurst and John Hopkins, both renowned playwrights; Colin Welland, then an actor but later to be honoured for the script of *Chariots of Fire*; and Stella Rickman and Sean Sutton, Head of Drama of ITV and BBC respectively. On an impulse I put *The Soda-Water Fountain* into an envelope and sent it off. I can say in all honesty that forty-eight hours later it had slipped from my mind.

It was summer, and Alex seemed better. We escaped to the hills when we could, but even being at home together was wonderful. When he was at the harbour, I would write. He liked to read the day's output when he came in, and in the morning I would find a scribbled note: 'This is the best you have ever done.' If the slightest mention of anything I'd written for radio appeared in the local paper, he would cut it out and carry it around in his wallet like a proud father with baby photos.

If only he hadn't had to work such unreasonable hours, life would have been perfect. I suggested he might ask for the occasional weekend off, but Captain Hudson could not be moved. On one occasion, when we were on our annual holiday, spent at home because we couldn't afford to go away, Alex was summoned back to work because Mrs Hudson wanted to go to the ballet. I say 'summoned' because it was not a request for a favour, it was a command.

Then one morning the phone rang. It was the BBC. I had made the short list with *The Soda-Water Fountain*. They would be in touch. I was still in my nightie and I sat down on the bottom step of the stairs to take in the news. There had been 2000 entries and I had made the short list.

Two or three weeks later I was told I had won. The play would have a stellar production on BBC2, I would get £1000 as a prize and go to London to meet the judges. Mark was suffering with tonsillitis that day, and I took him to the doctor. When we came back there was chaos: reporters at the door, the phone ringing, everyone wanting to see the County Durham housewife who had won a national competition. And suddenly it struck me that there was a nude scene in the play, a moving moment when a girl who has hung on to her virginity decides she must part with it in return for a favour done for her family. Writing a nude scene for radio was one thing, seeing it on camera quite another.

It seemed every newspaper in the land wanted to question me. I distinctly remember one, Victoria O'Reilly, who came from either *The Times* or the *Telegraph*. She came up from London on the train, with only a shoulder bag. I sat opposite her and wondered how she could possibly journey so far from home with so little luggage. If I went, I would need two cases at least. But she was nice, easy to talk to, and her pitch was flattering. I talked, she wrote, 'like Dylan Thomas'.

Her likening me to the Welsh genius made me laugh. Early in my days of writing for *Northern Drift* I had taken fright. I couldn't really write, I reasoned. Soon they would find out. Before that I must do some real writing! All I could remember from English lessons was onomatopoeia and alliteration, so I used them both – in profusion. That was the one script that came back. In the margin Bill Price Turner had written, 'I have several Dylan Thomases but only one Denise Robertson.'

Such a distinguished literary comparison had a startling effect. Marie Lawson, that millionaire cousin of my mother who lived in Mount Street in London, and whom I had never met, wrote to me. An old lady by then, she was interested in this unseen second cousin. When I was in London, would I visit her?

At any other time this would have been impossible, but things had now changed. The next week I was going to London at the BBC's expense to see the play in production. The director had already visited me, and outlined the cast: Paula Wilcox, a considerable TV star in the hit sitcom *The Lover*, Bryan Marshall, who had just starred in a play called *Stocker's Copper*, and Stephen Yardley, later to achieve stardom in *Howard's Way*.

I went down to see the last day of the production, carrying a case packed for every eventuality. The possibility of buying something if I needed it didn't occur to me. If I'd had one I'd have packed a rope ladder, the better to escape the White Slave Traders I was sure abounded in the capital city.

Alex saw me off on the sleeper train from Sunderland with a look on his face that suggested the possibility of my surviving the trip was doubtful. But I was safe in my little cabin, and would be home before bedtime the next night. I arrived at King's Cross at six in the morning, and took a taxi to the BBC. It was a strange world to me. Everyone kept talking about an imminent calamity called 'pulling the plugs'. This, it was explained to me, was a militant crew cutting off the power when their shift ended, even if there was only one minute of filming left to do. The director fussed and fluttered, anxious to extract the last ounce of drama from the play, but terrified of over-running and having to pay overtime – which was the aim of the crew.

Larry Adler, the harmonica player, had been engaged to provide the background music, a skilful reworking of the *High Noon* theme tune. He was in animated conversation with his girlfriend, and they were talking about her having to walk round the block. Seeing my puzzled face, someone explained. His wife was coming to visit, so the girlfriend must make herself scarce. This was a new kind of living to me!

The nude scene was easier than I had thought, thanks largely to Bryan Marshall's compassionate treatment of his co-star. In the play, he turns down her offer and wraps her tenderly in a coat. The actress was glad when she was decently covered, and the author was even gladder. What did distress me was the dog scene. The old father in the play has a dog, and during filming the dog behaved perfectly, raising and lowering its head to order. 'You have a way with dogs,' I told the actor later. He grinned, and showed me how he gripped the dog by the throat out of shot of camera, and made sure it did as it was told. On the train home I resolved never again to write about dogs or nudes.

When filming had ended, I was taken down to the bowels of the BBC to see the finished product. As I sat alone in the darkness, suddenly I heard 'Tara's Theme' from *Gone With The Wind* playing far off, obviously coming from another studio. My mother was with me, after all.

Two weeks later a film crew arrived to make a film about my life, which would be screened alongside the play. I had made valiant efforts to make the house look like a playwright's house should, including a bowl of fruit on the kitchen table. The director wanted to film us having breakfast. Never a good cook, I produced a burned offering that was virtually uneatable, but, intimidated by the camera and acres of cable around him, Alex munched bravely on. I offered Mark some fruit as the director had bade me. 'Do have a pear,' I cooed, in what I hoped were playwright-mother tones. 'You told me never to eat fruit that hadn't been washed,' Mark said accusingly. 'That fruit hasn't been washed.'

This was beginning to resemble that earlier film of life in

Seaham, where everyone we wanted to film had turned against me. Worse was to come. The cameraman was called Nat Crosby and was, the director told me, mega-famous. He had just come back from filming Omar Sharif in Afghanistan, where he had risked his life to get aerial photos of Sharif on horseback. This made my humble abode a bit of a comedown. Nevertheless, he was enthusiastic about his new assignment.

Before he came I had tidied the house by sweeping up all the toys and clutter and putting them in a cupboard which fastened with an old-fashioned sneck. It had been a struggle to shut the door, but I managed it. As he filmed me, Nat kept moving back to get a wider picture, back and back until he hit the wall. He looked round, desperate for more room. Seeing the door, he opened it before my agonised 'No!' could stop him. The clutter avalanched out, propelling Nat and his camera forward, and very nearly doing what Afghanistan had failed to do. When filming was finished, we adjourned to the local hostelry for a celebration supper, only to have the whole town plunged into darkness because of a power cut. It was certainly a night to remember.

Alex and I were still very short of money, but when the play was screened I would get the £1000 prize. It was a fortune, so, on the strength of it, I decided Mark and Alex and I would have a few days in London. And we would visit cousin Marie in Mount Street.

Two weeks later we three set off for London. I had got cheap tickets on a train called the Highwayman, but the special offer meant you had to alight at Finsbury Park and take the tube into central London. In eleven years of marriage we had had only two holidays, a honeymoon in Paris and a trip to Shetland. When Alex was at sea, being together at home was better than any holiday and afterwards there hadn't been money for holidays. We had never been away as a family, it was Mark's first time in a train, and a big adventure for us all. I had packed a bag of food because we couldn't afford to eat out, and I kept sniffing it anxiously throughout the next few days in case it had gone off. We stayed in a small hotel in Gray's Inn Road, three in one room, and with shared facilities. It felt like a Hilton.

We did have one meal out, in a Greek restaurant near King's Cross. In the middle of his apple pie, Mark had a terrible nose-bleed. Undeterred, he plugged his nose with tissue and carried on eating, while the Greek waiters applauded his courage. We showed him the sights of London from the top of a bus, and dreamed of the wonderful future we would have when I made us a fortune.

On our last night in London, we went to see Marie Lawson in her Mount Street home. It was huge and splendid, and there on the wall was the big family painting my mother had told me about, with the prosperous Victorian surrounded by his family, my great-great-grandmother dozing in the chair, a little dog in the foreground. We discussed our mutual ancestry. She told me she was proud of me, and described how she lived half her year in Menton. She also loved gambling in casinos. I was curious about her exploits during the war, and she talked of Brendan Bracken and Churchill as though they were bosom pals. She also talked about her early struggles to be allowed to function in a world dominated by men. 'We wanted to succeed,' she said. 'We still had sex, you know, even then, but success was the real goal.'

She shook her head over Aunt Phyllis. 'So much promise,' she said sadly, 'thrown away.' We dined at Scott's in Mayfair, quite the poshest place I had ever been in, but the waiters fussed over Mark and made the whole thing human.

The next day we caught the Highwayman at Finsbury Park and

went home, eating the last of the packed food on the train, a little whiffy now but still edible.

The play was to be screened in February, and I was to go down for the live presentation of the cheque. New clothes were needed, and I bought a brown Berketex dress at Binn's. It had buttons all down the front and long sleeves with buttoned cuffs. As soon as I got to the BBC, they showed me the film they had made in Seaham. To my horror, there was a zoomed shot of one of my neighbours, in braces and open shirt, peering through his curtains and muttering darkly about the carry-on in the street. He was an irascible man, but I didn't think he deserved to be pilloried. 'You can't show that,' I said – but I had reckoned without the director's artistic temperament. This was 'life' he told me. Authenticity. Actuality. 'It's trouble,' I told him. 'It's me never being able to go home again.'

By the time I had got him to edit the shot down to a few seconds, I was in a state. I went back to my dressing-room in the bowels of Shepherd's Bush. It had Ronnie Barker's name on the door, which had thrilled me on sight, but the inside was disappointingly Spartan. It also contained my minder, a lady given to me on arrival. She was the sister of a very famous TV personality, and would, I was assured, help me in every way possible. She was sitting with her nose in a book when I informed her that my distress had caused so much heaving bosom that the buttons had burst from the Berketex bodice. 'Oh dear,' she said and went back to her book. 'Is there a sewing room somewhere?' I asked, but received only a shrug.

In desperation I stepped outside into the corridor, and started accosting passers-by. No one could help me with my request for a safety pin. Eventually a tall, near-naked blonde wearing a feathered headdress appeared. No use asking her for anything: all she had on was a bra and skimpy G-string panties. She saw my face and stopped, towering over me. 'What's up, chuck?' I pointed to my gaping dress. She tutted and dived into her G-string, emerging with a huge nappy pin. 'There you are,' she said, and sashayed on her way.

I went to meet the judges, safely pinned, and found them charming. Except that Colin Welland took exception to the way the play had been produced. 'Cast out of bloody *Spotlight*,' he kept saying, which I took to mean going into a dark corner to choose actors. I had yet to learn of the huge book listing every actor in the business. He was also furious that the play had not been filmed in the north-east. 'Bloody sunshine,' he said. 'There's a grey cast over everything in the north – beautiful.' That, I suddenly realised, was true. Colours in the north were muted, greens just as beautiful but less lush.

John Hopkins was anxious I should show myself in a good light. He asked how I had come to write the play. 'It just wrote itself,' I answered truthfully. He shook his head. 'Don't say that. Tell them you worked on the structure.' I was going to have enough trouble spluttering out the truth, never mind making things up. I thanked him, and moved on. The rest of the night was a blur.

On the train home I kept taking out the cheque and looking at it. Could it be true? The reviewers were fairly kind, especially Nancy Banks Smith in *The Guardian* who said its tragi-comedy was very moving. It came, she said, from the same genre as Steptoe, and deserved an equally long sitcom run. The reviews may have been pleasing, but the neighbours were more forthright. One woman knocked on my door to tell me she had seen very little in the play, but her husband had liked it. A man who was a miner and a staunch Catholic, known to be strait-laced, was kinder. He had enjoyed it. What did he make of the nude scene? 'I liked it,' he said. 'He behaved well, that actor, covering her up. You did well.' What further praise did I need?

Offers for further plays rolled in, including the prestigious 'Play for Today', and I became an object of some interest in the town. One day I was walking down the main street. There were two women walking behind me, and I heard the first one say, 'You see her – she writes books, and she's never off the telly.' I preened a little, and then I heard her friend. 'I know who she is. I live beside her. She may write books and she may be on the telly, but she never cleans her fanlight.'

The first day it was possible we got in the car and drove to the hills. It was wonderful to get away from the telephone and the doorbell for a moment, and we spent a happy few hours on the hillside. On the way home, Alex was quiet. At last he spoke. 'I haven't said anything sooner, because you had so much on your plate. But I haven't felt well for a while. I think I have something wrong with me.'

10
CHAPTER

VERDICT

WE WENT STRAIGHT to the doctor, and from there to the hospital. Alex went in alone, and I sat and waited. In spite of the years I had spent working in a setting such as this, I was afraid. I had lost my parents and my sister, but as long as I had Alex I could cope. Without him I would have nothing.

When you are in a happy marriage, thoughts of being widowed occasionally occur. You know then that if, God forbid, it happened you would be brave – noble, even. You would live for your children and your memories. The reality is different. When Alex walked down the ramp into the waiting-room I knew from his face that the news was bad. He was admitted to hospital the next day to have his lung removed. He had advanced lung cancer.

He was to go into Seaham Hall, the place where Byron had married Annabella Milbanke, where I had done my first outside broadcast. It was a magnificent building with a sweeping staircase, former home of the Londonderry family and given by them to the people of County Durham as a chest hospital.

I was told I could not visit him the day of the operation, but I knew how afraid he would be. I went in at visiting time, and waited until the nurse left the side ward. Then I went in. He was lying amid masses of tubes and monitors, and our eyes met and flashed. 'You're going to be all right,' I mouthed. 'I love you.'

The nurse came back then and ordered me out, but I had achieved my objective. He knew he was loved. He wouldn't allow me to bring Mark in to see him, at first, fearing it would upset him; but as the days went by he grew stronger, until at last I could take Mark to see him. One day he told me he had requested a song on hospital radio. 'I chose it because it's what you have been to me.' It was Simon and Garfunkel's 'Bridge Over Troubled Water'.

When I knew I would soon be able to bring him home, I was relieved. I was sure I could build him up. Together we would fight the disease. A surgeon friend from my hospital days told me to keep his spirits up. 'We don't know why, but it does seem to have an effect if people are optimistic about recovery.' But in the car coming home I could see how frail he had become, and how difficult he found breathing with only one lung.

Once he was in his own home, things improved slightly. Mark was overjoyed to have his father restored to him. Alex had always spoiled him. I had had to put my foot down at times, but now I watched father and son together and exulted in their closeness. One day Mark came home from school full of the anti-smoking lesson he had just had. 'It's a good thing you gave up, Daddy. Cigarettes can kill you.' We both mumbled in agreement, afraid to meet one another's eyes and have to acknowledge that it was cigarettes which had caused his cancer. He had given up a year or two before, but too late. Another day someone came to visit him and smoked incessantly. When they left, Alex picked up a butt from the ash-tray. 'It's a silly thing to die for, isn't it?' he said.

A man who lived in a neighbouring street called one day. He

wanted Alex to know that he had had the same illness, accepted the removal of the diseased lung, and had survived. 'You will, too,' he said; but I knew that Alex didn't believe him. He never contradicted me when I talked of better days ahead, but he never agreed with me either.

And he was in pain, needing more and more of the painkillers the doctor was so unwilling to dole out. Looking back, I believe that doctor was cruel, even sadistic, demanding, among other things, that Alex attend the surgery each week to get his sick-note signed. It was agony to get him into the car, misery on the journey, and painful for him to sit in the waiting-room, for increasingly he was complaining of pain in his back.

I bought a new mattress, hoping it would help, but when I woke in the night I found he had gone downstairs, unable to sleep for pain. We were short of money, too. His low wage meant we had long since used up any savings, and the sick-pay from his employer had come to an end. Social Security was willing to pay him sickness benefit, and something for Mark. I was a writer, they decreed, and must support myself. In vain I protested that I couldn't write while I was nursing a sick man. They demanded a profit-and-loss account. I had declared the small amount I earned each year to the Inland Revenue, but profit-and-loss accounts were beyond me. I told them, politely, to stuff their money. We would manage.

I was contracted to write a TV play for the BBC based at Pebble Mill. The producer was a young woman called Tara Prem. I made visits to Birmingham, ostensibly to discuss the play, really to convince Alex that I was writing and all was well. Tara would sit with me in the canteen at Pebble Mill while I cried my eyes out. She never lost patience, and I will always be grateful to her.

One day I persuaded Alex to come out in the car. It was a lovely day and we drove to a field beside the sea. It was filled with corn and I coaxed him out of the car to see the rolling waves of gold. He tried a few steps but then he faltered and turned back. As I helped him into the car I saw that the field was studded with scarlet poppies, a Flanders field. Even now I cannot drive past that field when the corn is high.

He was in increasing pain, and would no longer take the weak painkillers prescribed. Sometimes I would go to a sympathetic chemist and beg for something stronger. He would give me two heavy-duty tablets and I would hurry home with them. A friend whose father was a doctor would get pills for me too – whether with his blessing or unknown to him, I dared not ask. I knew only that Alex was in agony and, in the face of the doctor's intransigence, I was powerless to help him. But I saved the tranquillisers given to me, and any other tablets I could get my hands on. I never confronted my reason for amassing this hoard, but I knew what it was. I could not let him die in unbearable pain.

Alex had always been immaculate in his personal habits. Shaving was an important ritual. Now it was becoming difficult for him to stand at the bathroom basin. I knew that it would defeat him if I offered to help him shave sitting down, so we began a charade. I would stand behind him, my arms locked around his waist, pretending to cuddle him, in reality holding him up.

It couldn't last. He was in so much pain and so short of breath that he was re-admitted to hospital. The doctor took me aside. 'I think you should tell your son his father is going to die.' And then, as he saw my anguished face, he hesitated. 'There's still –.' he held up his finger and thumb a quarter of an inch apart, '– a little hope, but I think you should talk to your son.'

I drove Mark to the hospital, and we stood in the field that lay between it and the sea. By arrangement, Alex was at the window, and father and son waved to one another until he got too weak to stand, and was helped away. That night, Aunty Eve came to see me. She had been fond of Alex, and was anxious to help in any way she could. 'I want you to do one thing for me,' I said. 'Buy the plot in the cemetery next to my parents' grave. We won't need it, but I want it just in case.' I did one other thing, something for which I still can't find a logical explanation. I went out, bought cigarettes and started smoking.

They say that the shock of a sudden death is worse than watching someone fail. They're wrong. The long decline doesn't give you time to prepare, because every moment you keep on hoping for a miracle.

The next day I visited Alex. He was sitting up, and seemed relieved to be back in hospital. 'I love you,' I told him, and smiled to show him all was well. 'I'm taking Mark swimming, but I'll be in to see you tonight.' I turned in the ward door and he was smiling as I waved goodbye.

I took Mark swimming. Before he fell ill, Alex had been taking him to the swimming classes at the colliery swimming pool, but as yet all he could do was splash about in the shallow end. On the way home I bought ice-cream, and parked in a lay-by. 'You know Daddy is very ill,' I began. He stopped eating his ice-cream and I saw terror spring up in his eyes. 'He's not going to die!' he said.

I knew then that it would be wrong to make him anticipate death. He was a child. 'No,' I said. 'He's very ill. I just wanted you to know that.' I started the car and we drove home. As I let myself into the house the phone was ringing. 'I'm sorry, Mrs Robertson, but your husband died half an hour ago. He had a heart attack. We did everything we could to save him, but we couldn't resuscitate him.'

'I would never have forgiven you if you had,' I said, but I said it under my breath.

I went to see him as he lay in the hospital chapel. He looked peaceful and I kissed his cold cheek, his cold and lovely cheek. I felt protective of him, a reversal of roles for he had always protected me. The nurse was kind. 'What do you want to happen?' she asked. I knew exactly what I wanted. 'I want him to come home.'

Mark ran screaming into the street when I first told him. Now he was subdued, a frightened little boy. Friends who came to the house kept telling him he must be brave and be the man of the house, and take care of me. Poor little boy, I thought. He's lost his father and now he's being told his mother is a bent reed. The crunch came when tears welled in his eyes and someone told him he mustn't cry. He was eight years old. If he'd been a girl he would have received sympathy. 'He can cry as much as he likes,' I said firmly. And once it was permitted it ceased to be so necessary.

That night I took him into my bed for comfort, but I knew it mustn't last. He must have the wonderful life his father had planned for him, and becoming his mother's comforter wasn't part of the picture.

I got up early the next morning, but already there was a hand-delivered letter on the mat. It was addressed to Mrs D. Robertson, not Mrs A. Robertson, as I had been before. That was the moment when I realised that I no longer had a husband. I was a widow, and the world acknowledged it.

Later that day, when Mark was at school, Alex came home to lie in the front room amid the scent of flowers, the door carefully closed. Mark never knew his father was there, as I tried to make life as normal as possible. We sat at the table although I couldn't eat, watched *Blue Peter*, picked out clean shirts for school, even laughed at a clown on the TV. I felt detached, as though it were some other woman sitting there, composed, even smiling, when in fact the end of the world had come.

At night, when Mark was in bed, I went to Alex and told him how much I loved him. The memories came flooding in. The time I had put my hair up on a date and he had begged me to unpin it because I didn't look like myself. The way he always brought me tulips back from Amsterdam, and once a single orchid in a jar. The night I had wept over Ingrid Bergman till he'd had to lead me from the cinema. The arguments we had had over Germany, arguments that always ended with a kiss; and the way he always, always believed the best of me, so that I became a better person so as not to disappoint him. And then, the night before the funeral, I asked him how I was going to live without him. There was no answer.

11
CHAPTER

FAREWELL

Alex HAD BEEN the Launching Officer of the lifeboat. Now lifeboat men carried his coffin, the same men who had visited him in hospital and tried to keep up his spirits. I can't remember the service but I do remember that I kept thinking about Mark, safe in school, where his father would have wanted him to be. The grave was lined with artificial grass but it did not disguise the clay; rather, it emphasised it. Those present drove away from the cemetery, without my saying goodbye, although I did thank the lifeboat men.

I had listened to friends' scandalised protests that there must be some kind of funeral feast. Had listened and shaken my head. I was remembering the meringues after Joyce's funeral. There would be no repetition of something so bizarre. I wanted to be in my own home, alone. I had work to do.

The coffin was gone but the flowers remained and there were damp petals, remnants of the wreaths, on the carpet. I picked them up one by one and tidied them away, restored the room to normal, and then fetched the small posy I had made up the night before. I wrote a note to go with it, using words from a poem by Elizabeth

Barrett Browning. 'I love thee with the breath, smiles, tears of all my life, And if God choose, I shall but love thee better after death.' No need to sign it. He would know it was from me.

When I reached the cemetery the grave had been filled in and covered with wreaths. I laid the posy among them, stood for a moment, and then hurried off to collect Alex's son from school. I made him sausage and chips, and stood with my back against the fridge while he ate. I couldn't sit down at the table because the three of us had sat there, and the table was unbalanced now. Better for Mark to sit alone.

When he had gone to bed that night, I took out the carrier I had collected from the hospital on the day of Alex's death. It held the few possessions he had had with him: his wallet, a book, reading glasses, some spare pyjamas, and a soiled pair, the pyjamas he had worn at the time of his death. They were still damp when I held them to my face and I inhaled the smell of him for a moment. Then I washed and dried them, and ironed them neatly. It was the last thing I would do for him, and I did it with care.

Afterwards I looked through his wallet. It held a little money – he had never carried a great deal of cash – a picture of me at the time we got engaged, and another of Mark. There were cuttings there, too, almost every word that had ever appeared in print about my work. I cried, then, because I would never again wake up to a note that said 'This is the best thing you have ever done.' Before I went to bed that night I put the bolt in the door. I felt safe, with the world shut outside, but I still kept the bedside lamp on all night, and the radio burbling away in the background for company as I lay, eyes wide open, through the night.

I never cried in front of Mark. Instead I cried in the car and in the bath. You can emerge from a steamy bathroom red-eyed and it's hardly noticeable. The car was more difficult, so I tried not to cry tears. Instead I howled aloud, until the day when I saw a girl on a horse looking at me through the windscreen, an expression of horror on her face.

When Saturday came, I suggested a day out, but I hadn't bargained for the weakness I felt once I got behind the wheel of the car. It seemed to have grown larger so that where once I had been in charge of it, it now seemed in charge of me, zooming along as though it had a life of its own. It was easier once I got past Middlesbrough, but I couldn't face Look-out Point. Not without Alex. We drove on to Helmsley, and I parked in the market square. I had switched off the engine but it seemed that it still throbbed in my thighs. Mark made to climb out but I stopped him. 'Let's just sit still for a minute,' I said. I felt as though I were holding my grief behind a dyke and at any moment it might crack.

We ate in a little café, or rather he ate and I watched. When I toyed with what was on my plate my throat hurt, and I gave up. When he was finished we walked out into the market square. 'I need a lavatory,' he said, and vanished into a public toilet. I stood watching the people come and go, busy, purposeful, laughing, and always in pairs. And then I realised Mark had been gone a long time. Too long. I moved forward, but there was the sharp odour of a men's urinal to hold me back, and when I called Mark's name he didn't answer.

I stared into the opening but all I could see was white tiles. My imagination worked overtime. What if someone had been lurking in there, waiting for little boys who had no dad to protect them? I started to go in, but couldn't. Nothing for it but to cry, then, out loud, and I wrung my hands. You never realise what these phrases mean until you find yourself experiencing them.

A man approached me. 'Are you all right?' he asked. I tried to explain, stumbling over the words, but he understood. He vanished into the toilet, and reappeared holding Mark by the shoulder. A blood-stained hanky was clasped to his face. 'I had a nose bleed. I thought I better stay there till it stopped.' I turned to thank the man, but he had vanished, anxious to get away from the mad woman making a scene in the street. Later that week I went to a function at Mark's school. The head announced that he was delighted to see so many fathers there. That hurt like hell because my son had no father, but never did I wish the words unsaid. It *was* good to see so many fathers there – that was a fact.

For the next week or so we tried to live as normally as we could. We walked to school as though the sun was still in the sky. I read the sympathy letters, which were both a comfort and a knife in my heart. I smoked, too, but never where Mark could see, and I drank. We had kept drink in the house since Alex's seafaring days, but neither of us had bothered with it much. Now I drank my way systematically along the bottles. When Aunty Eve called she asked me what was in my glass, and I had to look at the label on the bottle to find out. She was being kind to me in every way she could, and I was grateful.

All the time I played records, two alternately: Roberta Flack's 'The First Time Ever I Saw Your Face', and Diana Ross's 'Touch Me In The Morning'. I knew they would reduce me to tears, but I wanted that. When Ross sang, 'We don't have tomorrow but we had yesterday', I would have liked the stylus to stick in the groove and repeat those words over and over again. We had had yesterday, but the more I looked at that yesterday the more I saw how selfish I had been. Alex had done everything for me, and only at the end, when it was almost too late, had I done anything for him.

Bit by bit Mark and I developed some kind of normality, but some things were still difficult. Alex had always had grapefruit for breakfast. No one else ate it, but I couldn't stop buying it when I went to the supermarket. To do that would be to acknowledge that he was gone. For the same reason, I couldn't cut down the milk order, so the house filled up with rotting grapefruit and rancid milk. Periodically I would pick up the pulpiest of the fruit and dump it, and up-end one of the bottles over the sink, shaking it till the solid contents tumbled out. I was eating, now, though only cottage cheese spooned from the tub as I stood by the fridge.

But there were comforts, too. Bundles of sticks would be thrown over the wall so I need not chop sticks to lay a fire. Buckets of coal, too, were simply left at the back door. This was solidarity in grief from a community too well acquainted with death. Mark had been learning to swim at the colliery swimming pool. The children wore a belt that dangled from a long pole so that they were safely held while they learned. Holding the pole was the role of the father. Now there was only me. I struggled with the pole until a giant of a young miner shouldered me aside. 'Here, lass, let me.' Hereafter he held the pole until Mark became independent in the water. I never knew his name – only that he was a gentleman.

I needed comfort, for now fear of the future was looming large. Captain Hudson came to see me and told me there would be a lump sum of £3000, but no pension. The Department of Health and Social Security notified me about my widow's pension. I would have £10.50p a week to keep two of us. Unless I could get back to work, I would have to pay a mortgage and feed and clothe us on that.

But when I took my pension booklet to the post office for the first time, feeling about as low as it was possible to feel, the man behind the counter looked up and gave me such a kindly smile that at once I felt better. Such small acts of kindness can make the most enormous difference. And I made a will naming two friends, Ann and Douglas D'Netto, as guardians. When I asked Ann if this was OK her answer was prompt. 'I have four children. If you die I'll have five.'

The next morning a bulky envelope arrived from the BBC. Tony Staveacre, the producer of the film about my life had painstakingly selected shots of Alex and me together and had them printed for me. They made me cry, but they meant a great deal in an age before video. They were the only moments I had left of what had been a very happy day.

I went back to delivering Meals on Wheels. On that first day my legs threatened to give way – small wonder when I was not eating. My partner, a lovely woman called Olive Clifford, was forthright. 'You look washed out. You shouldn't be doing this, not yet.' But I wanted to do it. More doing meant less thinking, and thinking was uncomfortable.

I was trying to think about how I felt about Mark. My feelings towards him seemed to have changed. Where once he had been the centre of my life, now I felt quite flat about him. Outwardly I was as loving as ever, but inwardly I had little or no feeling for him, and I couldn't understand this. Did I feel that he was anchoring me to a life I no longer wanted? Even I knew that taking up smoking when I had just been told what cigarettes had done to Alex was bizarre behaviour. Did I have a death wish, or was I shirking the responsibility of bringing up a son on my own?

I spent a lot of time worrying over how I would cope when he first needed to shave, until I decided I would simply go to Boots, buy everything he had to have, and rely on their advice. God bless Boots. He was being bullied at school by children who had seen his tears for his father, and now thought him vulnerable. I worried over his increasing misery, but I didn't know what to do about it. I was still crying in the car and into my drink when he was in bed.

And increasingly I took out the milder pills I had saved when Alex needed stronger ones, pills I now realised I had half-intended to give him if his life became insupportable. The heart attack had freed me from that need. Now I took them out, and arranged them like flowers on the coffee table, stripping the petals one by one, he loves me, he loves me not, one back into the bottle, one into my mouth. It was a kind of Russian roulette.

By day I would get angry. If someone jumped in front of me in a queue, I wanted to attack them; a wrong word would cause my hands to ball into fists; I wanted a fight with someone, anyone. And at the same time I would see old ladies or gentlemen in the street and wonder if they would put their arms around me if I begged them to.

I warmed to strangers more than to people I knew. All too often, acquaintances who saw me coming towards them in the street would drop their eyes and scuttle past. Friends who did drop by to chat would urge me to take up golf or gardening, when I couldn't have wielded a single iron, and my garden was a two-foot strip at the front door which grew only discarded bus tickets. I found salvation in writing it all down, pouring out my grief and resentment on to paper in a novel.

We were becoming desperately short of money, and I paid a visit to the bank. I would be getting a job soon, I told the manager. Could

I borrow something to tide me over till then? The bank manager was surprisingly sympathetic. He had seen some things about me in the paper. I was a writer. Wouldn't it be better to concentrate on that rather than go back to a nine-to-five job? To this end, he gave me an overdraft and a Budget Account, which seemed to mean that I could pay bills as they came in whether or not I had any money.

When I came out into the street, the now familiar anger engulfed me. How dare he, a bank manager, recommend that I should adopt an insecure lifestyle? I had a child to support. I needed security. If there had been a brick handy I would have lobbed it through the bank window. With hindsight, I think he saw a woman who was in no fit state to apply for jobs and was simply postponing the evil day. Nevertheless, I took his advice.

A number of agents had contacted me when it was announced that my play had won, offering to represent me. I had written back, declining their kind offers. I had Alex for advice; what more did I need? Now things were different. I picked out three of them and made appointments to see them. The journey to London felt like a trip into shark-infested waters. I sat, knees together, hand eternally checking for ticket and purse, until we got to King's Cross. I closed my eyes as the train passed through Finsbury Park. It was less than a year since we had alighted there, but I had lived a lifetime since.

One agent talked big. *Coronation Street* would snap me up; I would be rich beyond rubies. Another I disliked on sight. The third, a woman, talked common sense. 'What do you want to write?' she asked. I remember the exact words of my answer: 'Something that pays weekly.' Then it would have to be short stories for women's magazines, she said. I never read those collections of beauty tips and recipes, but I bought six at W. H. Smith at King's Cross and read them on the way home. I wrote four short stories, and she sold them all. The wolf, if not banished from the door, had at least retreated to the gate.

I still didn't sit at the table to eat, and I had lost a lot of weight. I realised this when I put my coat on one day and the hem was almost touching my shoes because the whole garment had dropped. I went out to buy some new clothes, and bought my first pair of trousers. I had never before worn them, but now they made me feel safe, more in control. I have seldom since worn a skirt.

Mark was not happy, either. He was still being teased at school over missing his father, and had become very withdrawn. In desperation, I arranged a party for Hallowe'en. A friend arrived with her two children. 'I've warned them not to mention his daddy,' she whispered. 'Well, tell them they can mention him whenever they like,' I said. The last thing Mark or I wanted was to airbrush Alex out of our lives.

I was having domestic difficulties, too. I found mice droppings in a drawer, and screamed with fear. 'Don't worry,' Mark said. 'I know what Daddy did last time.' Last time? We had never before had mice. 'Yes, we did. Daddy said not to worry you. He just made them go away.'

I pondered those words that night. Alex had made anything unpleasant go away – so effectively that I had not even been aware. Now I had to cope with the mice, and a blocked sink. I poured stuff down it, used a plunger, anxious not to call out a plumber if I could help it. At last a neighbour's son came to help. He was trying to unscrew the pipe under the sink when it came away in his hand. The resultant tide of gunge almost covered the kitchen floor.

And then one day we were invited to Sunday lunch with friends.

The hostess suggested Mark went out to play with the boys next door. 'They're your age,' she told him, and a little reluctantly he went. While she made lunch I sat and worried. Was he all right? Would they bully him? Perhaps they had shunned him, and he was standing outside, too scared to come in. I couldn't sit still, and went to look.

The shrieks of glee could be heard from the front door. They were out in the street, each armed with an empty washing-up bottle filled now with water. All three were soaked, and Mark was getting the worst of it. But he had a huge grin on his face. I went back into the house and got a bottle for myself. With my back-up, Mark came into his own. The two boys, one dark and one fair, looked at me strangely, obviously unused to seeing a woman run around in the street, but I was having fun. At last the water ran out, and the bigger boy told the younger one to get some more. 'You know Dad said we couldn't have any more,' the little one said. And I thought: 'What a misery – doesn't like his children having fun.'

We were still slightly damp as we drove home, but I felt strangely peaceful. That burst of energy had done us good.

The following afternoon, both boys turned up at our door. I invited them in, and Philip, the younger one, immediately offered to make tea. He was obviously proud of his ability, so I let him. He was quiet and reserved. The other, John, the blond one, was full of energy, and restlessly curious about us, the house, the back yard, everything. I made some tea, and with them sitting at the table the unset place was not so obvious.

They told me they didn't have a mother, but that they had two other older brothers, Peter and David, who were away at school. John would follow next September and could hardly wait. My opinion of their father grew worse. Begrudged them a water fight, and packed them off to school. Nice man!

Now they arrived every day, and they were very welcome. They were capable too, eating up small jobs like plugs and loose screws. I thoroughly enjoyed their company and the sound of laughter in the house once more, but I knew now that I must move away. I wanted to go back to Sunderland.

One night, when the boys had gone home and Mark was in bed, I went up to check on him. He had fallen asleep, a book open on the bedspread. He looked like his father, and suddenly I felt afraid. Downstairs, I did the familiar ritual of pills and booze, and tried to work out what was happening in my head.

And suddenly it was clear. I had lost everyone, mother, sister, husband. Mark was all I had left, and I was resigning myself to losing him, too. I was so convinced he would be taken away from me that I had tried to blot out the love I felt for him, so that it would hurt less when the time came. Except that I wouldn't lose him. I would take good care of him, and keep him safe as his father would have done. I put the top back on the bottle, and went to bed. But not before I had put my half-written novel away in a drawer. Such outpourings of grief had no place in the future.

In the early days I had to go back and forth to London to secure work, and I dreaded the trips. I had to set off early in the morning leaving Mark alone in the house with instructions to go to school when the clock reached a certain point. All the way down on the train I imagined the house on fire, or a traffic accident on the way. Once there was a policeman standing at the barrier as I left the station, and I waited for him to say, 'Mrs Robertson? I'm afraid I've got some bad news.' Now, thirty years on, if I catch sight of a policeman in King's Cross, my heart still lurches. I counted the hours and minutes I was away, ticking them off until home-time. I still do it now. After school Mark would catch a bus to my aunt's house in Sunderland, and stay there until I collected him straight from the station.

It was a far from ideal arrangement, but it was the best I could do. Paid childcare was out of my range, and there was no one else. And this way I was at home nine days out of every ten. If I had gone back to a nine-to-five job, I would have been missing every day when he came home.

12
CHAPTER

GOING HOME

I HAD AN overpowering urge to move house. Now, I realise that it is a common consequence of bereavement. Then, I knew only that I must get away as soon as I could, and getting away meant going home. I would go back to Sunderland where I had always been happy, and everything would be all right. I found a huge terraced house in Valebrook with a bathroom upstairs and another down. My plan was that Mark and I would live downstairs, and I would let the upstairs. That would deal with my fear of living alone, for now I sat up in bed until daylight, afraid to close my eyes in the dark. If there were other people living in the house, however separately, I would feel better.

I was taking tranquillisers, and I hardly ever ate, but life was on the move. When you are widowed, everyone tells you you have only to ask if you need help, but it's hard to ask, and after the funeral very few actually offer. I longed for some man to take Mark to the places his father had taken him, but no one did, with the honourable exception of my neighbour, Tom Cartwright, who, while we still lived in Seaham, never took his own son anywhere without knocking to see if Mark wanted to come too.

When the boys came into our lives, it eased the disquiet I felt about Mark's loss. I took all three of them bowling, enjoying the freedom of my new trousers, listening to an endless stream of romantic music. David Cassidy's 'Cherish' seemed to play all the time – 'You don't know how many times I've wished that I could hold you' . . . If the boys noticed that my eyes were permanently brimming with tears, they never mentioned it. They were, in fact, the perfect companions, and I watched Mark gradually begin to smile again.

And then one night I was invited to a party by a couple I knew. Gillian said 'Go. It'll do you good.' I went to ask a neighbour's daughter to babysit, and her father answered the door in his stockinged feet. 'If she can't do it, pet, I'll do it myself. You need to get out.' He was only half joking. Such is the kindness of mining communities.

I went in a new grey dress, two sizes smaller than I had worn before, but first I had to put on make-up and jewellery. It felt strange, bizarre even. I had done those things for Alex. What was the point of them, now? I made up my face, wiped it off, made it up again. Jewellery went on and off, in and out. I felt like a fallen woman as I got into the car and drove to the party.

The hostess was kind, but I felt out of place among other couples, and even more so when one upstanding citizen, his wife a few yards away, whispered that I needn't be lonely in future unless I chose. His hand lingered on my waist and slid down. Two seconds later I was on my way back to the car, realising just how alone and unprotected I now was, and that widows were considered easy game.

I drove home without really thinking of what I was doing. I must have passed through two sets of traffic lights, but I wasn't aware of them. I was nearly home and then a police car passed me, blue light flashing. I pulled up and waited. The officer got out and walked back. I wound down the window and he bent down. 'Mrs Robertson, are you trying to kill yourself?' It was so gentle and so unexpected that I burst into tears. He sent me on my way with a warning, and thereafter I remembered that a car was a lethal weapon and I had Alex's son to take care of.

One problem was that I kept forgetting Alex was dead. When I sold a short story I would think, 'Wait till I tell Alex.' I would see a man in the street and open my mouth to greet my husband. He was everywhere, in crowds, down side-streets, always smiling, until he turned into a stranger and the truth struck home.

Around this time I received the best piece of advice I've ever had. It came from an elderly lady who had lost her husband in the First World War. 'Don't look down the future,' she told me. 'It's so vast it will frighten you. Just take life a day or a week at a time, and you'll cope.'

I was writing regularly now, turning out the short stories which were all selling. I had never regretted putting away the sad novel. I needed to make money, not indulge my grief. And to my relief the agent managed to sell the stories to foreign countries, sometimes as many as four or five, once twelve times, and each time it was printed I got paid. I also received a copy of the magazine, but it was hard to decide which story it was, for the title was in a foreign language and was sometimes changed altogether.

I had feared that I might have difficulty in getting a mortgage for the £7000 that Valebrooke cost, but it had been surprisingly easy. The bank helped me, and it went through without a hitch, the £3000 I had received when Alex died serving as a deposit.

As autumn turned to winter, it was time to pack up. A sink and cooker were installed in an upstairs bedroom of the Valebrooke house for the tenants-to-come; I furnished the flat from the auction rooms, and we moved. I said my goodbyes to the house, remembering how the previous owner had come and begged to look round after her husband died. I had been more than happy to let her check out her memories. One day it would be my turn. Till then I must drink it all in – the kitchen with its red tiles, the white wall in the yard with its mock flowers, the huge fireplace in the front room with the popping gas fire, and the little window in the hall where I had stood to take that fatal phone call. I stored it all up, and then I closed the door for the last time.

I had imagined that I would seldom see the boys once we moved to Sunderland. I was wrong. They went to prep school there, so Valebrooke became their first port of call after lessons. Philip was always the law-abiding one, John the rebel. One day I heard them arguing. Their father had told them they were not to come to me every afternoon, and Philip was afraid of retribution. As usual, John's will prevailed. They kept on coming, which pleased me but obviously displeased their father.

I had never met him, but I had long been ready to heartily dislike him, especially when John told me that his yellow, rather racy-looking car had reclining seats. I don't know why, but I took that as a sign of a dissolute life. When I drove them home one day, one of their older brothers, home from his public school, was waiting at the gate. 'You're going to get it when you get in,' he said. 'Dad was waiting to go out.' John simply shrugged, but Philip looked distinctly worried. 'Don't worry,' I said firmly, and got out of the car. I rang the doorbell, my fury mounting at this bully who threatened his children.

The man who answered the door was tall and thin and harassed-looking. He had a tea-towel in one hand, and at the sight of me in full flood he visibly shrank. 'I understand you're going to thrash this child,' I said. His mouth fell open. 'What for?' he said. 'For being late,' I answered. 'It was my fault, and they shouldn't be blamed.' I was beginning to feel foolish. Whatever he was, this man was no child-beater. He assured me I'd been misinformed, thanked me for taking his boys out, hoped they weren't a nuisance, and asked if I'd like a cup of tea. I said no, thank you, and beat a retreat. So the boys' visits continued.

When the house was full of children and the young couple were in the flat above, I was happy. During the day, when the children were all at school, I felt desolate. If I was in the house, I wanted to be out. Once out, I wanted to be in. Back in, I wanted out again. I could find no peace. Sometimes I walked down into town and bought something I didn't need with money I couldn't spare. One day I was crossing the main street with a dress bag in my hand when I asked myself: 'Is this all there is going to be to life?'

And I was finding taking care of everything on my own a difficult task. Valebrooke had a huge central-heating system that fed itself – but only after I had filled a vast hopper above my head with coke. Sometimes I would weep tears of fatigue and frustration as I missed the opening and coke cascaded around me.

The first Christmas without Alex came a few weeks after we moved. The couple living above went back to their family for the whole of the holiday season. Gillian, by now married, invited me for Christmas Day and I accepted gratefully, knowing she would be kind to Mark. But in the afternoon I left him there, and drove to the cliffs above the sea. I didn't cry. I sat and made a list of the twenty things I would do in the New Year to make things better for Mark and me.

I declined all invitations for New Year's Eve. I wanted to be alone with Mark. I let him stay up to see in the New Year and promised him that things would get better. His eyes were heavy with sleep, but he nodded his head, and I realised how much he resembled his father. I hadn't really lost everything, Alex lived on in his son, and I must make sure that the coming year was good for us both.

When the boys returned to school after the holidays, and resumed their daily visits, John filled me in on the riotous New Year they'd had. 'Dad's friends arrived half-drunk,' he said, 'and then, when they were fully drunk, David drove them home.' David was his eldest brother, and the proud possessor of a car. I kept my opinion of fully-drunk parties to myself. I'd jumped to conclusions before, and been left with egg on my face.

The following week I bumped into Jack Tomlin, the boys' father. 'John tells me you and Mark were alone at New Year,' he said. 'You should have come to us. We had some friends in.' I repressed the urge to say, 'Fully-drunk friends?', and explained that I had wanted to be alone that first New Year. 'I know how it feels,' he said. 'It's not easy.' His next-door neighbour had filled me in on the details, so I knew that Joyce, his beautiful young wife, had died of leukaemia when his sons were one, two-and-a-half, five and seven, and that he was bringing them up alone. Of course he knew how it felt!

A week later I took all three boys to see *West Side Story*. It wasn't as good as a James Bond film, but they enjoyed it. When we pulled up at their house, Jack was waiting in the porch, and for the first time I realised he was rather good-looking. He came over to the car. 'Did they behave themselves?' I smiled and nodded, and prepared to let out the clutch, but he stayed at the car window. 'Joyce and I saw that show in London.' 'So did we,' I said. 'Well, the film anyway.'

As I drove home, I was remembering the night we saw that film, and how Alex and I held hands and sang 'Maria' all the way back to the car park.

By now I was going out occasionally on dates. The first time a man took me out for a meal, I went through the same pantomime with make-up, and made a bee-line for the darkest corner of the restaurant. I didn't want entanglements but I longed for conversation. The trouble was that no one's conversation measured up to Alex's. I was bored. Only with the children did I feel in the least fulfilled.

One day I promised to take them to Hamsterley Forest, but a thick fog descended. We went anyway, the fog simply adding to the adventure. When it was time to come home I couldn't see the edges of the forest road, so John volunteered to hang out of the car and watch for the verge. And then suddenly, in the ghostly headlights, we saw a fawn, a tiny thing trotting ahead of us, obviously scared and anxious to get away from the car. I was afraid we would herd it away from its mother so I slowed down and we watched until it trotted off into the fog and was lost to sight. Such things are magic memories.

Jack was at the gate when we got home. 'The boys tell me Mark has to catch a bus to Sunderland when you're in London,' he said. I nodded. 'He goes to my aunt.' 'Well, the boys think he's a bit bored there. Why don't you let him come here after school?' I protested that I couldn't possibly foist yet another boy on to him, but he smiled. 'When you've got four, one more makes very little difference.'

So Mark began to go to Jack when I was in London. Jack refused my offer to come and collect him, and said he would run him home if I rang as soon as I got back. At first he brought John and Philip with him, then he came alone. The first time that happened he came in, and seemed disinclined to leave. At last he said, 'Would you like to go out for a drink?' I was tired after London, but it seemed churlish to say no. The people upstairs were prepared to watch over Mark, who had gone to bed, and we went to a nearby pub. He talked about his wife, I talked about Alex, and it was a relief not to have to watch my words. This man understood. I told him I had considered moving right away, at least for a while. 'It's no good running away,' he said, and I knew he was right.

The nights out became a fixture; and then Sunderland was gripped by FA Cup fever. Sunderland AFC got to the semi-final, then the final. The town went mad. All three boys demanded red and white scarves, and I started knitting, but the shops had run out of red and white wool, and I had to settle for a terrible fluorescent orange. Jack had a ticket for Wembley, and I offered to have the boys for the weekend. He was driving back on Sunday morning, and I invited him to lunch. It was only after he was gone and it was too late to withdraw the invitation, that I realised this meant I would have to make a proper meal. Moreover, I would have to sit down at the table. You could hardly stand with your back against the fridge when you had an adult guest, and I knew him well enough now to know that he was meticulous about setting table and giving his children a proper routine.

That morning I stood in the kitchen, unable to remember how you drew a Sunday lunch together. I knew how to deal with each separate dish, but I couldn't —or wouldn't – remember how you timed things so everything was ready at once. It was Philip who saved the day, standing in the kitchen, saying, 'Now do this,' and sometimes stepping in to do it if I didn't respond quickly enough. He had grown up without a mother, and he was as capable a little boy as it was possible to be, a testament to his father's upbringing.

We sat down together, my first proper meal in my own home, and toasted Sunderland's win with sparkling wine. Later that week we went to see the team's triumphant return with the cup. The crowd was euphoric, and I realised that I too was quietly happy. A month later we went out for a drink together. It was 9.30 at night when Jack said, 'It's the Trooping of the Colour tomorrow. I've always wanted to see that.' I was in a jokey mood. 'Let's go, then.' Ten minutes later we were speeding home to pick up the boys and bundle them sleepily into the car.

We drove through the night and joined the crowds in the Mall, taking turns to lift the boys up so they could see, until a stranger beside us took the third boy and hauled him up so all three were aloft. Coming home in the car, they were all moaning about hunger, and I promised food in ten minutes when we got back. I did it too, in Jack's kitchen!

I felt less lonely now. Often I found myself laughing out loud, and I ceased to feel guilty about it when I remembered how much Alex had always enjoyed a joke. I went down to Birmingham for the recording of my second television play, *The Medium*. It was the story of a house party held to celebrate the visit of a medium, and although it centred on a death it had some funny lines. 'I do admire you,' one of the crew said one day. 'I know you've lost your husband, and yet you can still see the funny side of things.' It was true. At first you think you will never laugh again but life reasserts itself, whether or not you like it, and humour returns too.

Jack and I were often in each other's homes. One night he came into the kitchen at Valebrooke and found me swigging down the pills I took each night. His eyes widened at the number, and then he said, 'I didn't think you were so selfish.' I knew what he meant. Knew, too, that he would never have done anything risky when he was still responsible for children. That was the last night I did my 'loves me, loves me not' routine. He took me to see his old school, where his two elder sons now were, and where John would go in September. Mark was still at school in Seaham, and each morning our cars would cross as he took the boys to Sunderland and I took Mark to Seaham. We watched for one another, and flashed our lights; and on the odd occasion when we missed each other, it was a disappointment. Something was happening, and we both knew it.

Eventually he asked Mark and me to go on holiday to Southport. I said no. I wasn't ready for such a step. We were friends. A holiday would mean something more than friendship.

The Friday before the holiday we said goodbye, and I wished them all bon voyage. The next morning, Jack arrived on the step, Philip in tow. 'Philip really wants you to come,' he pleaded. 'Will you change your mind?' We both knew who wanted me to change my mind. Philip was an excuse, but I could never resist Philip. It took me ten minutes to pack, and we were on our way. I shared a room with Mark, Jack with the boys.

Out on the miniature golf course, I got in the way of a swinging club and collected a black eye. That night we sat in the hotel lounge, me nursing my shiner, the boys playing billiards in the next room, and Jack proposed. I had known it was coming but hadn't formulated an answer. There would be advantages for all the younger children. A few days earlier, I had come out of the hairdresser's to see Mark waiting for me among a gaggle of women. Was that to be the pattern of his life: waiting for his mother? Jack could give him guidance and a ready-made family. I could certainly mother the two younger boys, and perhaps befriend the older two. I would ease Jack's load domestically; he would offer me the support I so badly missed. Who would lose? But Alex had been dead only a year.

I was struggling for an answer when John came in search of money for crisps. The tension was defused, and when we were alone again I said yes.

We decided to tell all five boys that weekend. We arrived home from Southport on the Friday night, and had just unloaded the car when the doorbell rang. It was a man who had done contract work for him, come to tell him that someone had applied to have Jack's business put into liquidation. When we looked, the notice was there in the paper, an application for winding up.

'I can't marry you now,' Jack said. 'I'll have nothing to offer you.' But if anything the news made me more sure of the rightness of our coming together. He needed me, and so did the children. I brought a little smile to his face by threatening to sue him for breach of promise, and then we set about working out how to turn a disaster into a triumph. Now I had something to do with my life.

13
CHAPTER

NEW BEGINNINGS

THE NEXT FEW days were a blur of solicitors and courts as Jack fought off the attempt to close his business. It had been brought by a sub-contractor frustrated by non-payment of a bill, but Jack was able to prove that his business was viable, and the order was withdrawn.

Nevertheless, it was obvious that his business was in a bad way. Our great ally was Jack's solicitor, Cyril Barker – a huge man, disabled by polio but the best person in the world to have by your side in a tight spot. I told him that it was my intention to sell Valebrooke, now worth twice what I had paid for it, and put the money into the business. He asked me if I had thought it through, and I said I had. 'Very well,' he said. 'I'm really glad for you both. You're getting a good man, but you need to make him tougher.'

He went on to tell me that Jack was a superb builder but bad at getting in his money. 'There are people in this town, people with money, who actually boast that they've managed to evade paying him,' he said. If I didn't believe that at the time, I certainly did later as the crazy world of house-building unfolded to me.

But if Cyril was glad for us, other people were not. One woman stopped me in the main street. 'I never would have thought this of you,' she said. Another, in Sunderland town centre, was more dramatic. 'Just tell me what I've heard isn't true?' Alex had been dead for only a year. But I had five children to consider. What was the point of denying them family life any longer than necessary?

And I knew that what I was doing would be good for Mark. If it was good for Mark, it was what Alex would have wanted, too. Mark would now have a father-figure and brothers. But it was hard to bear the distress in the eyes of one of the men Alex had worked with at the harbour. 'You must do what you think best,' he said, but he could hardly bear to look at me. Another, rather spiteful, young woman called at the door one day while I was at Jack's. 'So this is how you solved your housing problem,' she said, obviously meaning that I had needed a secure roof over my head and was marrying to get one. 'If you only knew,' I thought, but aloud I simply said something about the weather.

I know there is supposed to be a respectable length of time for mourning. In part, this is to protect you from rushing headlong into a wrong relationship out of loneliness and grief. But the idea that there is a moment when you stop loving the one you have lost and can therefore transfer that love to another is foolish. If you have truly loved, you never stop loving. The grief is endless. I have missed Alex every day since he died. I will miss him until I die, and for all I know beyond that. But another part of me has gone on to love again as deeply and lastingly. I wish people would understand that.

Two things sustained me through this time. One was a letter from Annie, Alex's sister. 'I know you would have given your life for my brother. Now I know he would want you and Mark to be safe and happy. If this is a good man, I wish you all the happiness in the world.' And with the letter came a gift of beautiful embroidered pillowcases. The other balm to my soul came from a vicar who was a fellow Rotarian of Jack's. 'When we have a meal at Rotary he doesn't eat,' he said. 'Frankly, I've thought he was going into a decline. You'll do him the world of good.'

We arranged to marry in November, the same month as Princess Anne. I wasn't sure how to conduct a wedding second time around. Who should send out the invitations? In the end we settled for 'Jack and Denise invite you'. I bought a cream Ossie Clark off-the-peg dress that Gillian assured me was just right, and decided to carry a single orchid. Gillian would be my bridesmaid once more, and wear pink. I had bought a wedding-etiquette booklet but it didn't cheer me. A second-time-around bride should dress soberly, it said. She should enter the church by a side door and there should be little fuss. If a man was marrying for the second time, however, there was no need for any such restriction. So much for equality.

A few days before the wedding we were asked out to a friend of Jack's. We were just leaving when the phone rang. It was a friend ringing to wish me well and tell me that Alex had told her, when she visited him in hospital, that he hoped I would marry again. 'So you see, he'd be glad about this,' she said. When I put the phone down, I felt as though my heart would break. I had tried so hard to make him think he would get better, and he had played along with me when, in fact, he had known all along that he was dying. I cried for an hour, while Jack stood by, uncertain what to do to help. When at last we reached the party I blamed my swollen eyes on hay fever, but I don't think anyone was fooled.

On the day of the wedding, I felt oddly calm. Aunty Eve and Gillian helped me to get ready. Mark wore a grey suit and looked strangely grown up. I had talked things over with him many times, and I knew he felt comfortable with what was happening; but doubts were assailing me. I was putting his inheritance into Jack's business. Did I have the right to do that? And then I thought of the companionship and security he would get in return. It was a fair exchange.

But my composure couldn't last. The car taking me to the church lost its way, and wound up at the entrance to the harbour. I thought of the nights I had sat there in the car, baby asleep on the back seat, waiting for Alex's blond head to appear under the lamp and to take him safely home. By the time I reached the church I was sobbing uncontrollably. The vicar, Roy Braine, had been a tower of strength to Jack when he was widowed. He took in my tear-stained face and seized my arm, saying firmly, 'Now we're going to have a happy time.' He acted swiftly, but not before a photographer had snapped me crying my eyes out. It ornamented the evening paper under the headline 'Playwright Marries'.

The first time I married I had worried about the dress, the veil, how I would look from the back when I knelt at the altar. Now, all I could think of was the responsibility I was taking on. Somehow I must make everyone happy.

We drove down to London to honeymoon, intending to stay for six days, but on the fourth day Gillian, who was looking after the boys, phoned to say that Peter had an abscess in his tooth, and we should come home. We arrived back to find the younger boys at the gate. As I got out of the car, John stepped forward, the spokesman as usual. 'Dad always said we couldn't have a dog because there was no one to look after it. You're here now. When is the dog coming?' It wasn't a request. It was a statement. I walked past him into the house, suddenly aware of just what I had taken on. There were seven of us now, and they wanted animals.

When I thought it over, however, it made sense to get them a puppy. They had been motherless for a long time. It was up to me to show them that having a mother came with advantages. Mitch arrived a week or two later. He was a black-and-white terrier, and I wanted nothing to do with him. 'I won't touch him, feed him, walk him or be left alone with him,' I said. 'You wanted him. You look after him.' A month later I was besotted, and one of the most rewarding experiences of my life was beginning.

But if the pup was a joy, other things were more difficult. I was moving into a house that had belonged to another woman and in many ways still did. Her name had not only been Joyce, it was Catherine Joyce, the same name as my sister. Her photographs were everywhere, her brushes with the monogram CJ were on the dressing table, I slept in her bed. Curtains hung shabbily at windows, but she had put them there – who was I to take them down? I would open books and see her name on the fly-leaf, so like that other name.

I had brought my furniture with me, but somehow it seemed sacrilege to cram it in. Pieces of it had to go, and parting was painful. I felt as though parts of my life were being hacked off. In addition, I was finding that second marriage was more difficult. The first time you marry you are green, and you bend. This time Jack and I both had established lifestyles – he liked to sleep with the windows shut, I had to have them open. Little things like that needed give and take.

In all this, Mrs Bates, who cleaned for Jack, was a wonderful comfort. When I first appeared, she put in her notice. She would stay till I settled in, then she was off. Now, as I struggled to make two homes into one I could feel comfortable with, she withdrew her notice. 'Now that I've had a look at you, I'll stay, if that's all right with you.' It was more than all right, it was wonderful.

She was with me when, trying to tidy the box-room because John wanted to move into it, I opened a cardboard box. There was a circlet of orange-blossom, yellow with age and attached to a grey mass. I picked it up, and the grey mass disintegrated and fragments swam in a shaft of sunlight. It was Joyce's wedding veil, and I let out a little howl of anguish. 'Give it here,' Mrs Bates said, and vanished. What she did with it I never knew and didn't ask. Ten years later I would write that scene into a novel, *The Second Wife*. The fragments of that veil, spinning in the sunlight, are still etched on my memory.

The first Christmas was a happy one. While the boys were in bed we laid out their gifts in piles, one for each boy. Later, as we sat with a drink, Jack told me of the Christmas his young wife had died. Her funeral was on Christmas Eve, and that night he had filled four stockings, for the first time alone. I could see it had affected him deeply, for he had loved her very much. But this knowledge only reinforced my feeling of being an interloper.

I took to looking through photograph albums, seeing her always smiling. Jack was smiling too, in every photograph. Often he was holding a baby – David, the first-born; then Peter; John next, always recognisable because of the yellow thatch; and Philip, born when his mother was already ill. And in those photographs where he was holding Philip, Jack looked ill too, with the pallor of a man who knows his happiness will soon end.

But none the less I was revelling in having a large family. I had wanted six children; now I had managed five, and it felt good. Philip was the great help, John the one who kept me constantly anxious and constantly amused. One day I was washing up at the sink when his face appeared at the window in front of me. Unremarkable – except that it was upside-down because he was dangling from the roof. Another time, I was driving home past a field with a six-foot hedge when he suddenly soared into view on his bike, ten feet in the air. He had rigged up barrels and planks in the field and was riding up them Evil Knievel style. He didn't always avoid the casualty department, but, considering his antics, it's a wonder they didn't offer him permanent residence.

And the boys all loved Mitch, dressing him up in a football shirt so he could join in their games. I watched Mark enjoying a family, and I knew I had done the right thing.

Valebrooke was up for sale, but it was taking time, and we needed the money urgently to shore up the business. I had never felt that I lived in Valebrooke, so parting with it was no strain. I just wanted to get the business on an even keel, and settle down. Worry prevented Jack from sleeping through the night. Whatever time I woke, he would be awake, staring down the dark, tuned in to the World Service beside him. I understood his tension. I came to dread Thursdays, pay-day, because it was always a struggle to meet the wage-bill. On Fridays, when we had managed it, I felt euphoric. I still like Fridays, thirty years on.

The building trade was under pressure, or rather the solid core of small builders was. Wimpey and McAlpine were doing well, and cowboys were springing up everywhere. Only middle-sized businesses like Jack's, paying their taxes, declaring their profits, were slowly being strangled. And I was beginning to see that building one-off rather posh houses, as Jack did, was a minefield.

One owner wanted gold taps. They were fitted and stolen. Fitted again, stolen again. Another ordered every room in the new house to be painted magnolia. Jack advised against it. She insisted. The house was handed over on a Friday morning. At noon she rang to say it was like a hospital, and every room must be painted a different colour by five o'clock. Architects told him to take short cuts. Clients objected —sometimes forcibly. When I told him to tell the client who was to blame, he pointed out that all his work came from architects. If he upset them, the work would dry up. And people lied. One house was built with a cellar. Jack advised proper lining to exclude damp. The client didn't want to pay, arguing that it wasn't necessary, so Jack went ahead according to instruction. A year later the client refused to pay the balance of his bill on the grounds of dampness in the cellar!

I tried to concentrate on the family. The boys had told me the thing they had missed most was home cooking. I was no cook, but I tried to oblige. They liked Victoria sandwich cakes hot from the oven so that the jam melted and ran down the sides. And when I made vol-au-vents they ate them hot from the oven before I had a chance to fill them. Eventually I would progress to biscuits, and would cook and freeze soup – anything to make sure there was something for them to eat. Jack was actually a better cook than me because he'd had plenty of practice, so between us we managed.

The regime in the house was looser, now. Jack was happy for me to decide things. Only once did he over-rule me. The boys were fond of watching James Burke's science programme. One day, reading the *Radio Times*, Jack discovered that the topic for discussion on that night would be VD. 'They can't watch that,' he said. In vain I argued that they were growing up. If we watched it with them, we could discuss it. I had always discussed things with Mark, and I could talk to the boys just as easily. It was useless. We piled them all into the car and went on a car-ride that lasted until

Jack could be sure that James Burke had departed the air-waves.

Although the boys had been loved and cared for, discussion had not been a priority. Quite early on in my marriage, one of the boys, by then living away, asked if I could tell him what his mother had died of. In all his growing up, it had never been mentioned.

Mark was due to go into hospital to have a small abdominal operation. I tried to spend as much time as I could with him, but then Philip started to be poorly, vomiting and losing weight. I took him to the family doctor, and he decided to do blood tests. A few days later I rang for the results, only to be told that we must come back to see the doctor. Once in the surgery, he asked Philip to wait outside. I licked suddenly dry lips as he toyed with the things on his desk. 'I'm afraid it's bad news.' I waited. 'It's as I suspected. His white blood-cell count is up. It looks like leukaemia.'

I felt bile rise up in my throat, and at that moment something twanged in my abdomen. I had felt that sensation before, when I was about to give birth. The doctor said he would contact the hospital, and I walked out to collect Philip, looking small and forlorn in the waiting-room. We walked home together, chatting about something and nothing, and all the while I was making plans. What I knew beyond doubt was that I would not let this child die. I loved him, and I had lost enough already. I was not losing him. We could sell the house and take him to Manchester, London even.

I didn't tell Jack. I muttered something about more tests, and then rang a friend of mine, a doctor. 'It's what his mother died of. Just tell me lightning can't strike twice in the same place.' There is always a pause before bad news. It came now. Then he said, 'I wish I could say that, Denise, but I can't. And you have to tell Jack. It's his child.'

I walked out into the garden where Jack was digging in a border.

He turned round and smiled at me, and I saw for once he looked relaxed. I couldn't wipe that rare smile from his face. Instead I said, 'The doctor wants to send him to hospital, but I think I'll take him somewhere privately.'

The next day I took him to the best paediatrician in town. He had treated one of the other boys and knew the family. He took a history from me, examined Philip and then asked him to wait outside. 'It's not leukaemia,' he said. 'In fact, I don't think there's much wrong with him.' I wanted to believe him, but didn't dare. 'What about the sickness and the blood count?' 'Children can have a rise in white blood-cells with a minor infection. The sickness is probably emotional. Has anything upset the household lately?'

I shook my head. 'No. My son's been in hospital, but apart from that. . . ' He was smiling. 'And you've been spending a lot of time at the hospital?' I nodded. His grin broadened. 'This little boy has had no mother for a long time. Then you come along, and things improve. All of a sudden your attention is elsewhere, and he feels abandoned. Is your son home now? Good. I don't expect we'll have any more trouble.' And we didn't.

But as the spring came and the garden was suddenly full of daffodils, I went back to perusing the photographs, a strange kind of self-torture that left me in tears. How could I measure up to that other life, filled with babies and gala days and obviously without a care in the world? There could be no babies for me, much as I wanted them. We had enough on our hands. And even though Valebrooke had now sold and the pressure had eased, life was still a struggle. The only relief I could get was turning up the thermostat on the boiler and then holding my hands under the hot tap till my fingers swelled and throbbed with pain.

14
CHAPTER

GHOSTS

JOHN WAS AWAY at school now, David already at university, and Peter on the verge of going. John had looked forward to going away to school; now I sensed that he was not quite so keen. But at last the summer holidays came. Jack loved holidays, and had enjoyed wonderful trips abroad in earlier years. We couldn't afford a lavish holiday, but he suggested we hire a mobile home and take the three younger boys to France.

I had been abroad only once, on my honeymoon with Alex, but Jack was enthusiastic, and the mobile home was duly hired. When, bags packed, we went to collect it, we were told that, as we hadn't informed them we were taking it out of the country, we couldn't have it. I wasn't going to have the children disappointed at this stage. 'We'll go in the car,' I said. Jack was dubious, I was determined.

A tent was hired, we piled everything on top of the Ford Cortina, and off we went. We were crossing London en route for Dover when the car groaned and came to a halt, right beside Churchill's statue in Parliament Square. There we were, two adults, three boys, a tower of camping gear, with traffic whizzing by: it looked like disaster. Until an angel in the form of a Cockney appeared. He was driving past, he took in the situation at a glance, and leaped from his car, holding a tow rope. He towed us as far as a garage, and then hurried off, waving aside our profound thanks.

The garage owner made a temporary repair, but shook his head at the folly of our expedition. 'It'll go again,' he said gloomily. He was right. We held our breath as we limped on, especially in the queue for the ferry, but we made it across the Channel to a camp site at Gravelines, which the boys christened 'Gravel pits', not without some justification.

Making that holiday work was not easy, but it was worth while. The car conked out more than once, but each time we got it repaired, and somehow the stress added to the enjoyment. All too soon, however, we had to return home to face the difficulties of workaday life – although we did manage to hire a Dormobile the following year and repeat the trip. This time we took Peter as well.

I had written my third television play. Like the second, it was about death, a sad tale of a young widow whose husband was killed in the pit. I hadn't enjoyed writing it. Somehow, plays were linked in my mind with the time of Alex's illness and death. It would be ten years before I attempted another, and twenty-five years before I actually completed one.

Another thing that may have contributed to my dislike of writing plays was the episode of the Birmingham bombs. In November 1974, the IRA blew up two Birmingham pubs packed with young people. Up to 120 customers had to be ferried to hospital by bus, ambulance, taxi – any vehicle that came to hand. I arrived in Birmingham, where the play was being produced, to attend final rehearsals. I had been miserable on the train, as I always was when leaving home. Now I emerged into the city's New Street

Station to hear carols being played on loudspeakers to people still obviously traumatised by what had occurred the night before. When I got into a taxi to go to the BBC, it was all the driver could talk about. 'I had to clean blood off the seat you're sitting on,' he told me.

For reasons I can't explain, I have never known fear of bombs, nor of the train accidents that have sometimes overshadowed my travels. But I felt a terrible grief that day for the people involved in that outrage, and an overwhelming desire to go home. And it brought back a vivid memory of my Grandpa Cahill crying, years before, over the actions of the IRA.

I was still writing short stories, and they were still selling. I was also writing the occasional feature for magazines. We needed the money desperately, as cash-flow in the business fluctuated. I wrote with Mitch's head on my foot, alone in a quiet house with everyone at school or work. When inspiration failed me, he and I would walk in the park until I worked out a tricky angle of the plot. He seemed to know when the writing was going well, and when I was stuck. Whoever says dogs don't understand human emotions has never owned one.

At his own request, John had come home from his public school, and I was glad to have him back. I was enjoying the business of step-motherhood so much that I wrote an article about it. The week after it had been published, the phone rang as I was getting tea ready. The man on the other end of the phone had got my number from the *Sunderland Echo*, and sounded desperate. 'I've read your article,' he said. 'You seem to be able to do this stepping thing. I can't and it's threatening my marriage.' He wanted to come and see me. He was willing to pay for advice, any sum.

'Where do you live?' I asked. He lived in Portsmouth, more than

300 miles away. I turned down his cash and his visit, gave him what help I could over the phone, and went back to cut bread with trembling fingers. I wasn't qualified to advise anyone else. I could only just cope with my own life.

As far as being a second wife was concerned, I wasn't coping at all. I spent hours agonising over those old pictures. I cried, scalded my hands under the hot tap, reproached Jack for not smiling – ignoring the fact that, with a faltering business and a neurotic wife, he had precious little to smile about. Eventually I went to see the doctor. He was a friend of mine, and had lost his wife at the same time as I had been widowed. We had even gone on dates together, sharing our misery, and had remarried within weeks of one another. Now he urged caution. 'People are waiting to criticise us,' he said. 'They don't agree with our finding happiness again.' He gave me tranquillisers, and advised me to keep my troubles to myself. 'I'll get you through this,' he said.

A dope-filled haze followed. I saw Mrs Bates, as ever a wonderful support, look at me strangely sometimes. I often took an extra tablet, anything to dull the pain; and when it was time for the children to come home from school I would have to force myself to get up and prepare a meal. When the children were there, I was happy. When the house was empty, I was bereft. I moved about in the house of that other Catherine Joyce and felt I had no place there.

One night I dreamed that I had been banished to the box room, and when I'd asked Jack why, he'd pointed to our bedroom. His first wife was in there, he said. I woke up crying. 'Was it better with her?' is the question that haunts you – after making love, and a thousand other times a day. It is the question that must never be asked, but can never be avoided.

I have a theory about second marriage. That it can be wonderfully happy I know beyond doubt; but if you come to it with a crack in your self-esteem it will get into it and never rest until the crack has become a chasm. I had always felt a 'second best'. Now it seemed to be confirmed. And it is particularly difficult if your rival – for that is what your predecessor is – is dead. She will never age, never rage; she is forever sanctified. You are merely mortal; you grow older, you lose your temper. You can never compete.

Jack did all he could to help me, but others were less kind. One frequent visitor to the house would say, when I brought in the tea, 'Now, you're doing that just like Joyce.' At first I thought she was well-intentioned but tactless. Soon I learned that she thought me a usurper. The digs went on for a while – I couldn't retaliate, and Jack was trying to ignore them – until one day she went too far. 'What do you do with the raspberries in the garden?' she asked. 'Not much,' was my answer. 'The boys eat them as fast as they ripen.' She sighed. 'Joyce used to make wonderful jam with them.' Jack had been hidden behind his evening paper but suddenly it was lowered. 'Joyce never made a jar of jam in her life.'

Feelings of hopelessness overcame me, but I knew I couldn't let them win. If they interfered with my ability to earn, we would all be in trouble, and a diet of Valium is not conducive to the creative talents. So I went back to the doctor and demanded action. 'I can't go on like this, I want to see a psychiatrist.' That early psychiatrist had opened doors for me: could I be as lucky again? At my doctor's urging, I agreed to be a private patient. I didn't know where I would find the money, but as I found unfindable money every day, this would be no novel experience.

The psychiatrist was young, Asian, and solemn. His first action was to tell me firmly how much he cost, and to request payment in advance. I had been having doubts about the wisdom of confiding in a psychiatrist, but looking at him I realised that he was more scared of me than I was of him. I set about putting him at his ease, which eventually led to my confiding in him. Later on in our acquaintance, he would tell me that I was his first private patient and that he had been embarrassed at having to talk about money. That had made him vulnerable, and his vulnerability had got through my defences.

For me it was a huge stroke of luck. For the next few weeks I was on drugs he prescribed, some of them administered by injection, others by mouth. They lifted my mood without the deadening effect of tranquillisers, but my initial difficulties remained. 'Why can't I be happy?' I asked him. 'Other people are happy with much less than I have.' 'You're a writer,' he said. 'Feeling deeply comes with the territory.'

It made sense, and it also had the effect of easing my guilt. What was happening to me wasn't happening by chance, it was happening because of who and what I was. He told me that even happy events take their toll. I had been widowed, married and gifted with four more children in a very short space of time. Now I was paying for it.

From the very beginning he recommended something called narco-analysis. I would be given pentathol, the truth drug, and this would enable him to see into my mind. I instinctively recoiled from this. Telling him how I felt was one thing; having no control over what I told him was another. I refused point-blank. We would continue with the drugs and the conversation.

While all this was going on, I tried to keep life in the home as normal as possible. John and Philip had joined Mark at his school and they came home each night. John was doing a study of the rise and fall of the Nazi party, and I was happy to help with this. He was still full of enormous energy, planning exploits, taking up new hobbies. Philip was steady, quiet and helpful. Mark had requested a second-hand drum kit costing £10 for Christmas, and now talked, thought, and made music. Alex had always loved music, and had a good ear for it. It delighted me to see this coming out in his son.

One Saturday afternoon, Jack and I were in the sitting-room when there was the pounding of feet outside. 'What's happened now?' I thought. But it was not one of our boys who burst into the room. It was a friend of John's, his eyes starting out of his head. 'John's been attacked,' he said. 'They're taking him to hospital.' Driving along the town's main street, I wondered what John had done to provoke an attack, but running down the alleyway from the car park, I saw his blood on the ground. My child's blood! I have always been against capital punishment, but in that moment I could easily have committed murder.

We found John in Boots, where they were stemming blood from a huge cut on his head. The backs of his hands were scarred and bleeding where he had put them over his face as he lay on the ground as his attackers had tried to kick his head in. As I rode with him in the ambulance, he told me that the attack had come out of the blue; but what upset me most was that, on that busy day in that crowded street, no one had intervened to stop it.

The staff at the hospital were cool and brusque as they stitched his head, one nurse informing me that they had better things to do than treat people who got into fights. I subdued my anger. Still at the back of my mind was the fear that perhaps John had been partially responsible. The sergeant who came to the house two days later dispelled that idea. The gang had been spoiling for a fight. They had picked John as a target for one reason only: his very blond hair.

'But they come from nice families,' the policeman said. 'The parents are devastated.' He asked if we would consider dropping the charges, and we agreed. The boys would receive a police caution, and that could sometimes be harsher than the juvenile court, he said. Later on, we were told that a senior officer had decreed the offence to have been too violent to permit of a caution, and it went to court; but we were not informed of the outcome. It made me realise that the victim's family is often overlooked.

Progress with the psychiatrist was slow, and he kept pressing me to try narco-analysis. 'I don't want you looking into my soul,' I told him. I meant to be flippant but in fact it was the truth. I liked keeping things to myself. I am enough my mother's daughter to want to keep some things hidden. If I went ahead, he would know everything about me, and I couldn't take that. And then I got a surprising offer. BBC North was planning a new television game-show called *A Likely Story*. It would feature a panel guessing the hidden secret of a contestant's life. There would be one celebrity guest each week, and the panel would be chaired by Mike Neville, anchorman of the BBC's *News Magazine* and the darling of the north. They wanted me to be a panellist. Was I interested?

I was interested in anything that would pay the bills, so I said yes, although my one and only experience of television hadn't endeared me to the medium. But with that ordeal coming up, I knew that I must overcome my depression. I agreed to the narco-analysis.

The psychiatrist said it would have to be done in hospital, because some people had an adverse reaction to the drug. Jack drove me there, and waited while I went into a small room and lay down on a couch. The drug was injected into my arm, and I began to feel pleasantly detached. At first the questions were innocuous, then they became probing. My head said, 'Don't answer that,' but at the same time I heard my own voice giving the answer. It was a weird sensation. At last the psychiatrist asked me, 'Do you think Jack's sons are your children?' and I heard myself say: 'No, they're not mine but I do love them.' Another question was, 'Do you think you're Rebecca?' and I answered, 'No, because everyone was unkind to her, and everybody is being kind to me.'

I don't remember thinking; the words came out as though spoken by someone else, and yet there was thought behind them. At times, I had indeed felt like Rebecca, trapped in a house that was much more another woman's than mine; but there was no Mrs Manders, the wicked housekeeper, in my story, only Mrs Bates who would do anything to help.

The questions went on for what seemed like twenty minutes, and then he asked me to count backwards from a hundred. 'You can sit up now,' he told me, and I got up, retrieved my coat and bag, and went to find Jack. 'That didn't take long,' I said, and thought he looked at me strangely. The psychiatrist told me he would come to see me the next day. When we were safe in the car, Jack told me I had been in there two and a half hours. Somewhere in the questioning I had lost consciousness – at least, I had not been conscious of the questions continuing. I tried to think back. He had asked me something about my father – did he ever touch me inappropriately? And I had laughed at such a ridiculous idea.

Try as I might, I couldn't remember anything else, so it was with some trepidation that I sat down with the psychiatrist the next day. He had a clipboard in front of him and he consulted it before he spoke. 'This recurring dream you had,' he said. I felt my face flush, and I began to regret that I had ever agreed to the pentathol. For years – ever since my teens – I had dreamed almost every night about being naked in the street. I would find myself there, and try desperately to make it home before anyone saw me. 'I know what that is,' I said, trying to pass it off. 'It's where I dream I'm naked in the street. I didn't tell you about it because it's sexual, isn't it? It's not really important.'

Freud has a lot to answer for. We all think we are psychiatrists, and we blame everything on sex. I had not mentioned the dream in our conversations because I was ashamed of it. But my psychiatrist was shaking his head. 'It's got nothing to do with sex. You were shabby when you were growing up. You felt ashamed of your clothes, and you blamed your parents, and that made you feel guilty.' Now it was my turn to shake my head. 'I never minded. I don't think clothes are important. I don't care about people who think they do matter. And I knew my parents did their best. I never blamed them.'

We argued for a while, and then he let it go. I was still convinced he was wrong, but I have never had that dream again, not once – so perhaps he was right after all, and bringing it into the open set me free. We talked about other things, things I had kept secret, things I had not thought important enough to tell him. And then he said, 'I owe you an apology. I was convinced that you were not as enthusiastic about your step-children as you appeared. Now I know I was wrong, and I'm sorry I wasted time on a mistaken theory.' I smiled wryly. He still didn't know how wrong he was. The children were the only thing that had kept me sane.

But he was not alone in his belief that step-motherhood must be an ordeal. Weeks later I would do an item on radio with a Relate counsellor, who would blithely tell me that I was in denial. No one could ever enjoy step-parenting as much as I said I did. And twenty-five years later, I would argue with that arch-advocate of unhappy stepping, Brenda Maddox, who thought it was impossible to love someone else's child as your own. I gave up in the face of her intransigence, but I felt pity for her.

Of course, like any relationship, it is fraught with difficulty; but so is parenting your birth children. I have had ten letters from unhappy birth parents for every one I've had from an unhappy step. One radio producer said to me, 'If your son and your step-son fell in the river, which one would you pull out?' I knew what she meant – that your own genes would demand first attention. But there comes a time with a child you care for when you bond as surely as you ever do in the labour ward. With Philip, it came at that moment when the doctor said he had leukaemia; with John it was earlier, when I saw how open he was to having me as a friend. With the older boys, it took longer, but now I look on them all as my children, and am thankful I had and have them in my life. Their children are my grandchildren, as surely as if we were linked together by blood.

I don't know what happened during the narco-analysis, but I know it spring-cleaned my mind. Gradually the need for drugs fell away. On the afternoon of the first broadcast of *A Likely Story*, the psychiatrist spent an hour with me. It was helpful, but not vital. I had girded up my loins, and I was going to cope. I found I was quite good at guessing the likely stories of the contestants. Somehow it would just come to me, in a way I couldn't explain. One evening it scared me – a middle-aged woman came on the show, and I suddenly could see a child on her knee. It so shocked me that I spluttered my way through it, and we couldn't guess her secret: she had been the nanny to the recently installed Cardinal of Westminster, Basil Hume.

Did I have a vision? No. But I do think she was thinking about the child she had cared for, and I somehow picked up on her thought waves. I was beginning to realise I had a fair degree of intuition. One night we went to a party at a friend of Jack's. When we left, he said one particular man had been in fine form. 'No,' I said. 'He's desperately unhappy.' Jack was scornful. 'He was the life and soul of the party. Your imagination will get you into trouble one of these days.' Within a month it was revealed that the man's life was in ruins, as secrets tumbled out. Jack was less sceptical after that.

The situation within Jack's business was getting more desperate by the hour, and I would have to do more to help there. But I used part of my *Likely Story* money to send Mark up to Shetland to see his Aunt Annie, and his cousins.

It was hard to let him go, and without Jack's support I could not have done it. We put him on to the plane at Newcastle, and Jack's cousin met him in Aberdeen and saw him on to the Shetland ferry. He was thirteen now and he had a wonderful time there, in his father's homeland. When he stepped off the plane at Newcastle airport on his return he looked older and more confident, no longer my little boy but every inch his father's son. 'See,' Jack said, uncharacteristically emotional, 'he's a man now.'

15
CHAPTER

HARDSHIP

OR CHRISTMAS IN 1976, Philip bought me a Johnny Mathis recording of 'When a Child is Born', because he knew how much I liked it. He gave it to me in advance of Christmas, and I played it over and over again. But as it echoed around the house, Christmas spirit was in short supply. Getting presents for the boys was difficult, and we were having terrible problems with both the car and the vehicles belonging to the business. If you have never pushed a lorry uphill, you can have no conception of the labours of Hercules. In an effort to boost the cash-flow, I was visiting clients who hadn't paid, which was a job I hated.

People's attitude to builders is a strange one. Denying them some portion of the whole bill seems to be almost a natural pastime. I sat in offices of tycoons, I knocked on doors of affluent homes, subduing my resentment at the necessity of chasing them, and sometimes – if I was lucky – I came away with a cheque. More often I came away with promises.

I had six hungry mouths to feed, there was no money to come from the business, and I couldn't be both writer and debt-collector.

Besides, the market for short stories was beginning to shrink, as fewer magazines featured them. I had two bank accounts, and sometimes I had to cover a cheque paid from one account with a cheque from the other, although neither account had funds in it of any consequence. It meant constantly keeping on top of what I had paid out and what I needed to pay in, but it also meant that I could keep us afloat and put food on the table. Years later I would work with Alvin Hall, the money guru. He told me that the process of passing cheques between banks is known as cheque-kiting, and is not illegal as long as the cheques are honoured eventually. It's also impossible in the age of the computer, but luckily for me it worked in the 1970s. I knew that once I could get back to work I could make everything good. It was just a matter of keeping the balls in the air in the mean time.

I was also selling possessions for whatever I could get for them. One day I saw an advertisement: a jeweller was going to be at a town-centre hotel to buy unwanted jewellery and silver. I went along, taking some pieces I could do without. He paid a pittance, but it was wonderful to come out with real money in my pocket. Thereafter I sold anything I didn't actually need: the silver teaspoons my father had always kept in a linen bag, dress rings, and eventually my wedding ring. Jack had bought me a wide wedding band, but it had begun to irritate my finger, and I had put back the thin ring I had worn as Alex's wife. In desperation I took the broad ring and sold it. When the ship came in, Jack could replace it, I reasoned. And, anyway, I had no option.

Each time I went there, I noticed a frail little old lady, clutching a battered handbag and looking mournful. My heart bled for her. I was in trouble, too, but at least I was young and healthy. And then one day I happened to be near enough to see what she was handing over. Out of the battered handbag came handfuls of chains, rings, brooches – obviously the product of theft. My little old lady was a fence, and the jeweller must have known it.

I could not face going back after that, and in any event I was running out of saleable possessions, at least possessions I could bear to part with. It grieved me that the boys were shabby, and that I couldn't afford better clothes for them But the real torture was the Thursday pay-day, and wondering each week if we would be able to find the wages.

One week, we were really up against it when Marge Barton, a friend of mine, called. Jack had recently built them a summer-house but the bill was not yet due. I didn't say anything, but somehow she sensed the situation. 'Would it help if we paid now?' she asked. An hour later we had the cheque. The value of such friends is above rubies.

I lived in a perpetual state of fear, but the fear of not being able to put food on the table was by far the worst. One day, I had a beefburger for each boy's evening meal. I'd been out, and when I came into the kitchen I could smell cooking. 'I've just fried myself a couple of beefburgers,' one of the older boys said blithely. I didn't say anything. Hungry teenagers need to eat. Instead I went into the bathroom, sat down on the edge of the bath, and cried until it was time to dry my eyes and perform the miracle of the loaves and fishes. You can always come up with something if you try, and this time it was eggy bread with beefburger garnish.

On another tight day, a miracle happened. I was contemplating an empty pantry when the doorbell rang. One of our affluent neighbours was standing there holding a cooked joint the size of a small barrel. She had cooked it, they had been called away, it was a sin to waste it, and we had a dog: could I put it to use? I managed to say thank you, and close the door soberly, before I ran whooping with glee into the kitchen to prepare a feast. I never told them where the meat came from, nor what it was intended for. And I never really worked out whether or not my neighbour was just covering up a kind act in order to save my feelings. The important thing was that, for one night at least, we dined like kings. And so did the dog!

Eventually I got a job as an agony aunt on Metro Radio, the north-east's new commercial radio station. I would do an afternoon slot, repeated through the night, and the fee would be £41 plus a mileage allowance. Riches! Now the experience I'd gained answering readers' letters would stand me in good stead. I had my hospital experience to draw on, and my work in the voluntary sector. Nevertheless, as the day of the first broadcast drew near I was terrified. Who was I to go on air and advise anyone about anything? More important, who would be foolish enough to ask my advice?

The format was that I would read out the letter, and make my suggestions. No names would be used and no calls would be taken. Just before the first show, I got cold feet. I needed cash desperately, but could it be right to make money out of the misfortunes of others? Some friends of ours had a Canadian psychiatrist visiting them, and I asked his opinion. 'I would rather you did it than someone else,' he said, 'At least you're frightened.'

So I went on air with a very good DJ called Steve King. I knew little or nothing about broadcasting, but he knew everything and made it easy. I can't remember the first letters, but I do remember feeling relief that at least there was something I could advise, and I could certainly offer sympathy. Nowadays there are hundreds of organisations offering help to anyone in trouble. Then there were only a handful. I could suggest Marriage Guidance, or point them towards the Citizens' Advice Bureau – but, as I was to find out, those two could not possibly cover the wide range of problems with which I would be presented.

This was driven home to me early on. I received a letter congratulating me on my tolerance with the people who wrote to me. I would not be so tolerant with him, the writer said, if I knew how wicked he was, evil beyond belief. Intrigued, I went on air, and told him I had broad shoulders: why didn't he try me, and see if I buckled under the strain? Back came a letter, thanking me and confessing his sin. He couldn't look at a woman, he wrote, without thinking improper thoughts. He was 39, and he had been like this since boyhood.

Guessing at a repressive upbringing, I told him on air that I frequently had impure thoughts about men, especially, I added, in lifts. This hadn't stopped me from being a faithful wife. Appreciating the opposite sex simply meant you were alive – no more. If he would let me get him some help, I thought we could make his life a whole lot better. His reply came by return of post: he would take help, gratefully. Now all I had to do was find some. Eventually I found a kind doctor at the Family Planning Clinic who agreed to give him some counselling. Six months later he was a freer and happier individual. I hope he still is.

I had made a public vow that I would read and answer every letter, and that no one else would see them. The letters began to flood in, a few light-hearted, most of them telling of years, even decades, of misery. Nothing had prepared me for the tidal wave of letters about sexual abuse which engulfed me. I had hardly ever heard it mentioned; certainly had never spoken to anyone who had endured it. Now I was hearing from people who had suffered abuse as long ago as fifty years, and who still couldn't overcome the pain of it. For years they had told no one. Now they could tell a voice on the radio, someone who wouldn't know them if she saw them in the street the following day.

There were men and women, too, who were hiding the truth of their sexuality and found it a relief to tell me – and, through me, explain their feelings to a wider audience. One young woman who wrote to me then writes to me still. We have corresponded for thirty years, and I am very fond of her, but we've never met.

At the beginning, I had been afraid that I would receive obscene letters. In fact, I never did. On the contrary, writers bent over backwards to explain things as delicately as they could. I'd also thought I might receive hoax letters, and early on I received a letter that I thought might well be sending me up. It came from two university students in Newcastle. They had, they wrote, so perfected the art of making love that they felt it their duty to give demonstrations to the less able. If I would identify people who needed this help, they would be happy to oblige.

I thought about this for a while. I was pretty sure it was a wind-up, but what if it wasn't? At last I replied. I was delighted, I said, that they had achieved such a high level of proficiency in the art of sex. Unfortunately, all the people I knew were too busy practising it themselves to watch a demonstration. I never heard from them again.

In time I acquired some fans. One man had to have a photo despatched to him periodically, because he kissed it so enthusiastically that it soon wore out. Another wrote begging me not to take cough medicine when I had a cold, because my hoarseness was a huge turn-on. Yet another man named his greyhound after me. Poor thing, it never thereafter won a race.

I had been at Metro for about a year when the first real crisis occurred. I came downstairs at the end of the show to see a tall, familiar figure coming through the swing door. It was T. Dan Smith, a Labour politician who had been sent to prison for his involvement in the Poulson corruption affair. This was his first day out of prison, and he was coming to do an interview. As if he were the Pied Piper, anyone who was anyone at Metro fell in behind him. He was a charismatic figure, a man who had been powerful and – judging by what was happening – was continuing to wield influence. He had been known as 'Mr Newcastle', though his political opponents called him 'The Mouth of the Tyne'.

I stood back to let his now considerable entourage go off towards the studio, and, just as I was about to leave, the receptionist said there was a telephone call for me. When I took the phone, I could hear a baby crying; and a woman's voice addressed me. 'I listen to you every week, and I trust you. I've just taken a lethal dose of pills. I won't tell you where I am until it's too late for you to do anything about it. Then I will tell you, because I want you to come and take my baby.' For a moment I was lost for words, but only for a moment. 'Look,' I said, 'I'm in reception. I can't talk to you here. Hang on while I find another phone.'

I ran along the corridor, flinging open the office doors, looking for help. All were empty – like lemmings, the occupants had followed T. Dan Smith. At last I came to the office of the MD, Neil Robinson. No one, but no one was allowed to burst in on him – unless it was an emergency! I threw open his door and blurted out the problem. In that moment I knew precisely why he was the boss. He stood up, took off his jacket and folded it over his chair, at the same time motioning me to sit down. He picked up the phone and told the receptionist to put through the call. 'Keep her talking,' he said to me, 'and we'll find out where she is.'

For the next half-hour I tried to coax information out of her. Her husband had walked out; she couldn't face life alone with a baby; this was the best way out. In vain I argued. But as the pills took effect I began to get the upper hand. I got her Christian name, and then there was a breakthrough – she mentioned her doctor, Dr Black. In a second, Neil was leafing through the telephone directory. But on the B page there was long list of Dr Blacks. Now we had something to go on, though, and I weaved my way round detail after detail until we had a rough idea of where she lived. Neil left, then, to ring the man we hoped would be her doctor.

He came back holding a thumb in the air. The doctor had given anti-depressants to a woman with that Christian name, a woman who had a baby and whose husband had left her. The doctor was on his way. Ten minutes later he walked into the room, and took the phone from her. 'I'm here,' he told me. Panic over!

When I got outside and into my car, I felt the same tremor in my thighs I had felt on that day at Helmsley after Alex's funeral. I felt guilty, too. What if she hadn't wanted to be saved? What if I had condemned her to a life of misery? A week later I got a letter from her, thanking me and setting out her plans for the future. It came as a great relief.

Sometimes, though, there was no such reassurance. On one occasion I received a letter from someone who was clearly deranged. They had not signed the letter so I didn't know if it was a man or a woman although instinct told me the writer was male. He – if indeed it was a man – had been cursed, he said. A Bible had burst into flames in his hands. He intended to end his life that night. Special arrangements were made for me to go on air immediately and plead with him to make contact. He never did.

Wherever I have worked as an agony aunt, I have had many letters from young people. I also receive quite a high percentage of letters from men, especially at the newspapers I've worked for. At Metro I got a letter from Desperate Mr C aged 14. He enclosed his £2 pocket money, and requested that I purchase a packet of Louis Marcel strip wax for him. Hair was growing on his body, and he couldn't let anyone at school see it. He'd tried shaving, but the stubble betrayed him. His mother's magazine said wax was the answer, but he daren't go in a shop and ask for it. Would I get it and pass it on?

This was a real dilemma. Quite apart from the ethics of my interfering with another woman's child, we couldn't go on with Louis Marcel forever. Sooner or later he had to accept being hirsute. I begged him to tell his mother. He refused. Eventually a bargain was struck. I would supply Louis Marcel strip wax until the summer holidays. During the six-week break, he would allow the hair to grow, and go back to school in September looking like a normal teenager.

For several weeks I met him at Newcastle station. He came and went like wind, snatching the package from my hand with a muffled thank-you. He was thin, bespectacled and – strangely – he had a distinct growth of hair on his upper lip. One week I couldn't go, so I asked Mark to go for me. He had left the house when I realised that he was in his hippy phase, wearing a long green coat, with masses of hair and a Dr Who scarf. If a policeman saw such a figure handing over a brown-paper package in the station, a drugs bust would surely follow. It was a relief when Mark came home safely, and a greater relief when the summer took Desperate Mr C beyond my ken.

That summer, I knew, would be the last time we would all be together. The boys were growing up, and would go their separate ways. The two older boys were already both at university, studying building engineering. I rented a house in Newlyn for £50, and Jack drove me and the three younger boys down to Cornwall. It was a magic week, during which we both tried not to think about the future. At night we ate our meal as lights sprang up in the harbour below. By day we enjoyed sun and sand; but even though I loved every minute of it, I sensed that it was the lull before the storm.

16
CHAPTER

DOWNFALL

1975 HAD BEEN the worst year for financial failure in British history, and the situation had not improved since. In 1977 Britain was rife with strikes and bankruptcies. Many people blamed the Inland Revenue and the VAT man, but strikes and inflation were making everyday life difficult. Prices had risen, and things were hard for everyone – although I can't say that made us feel any better. The Prime Minister, Jim Callaghan, was threatening strikers with the withdrawal of government subsidies to ailing businesses, but it had no effect. Miners were demanding an end to the Social Contract; pickets were out at Grunwick; railwaymen wanted a 63-per-cent pay rise, and corpses remained unburied in London as undertakers struck. A pay-rise avalanche was looming.

Suddenly, amid all this national gloom, there was a ray of sunshine. A workmen's club gutted by fire needed rebuilding, and Jack got the job. The insurance was paying for it, and the committee wanted a first-class job. There was to be expensive wood panelling, and only the finest fittings. Best of all, the job was on our doorstep, so transport costs were low.

Jack threw himself into it with gusto, coming home each night with tales of amboyna pine and other rare woods, and of the breadth and scope of the lay-out. It was a plum job, and we felt a huge sense of relief. If the weather held and the job was done on time, we would be OK.

In November firemen went on strike, demanding a 30-per-cent pay rise. I took little notice. The army stood by with its Green Goddesses; and, anyway, you never think fire will happen to you. I was more occupied with the fact that John wanted to leave school once he'd taken his O levels, and join the Royal Navy. Jack was against this. His older brothers had gone on to further education; John should do the same. I had sympathy with John. He was as intelligent as his brothers, but he had always wanted more outlet for his energies. His eyes lit up when he talked of the Navy, and that was good enough for me.

The club was half finished when disaster struck. It caught fire. How, no one knew. No one came to put it out, either, and the half-constructed building burned to the ground. The insurers promptly declared this second fire a matter for investigation, all work stopped, and payment stopped too. Jack had ordered the timber, bricks and fittings. The debts were in his name. On top of that, the workers, some of whom had been with the firm for years, must continue to be paid.

Our lives became an even greater nightmare. One day we hid in the house as a bailiff knocked on the door. Then he simply sat in his car at the gate, obviously there for the duration. Eventually, Jack walked out to face him, and I watched him go. I had always admired his powers of endurance. Now I admired his courage.

I remember the one moment when I felt desperate. There was thick snow on the ground, and we had been out somewhere in the car. It broke down. We got out and began to plod homeward, each of us knowing that there was no money to pay for having it towed home or repaired.

Eventually, the papers landed on the doormat: the Inland Revenue was putting the firm into liquidation. The next day the Official Receiver arrived, barring Jack from his office, laying off the workers, removing all vehicles, and leaving my car only after I proved I had bought it myself before our marriage.

Our solicitor, Cyril Barker, was a huge support. 'If it's any comfort,' he told me, 'my experience is that these things never turn out to be as bad as you fear.' It was spring now and the daffodils Jack had cultivated over the years were nodding yellow heads in the garden. I found him one day, just standing watching them. I knew what he was thinking. The house was in hock to the bank. We would have to leave the home in which he had reared his children and watched his beautiful wife die. So many memories soon to be swept away.

It was in the garden, too, that Aunty Marian came to give me comfort. She was the aunt of Jack's first wife and, as she had no children of her own, she had doted on her niece's boys. When I first came on the scene, she had come to inspect me, an expression on her face like the wrath of God. Now, though, we were good friends. She came as soon as she heard the news. 'I'm glad you're here with Jack,' she said. 'You'll cope with this better than Joyce would have done.'

I knew what she meant. Before her illness Joyce had never known adversity. I had known very little else. Of course I would cope. 'But I'll help you,' she said. 'When you came, I thought you would keep the boys from me, but in fact you've drawn us closer together. You can count on me.' She offered to lend me money as long as I didn't tell her husband, who wouldn't approve. I thanked her, and promised to call upon her if we were absolutely stuck; but in fact I never needed to do so. What I did need, and received in abundance, was her love and support.

The next day the phone rang. It was the chairman of the club. 'Good news,' he said. 'The insurance are paying up. I've got a nice fat cheque here for Mr Tomlin.' I resisted the impulse to tell him what he could do with it and simply broke the news that he would have to find another builder.

Now the process of receivership began – or, rather, didn't begin. Each day Jack used my car to drive to the several sites where he had been working. They lay idle now, but each day another piece of equipment had disappeared, another pile of bricks or cement had vanished. The sites were being picked clean of anything of value. We went to see the representative of the Official Receiver. He didn't seem to care about the vanishing assets, but told us our business failure represented a plush job for some accountant. He was deliberating which lucky accountant should get it. He also told us he would be leaving soon to work for – you've guessed it – a firm of accountants. I was beginning to see the whole thing as a terrible charade. A business that had given employment for half a century was being brought to its knees. There would be unemployment for the men, and penury for us, but others would grow fat on its corpse.

Creditors now had to put in their claims. Stanley Carpenter, our bank manager, was another person who was doing his best for us. 'How can you bear to leave that lovely house?' he asked me. I didn't tell him that I could hardly wait to get away from its ghosts. Instead I asked him what help, if any, the bank would give us towards putting a roof over our heads. He told me they would advance the money for a deposit on a cheap house, and give an initial mortgage, but as soon as possible it must be transferred to a mortgage company. 'We can do this only on the strength of your earnings,' he said, and he advised me to put in a claim against the business for the money I had put in when I married.

I'd already decided that I wouldn't do this. If I did, it would make the debt huge, and I knew how deeply this would hurt Jack's pride. Instead I claimed for a couple of thousand pounds. At the rate things were going, the best the business would pay would be a few pence in the pound. Why shame a good man for a few thousand more pence?

The sale of the firm's assets was another farce. Most of the good stuff never appeared, having been sold 'under the counter'. Vehicles had been immobilised by removal of the rotary arms; these could not now be found, so the vehicles could not be tried out, and this made bidders understandably reluctant.

But the real shock came when Jack was asked to agree creditors' claims. He looked down the list with horror. 'They're all claiming ten times what they're owed,' he said. I was quick to reassure him. 'Don't worry. You've got the books. You can prove what you owe.' But the Receiver had taken the books, and now they were with the accountants handling the liquidation. I rang them. 'My husband can't agree this list without the books,' I said. There was an audible chuckle from the other end of the line. 'We don't bother with books much. They've usually been kept badly in the weeks leading up to the crash.'

I pointed out that Jack's excellent book-keeper had kept the books up to the last day, but I was wasting my time. The books were lost, and no one was going to look for them. A week later I saw one of the sub-contractors in the street. 'Why have you claimed ten times as much as we owe you?' I asked. He had the grace to look embarrassed. 'I had to,' he said. 'You see, that's the only way I can get my money, if you only pay 10p in the pound.' I gave up, then. Receivership was a farce, and a dirty farce at that. The sooner it was over the better.

When the final creditors' meeting came, Jack asked me to stay away. I think he was afraid I would erupt and say unpleasant things, and he was probably right. As a director, I was criticised for staying away by the man chairing the meeting, but I couldn't have cared less. He was presiding over a shameful system. His opinion counted for nothing.

Now we put the house up for sale. No decoration had been done for years, and we tried to tickle up the worst disorders. It was a lovely house with a terraced garden, but I could hardly wait to get away. I was also feeling a new ease. Thursdays were no longer days of terror. But I felt guilty about my relief, for Jack was suffering terribly. He had inherited a prosperous business: now it was gone. In vain I pointed out that every other medium-sized building business had already vanished. He was inconsolable.

He was also afraid. I, on the other hand, was excited. We had a hill to climb, and I could hardly wait to begin. I had two goals: a home, and ensuring that every one of the boys achieved whatever potential he had. If that meant university, so be it – although quite how it was going to be done I couldn't yet see. Our only income was my earnings from Metro Radio, and the little writing I could fit in, together with Jack's £19 a week unemployment benefit. The allowance for our approaching-six-foot teenagers was £1.75p each.

But selling the house proved difficult. People came to view, and went away. In addition, the boys' grandfather, their mother's father, was suffering transient ischaemic attacks, mini-strokes, and we were having to help care for him. As we at last found a buyer for the house, a new worry emerged. Aunty Eve, with whom I had always had a chequered relationship, was behaving strangely. For years she had shared a home with a friend. That friend had died a few months earlier, but she had appeared to come to terms with the death. Now she seemed desolate.

At first I thought it was depression, and urged her to see a doctor. She was admitted to hospital for examination of stomach symptoms, but no one did anything about her erratic moods. She would suddenly crave company and demand that we visit; then, when we got there, she had forgotten we were invited. One day she rang in distress. I jumped in the car and drove through to Sunderland only to see her wandering in the middle of the road, beautifully dressed as usual but obviously without any idea of where she was. And that stirred a terrible memory of that elderly man with dementia who had died in the road outside my parents' house all those years ago.

Aunt Eve had always boasted about her friends, pitying my mother for only having a husband. Now those friends were curiously reluctant to be involved. One day she arrived at my niece's home with a suitcase and no idea of where she was going. Gillian rang me, and I drove over. It was obvious that something was horribly wrong. My dominant, violin-playing, social aunt was a frightened elderly lady who bore every resemblance to a refugee. Her private health insurance, of which she'd always been proud, was now a god-send. The psychiatrist who had helped me saw her straight away.

I had every faith in his ability to sort her out, but when he said he needed to see me I knew it was bad news. 'I can't be sure till we do some tests, but I think it's Alzheimer's. Your aunt has had a very stress-free life – two pensions, no family to worry about. A little stress is no bad thing …' He looked on amazed as I burst into hysterical laughter. If stress protected you from Alzheimer's, I could be sure of keeping my marbles for a long, long time.

Gillian and I were Aunt Eve's only relatives. Now we tried to work out what to do for the best. Gillian was divorced, teaching full-time, and caring for a little boy. She couldn't be expected to do more than help. There was nothing for it but for Aunty Eve to come to me, at least for the time being.

She agreed, but with one proviso: none of her friends must know where she was. She didn't want to see them. Privately, I didn't think she needed to worry about their flocking round, but I agreed. She moved in, and Gillian and I went to collect some things from her flat. What we found there was a revelation: expensive boxed chocolate cakes were everywhere. You opened an underwear drawer and there, among the waist slips, nestled two iced chocolate cakes. More were in the store cupboard, more in the wardrobe, the cutlery drawer, the record cabinet. How could all this have been going on without our seeing that something was wrong?

The next two weeks were torture. She was aggressive with the boys, turning off the TV if they were watching, complaining about their clattering on the stairs. They were already having to maintain an unnatural tidiness because of people viewing the house, and she was making their lives unbearable, but they didn't complain. In addition, I was having to lie to anyone who rang up asking where she was. This made me uneasy.

I turned to the psychiatrist for help. It was only a matter of months since he had seen me suffering from clinical depression, and I could tell that he was apprehensive about the strain of the present situation. He needn't have feared: I was feeling stronger than ever. Too much depended on my holding up. He suggested an exclusive nursing home some hundred miles away. I took her to see it, and she loved it. It was palatial, with spacious grounds, and, above all, her health insurance would pay for it, something that gave her huge satisfaction.

Getting her out of the house was a relief, but it meant I had to go backwards and forwards several times a week. She was also liable to ring me up at odd hours, but I had made a decision that lying about her whereabouts couldn't go on, so that was one thing fewer to worry about.

In an interview I had with the medical director of the home, a question shocked me. 'Is your aunt a lesbian?' I was lost for words. It had never occurred to me that she might be, and on reflection I was sure she wasn't. Not that it would have mattered if she had been, but I knew that the friend she had lived with had had men friends, and my aunt had always seemed to like men. I said a firm no, but he seemed disappointed. I decided that he was someone who formed a theory and didn't like it disproved. The place was full of what seemed to be affluent young men, who, a nurse told me, were recovering alcoholics. I was beginning to have my doubts about the home, but for the moment it was the best I could do and at least she was safe there.

Safe she might be but she became increasingly unhappy in the nursing home. The nurses reported that she had delusions of grandeur, writing cheques for other patients and ordering still others to carry out menial tasks for her. On one visit, she complained that people were unkind to her. I mentioned it to a nurse in the hope that a solution might be found. 'I'm not surprised people are unkind,' was the reply. 'The way she speaks to people, what else do you expect?' For a moment I contemplated pointing out that Alzheimer's didn't make for considered conversation, but, with that reticence you develop in a hospital situation, I let it go. Aunty Eve was free to make telephone calls, and had every amenity; but I liked the home less and less. There was something decadent about it, a veneer of splendour covering up the real unhappiness of the patients.

One day she rang me up, saying she was locked in a room and frightened. 'Come and get me,' she said. 'I can't write. I've been trying to write a letter but the words won't come.' She sounded distraught, and I couldn't bear her distress. On the other hand, I couldn't bring her back here to a houseful of boys taking O levels. I rang my friend the psychiatrist. He had suggested the private home in the first place. Now he suggested I bring her back to the National Health hospital where he was a consultant.

So Jack and I set out on the two-hour journey to collect her. The drive back was a nightmare: I don't know how Jack kept the car on the road. She was in a towering rage with me because, she said, she was mad and I hadn't told her. 'They told me,' she said, 'but you lied.' I delivered a distraught old lady to the new hospital, trying hard to remember the composed, clever woman she had once been.

They advised me not to visit for a few days, and when eventually I drove through the grounds to the grim Victorian building, I feared what I would find. To my relief, I found her composed and almost cheerful. What's more, she could write again, and this was giving her enormous comfort. The doctor told me that she had been filled with drugs in the other home. Now that they were out of her system, she was more like her old self. But he warned me not to expect too much. 'She'll get worse,' he said. And when I asked him about the future he was quite precise. 'Two years. She'll cease to move about eventually, and that will be that.' I didn't believe him. Physically she was still vigorous, almost unable to sit still. I felt as though she would live forever. I was also worried about Jack. Normally gregarious, now he never left the house. Eventually his friend, Bill

Hoare, telephoned. 'He won't cone out' I said ' he doesn't want to see anyone.'Bill knew what to do. 'Get him in the front garden, Sunday at noon sharp, and leave the rest to me.' On Sunday I lured Jack into the garden on the pretext of inspecting an ailing plant. Bill drew up in the car and the next moment Jack was in the passenger seat and they were speeding off to meet friends for a pre-lunch drink. The ice was broken.

At long last the house sold, and we found a new one. It was in a graceful terrace quite nearby and was owned by the council. Bidding had to be by closed tender, and we agonised over what price would secure it. It was going cheap because it had been lived in by transients for a long time. The front window had been put in, and was boarded up. I picked up the stones that had broken it from the floor when I viewed. It was painted throughout in obviously purloined paint – khaki, black, cerise – all in gloss paint over paper, so it was dark and gloomy. But I could see its possibilities, and although it only had a back yard there was the most wonderful rambling rose growing there, weighed down with blooms.

Our bid won, and the house was ours. We moved and Mrs Bates and I went back to do a final clean on the house we were leaving behind. When at last we came out and clashed the door, she looked at me and sighed with relief. 'Thank goodness you've got out of that house,' she said. I raised my eyebrows. 'Every woman who lived there died,' she said simply. 'I didn't want it to happen to you.' It was true. Jack's wife had died, then his sister, then his mother-in-law, then his mother. But I had lived, and furthermore I had every intention of continuing so to do. 'Come on,' I said. 'Let's go home and put the kettle on.'

17
CHAPTER

STARTING AGAIN

FROM THE START I felt happy in Maureen Terrace. Shabby as it was, it was a fresh start, and it was a spacious house: four bedrooms, two living-rooms and a roomy kitchen. After two or three weeks, we were able to replace the glass in the front window, and although increased light showed up the ghastly décor, it made us all feel more cheerful. Jack, however, was inconsolable. He had lost his business, his income, his house, and his garden. Outwardly he went on as usual. Inwardly he mourned what he saw as failure.

I pointed out how the cards had been stacked against him, but I also knew that he was scared. He was in his fifties, he still had children to support, and a lifetime of running his own business had not exactly fitted him for job-hunting. He went to the weekly ritual of signing on, and came back looking grey. Eventually he suggested he went to work abroad, where his building skills would be in demand. I knew that his home and friends meant everything to him, and exile would break his heart. I told him he must please himself, but if he went he should pack a big bag because he wouldn't be coming back home. He shook his head in doubt, but I knew he was secretly relieved.

I was determined to get the house right, and together we set about a process made slow by lack of money. The house had been horribly hacked about. A plaster cornice in the hall looked a little strange – examination revealed it to be a cornflake packet tacked over a hole and painted. The manhole in the back yard revealed a television and stand, and there were seven layers of paper under a veneer of gloss paint on most of the walls. Each night I would put on my nightie, clean my teeth, and attack the walls with a table knife. Slid under the layers of paper and then tilted, it would bring off huge pieces of compounded paper, each layer charting an era. When I had cleared a big enough section, I could put out the light and go to bed knowing we had moved a little nearer our dream home. As often as I could afford it, I bought a small tin of magnolia emulsion and began to spread it through the house. Bit by bit it was becoming home.

John had been accepted into the Royal Navy, as he had hoped. One dark morning we put him on a train for the naval establishment at Portsmouth. He had always had a mania for sausages. As the train chugged out, his face bright with anticipation in the window, I suddenly realised that he was going out of my life as a child. When he came back it would be as a man. I started to cry, and Jack looked at me in amazement. 'I won't be cooking his sausages any more,' I said. Of such small things is motherhood made up.

During all this, Mitch had been the most enormous comfort to me. Walking with him, I could always forget my troubles. As I wrote, he would lie beside me, never complaining, always loving. Now, though, he wasn't well. I took him to the vet, and left him there so the vet could take a closer look. I went home, telling myself

Mitch was young and healthy, and this would be something simple, easily put right.

An hour later the vet phoned. He had found a tumour. The kind thing would be for Mitch not to come round from the anaesthetic. I felt I was losing everything. When Jack came home he found me sitting on the bottom of the stairs and when I told him I knew he felt the same. Breaking the news to the boys was difficult. He hadn't been just a dog, he had been a source of joy through bad times; and now he was gone. Not even the tide of magnolia emulsion spreading through the house could cheer me.

I was still working at Metro, and churning out short stories and articles for anyone who would buy them; but there were fewer openings and debt is a bottomless pit into which you throw money and never hear it hit the bottom. It was nearly a year, now, and Jack still had no job, largely because he hadn't applied for any. I felt really sorry for him. He had never applied for a job in his life, and the prospect terrified him. He had gone straight from school into his father's business, and had taken it over on his father's death. Nothing in his life had prepared him for being out of work.

But miracles do happen. One day there was a knock on the door and I opened it to find Arthur Brown on the doorstep. He was a local businessman with a strong sense of community responsibility. Together with another good citizen called Derek Mercer, he was starting up a government-backed scheme to train the young unemployed. He and Derek considered Jack would be the perfect man to run it. Was he interested?

When I told him, he didn't speak but his eyes said, 'Could I do it?' 'With one hand tied behind your back,' I said firmly. And so it proved. Young people flowed through the scheme, some going on to further training, others being a headache, but Jack coped with it all. In fact, he enjoyed it. He had responsibility once more, but without the strains that had accompanied the building trade. He would stay there until he retired.

To celebrate the job we got a new puppy, a tiny, brown whippet cross who was in a refuge. I fell in love with her on sight. She was intelligent, wilful, and still wobbly on her legs. We christened her Tipsy. We had had her only a day when she went down with some kind of gastro-enteritis. Everyone declared her doomed, but I wouldn't accept that. She couldn't eat or drink, so I fed her glucose and water from a syringe, at times forcing it into her as her head lolled in my hands. It worked. A week later she was back on her wobbly legs. We had a dog! She became my constant companion, even coming with me when I went to Metro. I was now doing a late-night show, and the drive to the radio station over icy roads was scary; but she lay on the front passenger seat, and I felt safer with her there.

Jack had just settled into the job when Marie Lawson rang me from London. Aunt Phyllis had eventually lost the job with the new towns corporation – why, I never found out – and had retired to the wilds of Northumberland, presumably subsidised by her Aunt Marie. Now she was dead, and Marie did not want to come north for the funeral, so would I go and represent the family? Jack came with me, and we drove through the beautiful Northumberland countryside to a church in a tiny village. Apart from the vicar and his wife, there were one or two others there out of duty. They told me of excesses of drink, of stacks of bottles that they had disposed of – and all the while I was remembering her progress through the town, tall and stately, a woman of substance. When I got home, I rang Marie Lawson and lied through my teeth. It had been a beautiful service I said, well attended, and everyone had told me what a pillar of the village Phyllis had been. There was a sigh of satisfaction from the other end of the line, and I put down the phone, counting my job well done.

John was now through the induction period and about to pass out from HMS *Raleigh*, the naval training school. We decided to go down for the parade, taking the younger boys with us. We booked into a hotel in Portsmouth, and Jack and the boys went in search of John. I had a short story to finish, so I stayed in the hotel room. I felt really happy that day. Things were working out. Maybe our luck had turned.

An hour later they were back. 'He isn't there,' Jack said. After many phone calls, we traced him to Haslar Naval Hospital. It was a vast place, and appeared to be completely empty. Eventually we found him in a huge and echoing ward, alone except for one elderly man, obviously a veteran, in a bed at the opposite end. John looked young and scared. He didn't know what was the matter. He'd had a cough, and they'd X-rayed him. No one was telling him anything.

A doctor came and uttered some platitudes: it was sure to be nothing, etc., etc. I didn't believe him. And I didn't like it. We had to go home the next day, but we promised to come back as soon as we could. We left him supplied with comics and drinks, but I turned in the doorway and saw him, a lone figure in a place built for the casualties of world wars.

Two days later a doctor rang. He was helpful and informative. They were doing tests, beginning with a bronchoscopy. As he reeled off the names of the tests, I felt a sense of *déjà vu*. I had heard that list before. 'You're testing my son for lung cancer,' I said. There was a long pause, and then the voice came down the line. 'It would be wrong of me to give you false reassurance.'

I was standing in the hall again, as I had done when Philip was ill, making the decision not to tell Jack the truth. The doctor was describing another possible prognosis. 'It might be TB,' he said cheerfully. 'I hope it is, because we can treat that.' There was no keeping from Jack that the situation was serious, but I didn't mention cancer. For a week or two we went backwards and forwards from Portsmouth. All John wanted was to come out and go home, but it couldn't be. Eventually they said we could take him out for an afternoon, but all he had to wear was his uniform, and it was hot and uncomfortable. God bless plastic! An hour later he was in civvies, and his uniform was in a bag. He looked a little better, and I began to feel hopeful.

The diagnosis, when it came, was neither TB nor cancer. He had sarcoidosis, a condition that can affect the young. He could go back to work, but must stay on shore and have regular X-rays for a while. These were minor things: he was going to be all right, and that was all that mattered. But his recovery presented us with a problem. His passing-out parade was on the same day and at the same time as Peter's graduation ceremony. They were 200 miles apart. We couldn't be at both. We discussed this endlessly. Should we each go to one? But whom would Jack choose? He was their father, and obviously the one they would each prefer to have there. In the end, we explained to Peter that John's illness meant he took priority. Peter took it well, but it made Jack and me unhappy. We wanted to be with Peter on his big day. It was just impossible.

Now that we were safely installed in Maureen Terrace, Mrs Bates wanted to retire. She had seen us over the loss of the business, and the move. Now she could go. Her replacement was Dorrie, younger but very much like her. She was building up her home after a divorce, and needed to work to keep her four children. This meant we had a lot in common, and our friendship would grow firmer with the years.

A group of businessmen had formed a consortium to bid for the Tyne Tees TV franchise and asked me to join them. At the moment it was held by Yorkshire Television, and the consortium's feeling was that the north-east lost out through this link. If it became an independent station, the area would benefit. I had some experience of broadcasting, so my brief was to work on programme ideas. I enjoyed it enormously, but it meant trips to London and much hard work as we hammered out a sample schedule. Our bid failed, but we did put pressure on the existing owners to step up their north-east coverage, so it had been worth while. And I made some good friends, notably Paul Nicholson and Tom Cowie, two entrepreneurs each running enormous businesses in their native north-east.

Whether or not as a result of this venture, I received an invitation to a Buckingham Palace garden party. Buying a new outfit was out of the question, but my wedding outfit fitted the bill, and we would drive down to London and save the train fares. We were loading cases into the car when one of the boys opened the front door and Tipsy shot out across the road, determined not to be left behind. There was a screeching of brakes and she was flying through the air. By the time I reached her she was dead, but we still put her in the car and drove to the vet. We knew it was useless, but as I cradled her in my arms I wanted to be sure beyond any doubt. I had loved her for her wilfulness, and in the end it had killed her. We brought her home and buried her in the tiny strip of garden.

It was then that Mark made a singularly comforting remark. 'Remember,' he said, 'she's been loved every day of her life.' And in a moment I realised that that is what matters – not the ending of your life, but the quality of it. She had indeed been loved, and still is, so her short life was not meaningless.

The journey to Buckingham Palace was a blur, my eyes half-closed with crying. Jack was embarrassed, but I had this strange fellow-feeling with the Queen, another dog lover. 'If she knew why I was crying,' I said, 'she would understand.' The garden party was very much what I had expected, the best bit being the walk through the palace to the gardens beyond. There were cabinets along every wall full of the most wonderful porcelain. I would happily have forgone the garden just to inspect the china!

Mrs Thatcher was there, very pretty in white, with Dennis the perfect *aide de camp*, fending off unwanted attention, finishing conversations when time was up, and generally easing her path. Most of the guests seemed to be in uniform, or to be grey-suited royal attendants as the Queen moved around. When at last she waved from the terrace and re-entered the palace, I suggested we wait till the crowds had departed. We were almost the last people to leave, and as we did so a stream of corgis appeared from a far-off door. I had a vivid picture of the Queen going in and saying, 'There now, darlings. All the nasty people have gone home. You can have your garden back.'

That summer was clouded by the loss of Tipsy. I was also still worried about money: we couldn't seem to catch up, and paying the mortgage, transferred from the bank to a society now, was getting more and more difficult.

I sought for ways to earn more, and began to plot a sit com, based on an idea I'd had for a while, about a house full of people living on social security and by their wits. Heaven knows, I was well qualified to write it. But as I conjured up the characters, John Lennon was assassinated in far-off New York. The airwaves were jammed with distraught young people. As I spoke about their fears on Metro Radio, I was learning something about the nature of communal grief which would serve me well in future.

18
CHAPTER

TWO FOR THE PRICE OF ONE

I WAS WORKING now with James Whale at Metro. He was a charismatic character, a brilliant DJ, and a good friend – but he was tough. Occasionally, if I had had a very sad letter, I would shed a few tears while a record was playing. James was having none of that. As I entered the studio, he would glare at me. 'If you cry tonight, I'll cut your mike off.' Now, without Tipsy, I was tearful even before I'd opened a letter. I couldn't come to terms with her death. She'd been more than another dog to me: there had been a kind of desperation about her that I understood.

He stood this for a week or two and then he pounced. 'You sit there mourning one dog while there are dozens of them being put to death every day. If you love dogs so much, save one of them – don't weep over me.' It was good advice and kindly meant, for underneath Mr. Whale is a softie.

The next day we went to a refuge. I knew what I wanted: a black Labrador cross. A puppy, preferably, but an older dog would do. They told me that they had just such a puppy. It was there in a huge concrete pit, black as coal, with beautiful eyes, obviously just weaned but sturdy. There was one snag. Snuggled up to it was a bundle of brown and gold fluff that whimpered constantly and looked about to die of fright. Jack picked up the black puppy, and the other went into a panic. I picked it up and cuddled it, but it wouldn't stop crying until we put it back beside the other pup. 'What are we going to do? I asked, mentally totalling up how much another dog would cost – collars and leads, food . . .

There was only one thing we could do. The boys were looking at us sternly, quite ready to invoke human rights if we put one back. We carried them both out to the car and drove off. I called the black one Poppy, and the fluffy one Daisy. When I asked the vet her breed, he pondered. 'She's a sensation,' he said, and so she turned out to be.

The two of them were a joy. Never separated, they ate, slept and played together. Daisy never lost that initial nervousness, but the whimpering ceased and she seemed happy. The only problem was that each morning when we came downstairs there was plaster on the kitchen floor: one of the pups was working her way through the wall. The one that was shivering with guilt was Daisy. Poppy, on the other hand, looked as innocent as an unborn babe. So Daisy got the blame – until the morning there was a telltale smudge of powder on Poppy's black nose!

Aunty Eve's Alzheimer's was worsening. One day I took in her beloved violin, anxious to awaken some chord in her. She looked at it without comprehension. And, just as the psychiatrist had predicted, she was ceasing to move about. One day I decided to use her love of the outdoors. 'If we can get her outside,' I told Jack, 'she might remember how much she likes walking.' I took one arm and motioned Jack to take the other. She walked a few steps towards the door, but as we neared the open air she began to resist, letting her body sag so that her legs dragged as we moved her forward. We took her back to her chair. That week I assumed legal responsibility for her affairs. It was a responsibility I could have done without.

Soon after that she developed pneumonia. She was unconscious when I arrived to see her, and as I sat by her bed I tried to analyse my feelings. As a child I had been afraid of her and resented her attitude to my parents. Now, though, all I felt was pity and, yes, love. She had been brave throughout her life, loving her music, paying her own way, treasuring the friends so noticeably absent from her later years. I sat on beside her, remembering my father buying marguerites on the Sunday walk to Mainsforth Terrace, and Radio Luxembourg and the Ovaltineys, my first experience of the magic of the airwaves. And in the last few years, when I had seen hard times, she had done everything she could to help me. Whatever the conflicts of the past, she needed me now. I was glad that she would soon be released from the prison of Alzheimer's.

On reflection, I think that disease is harder on the onlooker than on the sufferer once the initial stage has passed. The memory of her prowess with the violin had quickly passed from her recall, and I regretted it more than she did. Only once, since she had come to this hospital, had she displayed emotion. We had been out walking in the grounds, the last time she went outdoors. Suddenly she said, 'There is no God, you know.' I asked why she thought that. 'Because, if there was, He would let me die!" It was said with vehemence. Now she lay in bed, flushed but peaceful. After a day or two she died, looking suddenly more youthful, and relieved.

She left the little money that remained to Gillian and Paul and me, along with those pieces of furniture she had bought from my mother and father when they were hard-pressed. So she had preserved our heritage, and passed it back to us. And soon after the boys' grandfather died, too, an indomitable little man who had never quite got over the loss of his daughter – much as he loved his son and grandchildren. I stood dry-eyed at his funeral, although I had been fond of him. I was becoming inured to funerals.

Ever since he had got that first second-hand drum set, Mark had lived and breathed making music. At first I had thought it was just a flash in the pan, but as time went on his dedication became a little scary. He paid for better instruments by doing a paper round, slogging it out in all weathers. One day we went to buy a cymbal, a Zildjian, which he said was 'ace'. I saw the way he handled it, and realised that to him it was not a toy, more an object of veneration. The time he spent trying it out in the shop to see if the timbre was exactly what he wanted proved that. We could have grown a field of corn in less.

Shortly after that he was playing in an open-air event, and I went along to listen. As I was walking across the grass, I could hear that the music was good, especially the drumming. When I got near, I saw it was Mark playing, and the realisation was both gratifying and scary. I had always believed he would go to university and get a secure job. A life in music would be far from secure. In the end, we struck a bargain. He would go to university and get a degree, but it would be in the nature of a parachute, something to use if it were ever needed. Once that was done, he would devote himself to doing what he really loved, playing drums.

On 2 April 1982, Argentina invaded the Falklands. Three days later the task force that would eventually recapture the islands set sail. I had accepted, from the moment John joined the Navy, that one day he might go to war, but war had then seemed a long way off. Now it was very real. His ambition had been to serve on an aircraft-carrier, and now he was on HMS *Bulwark*, an old ship but still serviceable. Would it be sent? If the war lasted for any length of time, that would be inevitable.

The war had aroused tremendous emotions, sometimes in the least likely people. There was a convent between Seaham and Sunderland, and when I was driving past I would often pick up a nun waiting at the bus stop and give her a lift into Sunderland. One day I picked up a tiny sister with a strong Irish accent. I folded her into the passenger seat and set off. Her face was serene as a baby's under the wimple, but she obviously had something on her mind. 'I've been praying,' she said. I smiled my appreciation until one tiny fist was thumped into the other palm. 'I've been praying for that General Galtieri to get his!' How I kept the car on the road I will never know. But watching the newsreels and listening to the radio, humour was hard to find. I bit my nails until the moment the radio announced that white flags were flying over Port Stanley.

The last boy had gone off to university now, and the house seemed empty. I found myself wandering around fingering the neatly made-up beds which had once resembled rats' nests, heard the unnatural silence, and enjoyed it not at all. At first there were traces of the boys everywhere – lost socks under beds, open books laid face down, record sleeves, shampoo bottles, and sweet-wrappers – but at last everywhere had an almost supernatural neatness. The birds had flown.

Philip came home at weekends occasionally, and it was a joy to put the washer on and live as though everything was normal for a while. John racketed up in his old car whenever he had weekend leave. They were out with their friends within seconds of hitting the house, but that didn't matter. They were home. I had urged them all to go far afield and not choose establishments near to us, wanting them to have a wider experience than my own. But I hadn't bargained for the utter, aching emptiness of life with no child in the house.

Mark seldom came home. Half of me was glad he was enjoying life, the other half was gutted. I reasoned with myself that he needed to break the bond between us, which had been made stronger by his father's death. But it didn't help. I began to feel physically ill, short of breath, and panicked each weekend as the time came for them all to go away again.

Jack was not sympathetic. 'This is what you wanted,' he said. 'You've done everything to make their going away possible; now you're devastated at their going. Make up your mind.' I had not heard of empty-nest syndrome at that stage, but I was going through it! When I said goodbye to them, I would smile until I closed the door, and then make for the back door, panting for breath, wondering if this was heart-attack country. I contemplated asking the doctor to help, but I wasn't going down the pills route again. Somehow I had to solve it for myself.

In the end the answer was simple. I used the open-door technique that had worked to get me back to school. I told myself that if the pain got too bad I would simply get on a train and go to one of them. Never mind what it cost or where I found the money; never mind Jack's reaction; never mind that whichever boy I went to would be mortified at the sight of his mother – if I needed to go, I would go.

From that moment on it grew easier. I still missed them, but the fear, the aching void in my life was no more. That experience has made me very sympathetic to women who experience the empty-nest syndrome. On the face of it, I was not a prime candidate. My life had not revolved around my children, I was not a full-time wife and mother, I had a busy career, interests galore, and a looming money crisis to occupy me. The trouble was that none of those things obliterated my liking for having the children around. I didn't want to limit their lives, nor to tie them to my apron strings. But the art of not missing them was beyond me.

My postbag at Metro Radio was getting bigger by the week. The vow of confidentiality I had made meant no one could share the load. The promise I had made to write back to everyone meant hours composing answers. One day Jack came home to find me surrounded by opened envelopes. 'It's getting a bit much,' he said, and I had to agree. But the £41 I earned for two shows was only just keeping our heads above water.

Our debts were refusing to budge – the most we could do was nibble at the interest on them. The boys were on grants, but they had to be kept in the holidays and at weekends. Buying birthday and Christmas presents was the limit of our abilities, and those went on to the overburdened credit cards.

The situation was made worse in that Philip, who was studying mechanical engineering on a sandwich course, had to spend his third year in industry; but the recession was now biting hard, and no engineering works could take him on and pay him. It was a dilemma faced by everyone taking an engineering course at that time, but the Government had made no provision for it, and there was no grant to cover that year.

Eventually we found a firm in Peterlee that was willing to give him the work experience, but without pay. This meant that he came home for a year; but it was hard for him, surrounded by friends who had gone straight into paid work and had money in their pockets. And hard for us to watch him struggling, and to be unable to help him except in the most minor of ways.

19
CHAPTER

THREATENED

THE LETTERS WERE pouring in to me at Metro now, covering every subject under the sun – incest, possession by the Devil, sex (and the lack of it), anxiety over sexual orientation, bad neighbours, petty crime, loneliness. Until you opened the envelope, you hadn't an idea what to expect.

One night I brought my letters home from the studio and began to open them as I sipped a nightcap. One letter was written neatly in an educated hand and bore a Sunderland address. It congratulated me on my contribution to the show, admired my common sense, and then went on to pose a question. Could it ever be right to commit murder? The writer, who said he was in his twenties, had always wanted to take a life, and had kept himself aloof from relationships with that in mind. He would be interested to know if I agreed with his view, which was that he did indeed have the right to kill.

The letter chilled me. Or was it a wind-up? The next night, on air, I answered it. Violence was never justified unless in self-defence, I said. I hoped he would talk to someone and get his feelings sorted out.

A reply came by return. He thanked me for my advice, but disagreed with it. He thought he was entitled to commit murder, and with this in mind he had obtained a position as a trainee mental nurse in a London hospital, which he named. Such a hospital would be the perfect place to kill and get away with it. He also thought he might find an accomplice there.

Now I was really frightened, but was unable to decide what to do for the best. From the onset I had said that no one else would see the letters. How could I now take the letter to the police? On the other hand, how could I not? If I did, and it was a hoax, I would not only look a fool, everyone would believe my promise of confidentiality had always been a sham. If I didn't, someone might die.

In the end I copied out the letter, omitting the name and address, and asked my friendly psychiatrist for an opinion. Was it a hoax?

He had no doubt. 'It's real,' he said, 'and you must notify the hospital. You have a duty to the public who trust you, but you have an even greater duty to the vulnerable people in that hospital.' I knew he was right, and that the writer needed help before he did something that could see him incarcerated for the rest of his life. I asked what would happen if I told the hospital. 'They'll help him,' he said. 'When he turns up for the job they'll tell him they do standard personality tests, and that leaves the way open for them to suggest treatment.'

So I telephoned the hospital's Chief Medical Officer. Getting through wasn't easy. They didn't want to put through an unknown woman who might be a crank, and I wasn't prepared to divulge the reason for my call. It took half an hour, but at last he came on the line and I told him. He recognised the man's name and, yes, he was due to start work there next week. He thanked me for the information, and then said something so chilling it scares me still. 'You'll need to take steps to protect yourself and your family.'

I didn't speak for a moment, and then I asked what he meant. 'We'll have to tell him you telephoned when we tell him he can't work here. It may make him angry.' In vain I pleaded that I had a houseful of teenagers and animals. If he really wanted to hurt me, he'd hurt them. He was adamant. They didn't want to employ him now, and that was that. In a panic, I telephoned my psychiatrist. He was horrified and promised to intervene. An hour later he came back. 'They won't budge, and I think you should do as they say. But you still did the right thing.'

I sat down on the stairs, suddenly shaking. But it was with anger not with fear. It was bad enough that they were endangering my family, but they weren't going to help the man at all. He was being thrown back into whatever psychosis possessed him, and they didn't care. That night I wrote the man's name and address on a piece of paper, folded it and gave it to Jack, who was reading the paper beside me. 'If anything happens to me, that's who will be to blame.' 'OK,' he said absently and popped it down on a side table, all without taking his eyes off the paper. Obviously he thought my imagination was working overtime again.

A week later I got a letter from a firm of solicitors. I had betrayed the confidentiality of their client, as a result of which he had lost his job. He was taking legal action against me. When the circumstances were explained to them, they withdrew from the case: but a second letter, from a second firm of solicitors, followed. Again these backed off, and I heaved a sigh of relief – until my psychiatrist rang me to tell me that, by an odd chance, the man had been referred to him for treatment, that he saw me as the author of all his misfortunes, and that my life was in danger.

I went to the MD of the radio station. He said we must call in the police, but that turned into a pantomime. I lived in one police area, he in another, and the radio station, which was reporting it, was in a third. Eventually two detectives turned up to interview me. They frankly did not believe that anyone who wanted to commit murder would put his name and address at the top of a letter. Besides, they had no proof that he had threatened me. At last I asked a blunt question. 'Do you mean that until he sticks a knife in me you can't do anything?' The officer who said 'Yes' had the grace to look ashamed.

The other one had a brainwave. The hunt for the Yorkshire Ripper was in full flow, based on the letters from 'Wearside Jack', who later was revealed as a hoaxer. 'We're doing house-to-house in some streets,' he said. 'We'll do his street. That means we'll get a look at him.'

That night I tried to explain to Jack and the boys why they had to be careful. They seemed more interested in getting back to whatever they were doing, and I was torn between wanting them to be careful and not wanting to frighten them. I was frightened enough for all of us. Every man I saw walking towards me could be him. If I heard a step behind me, I froze. Opening the door to a knock was an ordeal. But driving at night was the worst thing. When headlights appeared behind me I was sure it was him following me – any moment he would pull out and overtake, forcing me to halt.

At last I cracked and rang the psychiatrist. 'Tell me what he looks like? Otherwise I'm afraid of every man I see.' 'Oh he's quite distinctive – you couldn't miss him. He's abnormally tall!' He must have been puzzled at my hearty laughter. That was the story of my life. If I was going to have trouble with a stalker, you could bet it wouldn't be a small one and easily dealt with.

The police came back puzzled. They had interviewed the man during house-to-house enquiries. He was polite, a graduate, thoroughly charming, and inoffensive. Was I sure I was right? That was when, for the first time, I showed them the actual letters, and saw their faces pale. 'We'll do what we can,' they promised, but it didn't look hopeful.

For the next few months I heard nothing, and lived in fear. If one of the boys was a minute late, I had prepared his funeral. If a dog failed to come at a whistle, I was whimpering in seconds.

This went on for several months, and then one Sunday I opened a newspaper. 'Man Planned Murder' said the headline, or words to that effect. He had been found behind a wall with a brick inside a nylon stocking. Challenged by the police, he had confessed he was waiting to kill. Then came the *pièce de résistance*: psychiatrists from the London hospital gave evidence that they had detected homicidal tendencies in him when he came for a job interview, and had tried to help him. It was such a blatant lie that it was almost laughable.

He was sentenced to be detained at Her Majesty's pleasure, and I could breathe easier. I don't know where he is now. I was asked to give his letters to the doctors treating him in Leeds prison, in the hope they would be useful, and I did so gladly. But I worry that he did not receive the help he deserved at the beginning, and, for all I know, still needs to this day.

When news came that Mills & Boon wanted me to write a series of novels for them, it seemed like a god-send. I had never read a Mills

& Boon book, considering them romantic rubbish. Now I devoured as many as I could lay my hands on. Could I do it? Could ducks swim?

'It's a pension plan,' my agent said. 'They bring them out again years later. You'll make a fortune.' The advance was large and welcome, causing the wolf to retreat as far as the gate, and I settled down to write a doctor-and-nurse romance, based on my hospital experience. But not before I had said goodbye to Metro. The MD had suggested I should answer letters with prepared statements, but I knew that wouldn't do. It was better to go. I asked them to forward any letters that came in, and said I would reply to them at my own expense. The letters continued for six months or more after I came off air.

The trouble was, though, that I couldn't write the romances. The books had seemed simple, but they were deceptive. How did you convey passion when sex was taboo, or express anger when 'bloody' was a step too far? I walked Poppy and Daisy in the park, praying for inspiration, but in vain. Years later, in my first novel, I would have the heroine walking in the park praying for an answer to her problems and wondering if somewhere, someone has a spyglass trained on her as she argues with the dog. The pups would have done anything for me, but plot lines were beyond them.

I squeezed out one romance, called *Nurse in Doubt* on the cover, but imprinted in my mind as *Author in Agony*. By mutual consent, Mills & Boon and I parted company. I now had no job, no prospects, and no money. The outlook was bleak.

20
CHAPTER

THE STOCKING GAME

I SPENT A lot of time trying to work out what to do next. At the
moment, all I could do was think of what to sell, and we were past
the stage of getting rid of things I could bear to part with. One day
we loaded the Wellington chest into the boot of the car and took it
to an auction room in Darlington. It was the same Wellington chest
that Granny had kept her laying-out clothes in. My mother had sold
it to Aunty Eve; she had left it to me; now I was parting with it, and
not without a pang.

It was a handsome piece, and the auctioneer was enthusiastic,
especially when he found the date 1844 scratched inside. It fetched
£440, a windfall of gigantic proportions. I'd pay ten times that
amount now to have it back, but the resultant lull in anxiety enabled
me to start writing again.

I got out the novel I had started after Alex's death, but it was
page after page of tears and sadness, and by now I knew that no one
is really interested in someone else's unmitigated grief. Instead I
started to sketch out the comedy sit-com about a house in a
northern city populated by characters all 'living on the Social'. Later

a critic would say, 'It was written with the knowing wit of one who has herself escaped the poverty trap.' A truer word was never written.

Eventually I completed what I thought was an episode and sent it off to the BBC. Back came a letter from the great Richard Waring, no less, himself author of some of the BBC's most successful sitcoms, and now in charge of new writing talent. He had good news and bad news to deliver. He considered the writing brilliant, but the episode, as it stood, was only half the proper length. Would I come down and discuss it?

How we scraped together the train fare I will never know, but I found myself back in the television centre. It was only six years since I had been there for the production of *The Soda-Water Fountain*, but my life had completely changed. Alex was gone, and I had responsibilities that would have terrified me in those days when writing was for fun, not for money.

Richard was complimentary and reassuring. I would have to lengthen it and write synopses for all the episodes, but he was prepared to pay me £1300 for the first one. I came back on the train scarcely able to believe my luck.

Around me, as I settled down to write, I could sense the discontent in the Durham coalfield. Unemployment now stood at a record three million, and the national mood was getting ugly. Miners had a new leader now: Arthur Scargill had replaced the unflappable Joe Gormley, and Yorkshire and South Wales's miners struck in protest at planned pit closures. Seaham depended on its three pits. Already it was difficult for youngsters to find jobs, although valiant efforts were made by Jack and his colleagues at the training centre. On my occasional visits there, I looked at the young faces, male and female, and wondered what would happen to them if the pits closed, and the many other firms that depended on them went to the wall.

Aunt Marian and I had grown very close by now. Watson, her husband of more than half a century, was an amazing character, but his health had failed. Blind and bedfast, his sense of humour never left him. One day, as we laboured to turn him in bed and get him into clean pyjamas he began to recite 'Gunga Din', and the three of us collapsed into laughter on the bed.

When eventually he had to be admitted to hospital, Marian didn't want to let him go. I was afraid for her, and I knew, too, that we could no longer keep him comfortable. This was what convinced her in the end. But once he was in the hospital she didn't want to leave his side. Eventually I half cajoled, half dragged her into going home. He seemed stable, and I knew she needed sleep. She kept insisting he was near death. But I wouldn't listen.

She rang me at six the next morning to tell me he was dead. I drove to pick her up, and we went to the hospital. 'I knew he would die,' she said. 'I should have stayed.' I feel guilty still that I made her leave. Now I believe that people's instincts should be obeyed, even when they seem to go against common sense.

In the aftermath of her loss, we grew even closer, because I understood what it meant to lose the man you loved. She had never had a daughter, and would tell me fondly that I felt like one. She knew I loved spring flowers, and her garden was an amazing place, so she produced two china baskets. Whenever I visited I would receive one of these beautifully filled with tiny flowers. The next time I would return the empty one and receive the other, filled, in its place.

We also invented the stocking game. She came to us each Christmas, bringing me a stocking packed with gifts all wrapped and fastened. One might contain a piece of china from her cabinet, another a toilet roll. Her favourites were cheeky pictures or headlines cut from the newspaper, appertaining to some idiosyncrasy of mine. When Jack and I first-footed her at New Year, I would take back the repacked stocking, with some little gifts and jokes, but I was never as good as her at selecting cuttings.

She was well into her eighties by now but her mind was razor sharp. She lived in a fair degree of chaos, but robins came in through the French window to take cheese from her hand, and she was the one person in whom I could confide my fears. She was elated by any successes I had; and news of the sit-com sent her into paroxysms of delight. 'Something on the television' was big news to her, although she only watched *Countdown*, snooker, and sports programmes. Once she got up at 3 a.m. to watch a boxing match in America.

I finished the second sit-com episode, and went down to discuss it with Richard. The trip was expenses paid, and therefore carefree. I sat in the train and luxuriated in the passing countryside and the ideas leaping around my head. Richard met me at the lobby and took me up to his office, but on the way we called at the bar. He bought two bottles of whisky and collected a cup of water from a cooler in the corridor. Back at his desk he offered me a drink: whisky, or wine that he produced from a drawer. He then poured a huge slug of whisky, picked up the cup of water and, with scientific precision, diluted it with five measured drops of water. This process was repeated at intervals, but his patience with me, the novice, never wavered. It was a convivial discussion!

Eventually I completed the second episode to his satisfaction, and was paid; but there was no definite word about production – and I knew very well that unless you had mega-hits you couldn't rely on writing for television.

One day I saw something in a newspaper about a competition for the best so-far unpublished novel written in or about the north. It was sponsored by a prestigious publisher, Constable & Co, and the prize was £1000 and publication. I got out my half-written novel, deleted page after page of tears, finished it, and sent it off. It was about a woman who finds herself widowed young, in a mining community in which she is a newcomer, and, like most first novels, it was semi-autobiographical.

Around now I was approached by several local businessmen who were worried about rising unemployment in the town. Derek Mercer and Arthur Brown, who had set up the centre for youth training that Jack managed, now wanted to do the same thing for adults. They were to be joined by the same Billy Hoare who had befriended Jack after the business went, a businessman named Eddy Pearson and a miner and local councillor, Matthew Burdess. Would I join them? I said yes.

We knew we could get Government funding to support the project, but first we needed premises. The old Water Company offices in the centre of town were vacant and derelict. If we could get a mortgage, they would be ideal. The men contacted the bank of which most of them were clients, and received a flat refusal. No one, it seemed, would take the scheme seriously. We held a meeting in a mood of despair. I suggested trying another bank but they shook their heads. If one said no, so would the others. I wasn't prepared to give in so easily. 'I'll try Barclays,' I said. Barclays was where my overdraft was housed.

How I got the cheek to go in there I'll never know, especially as Stanley Carpenter, the man who had helped us through the business collapse, had retired, and I didn't know his successor. I could only hope he didn't realise the parlous state of my personal finances as I set out the case. To my relief, he said he'd consider it. Within a year, the Seaham Adult Training Centre was putting a large payroll through his bank. Today it still thrives, and hundreds of men and women have passed through its horticultural, motor-maintenance and other courses, all thanks to the work of Derek Mercer and his fellow committee members. Such men as Mercer and Brown are the yeast in the loaf of any community. Seaham was lucky to have them.

But as the training centre began to flourish, my fortunes, and those of Seaham itself, were getting worse. In March 1984 a national strike by mineworkers began. It would last a year and bring the town, like every other mining community, to its knees. And I was becoming uncomfortably aware that we were likely to lose our house. The mortgage was becoming harder and harder to pay, and I couldn't shift the backlog of debt that was sucking up what money we had.

Marie Lawson died, and left me £500 and two family pictures. One was her portrait, painted when she became a Freeman of the City of London. The other was the portrait of my forebears, the wonderful Victorian oil painting, huge and detailed, with my great-grandmother in her chair and the little dog coiled in front of the assembled family, which I had seen hanging in Mount Street. Now I had no option but to let it go. It sold at Christie's for £400. I needed the money.

News came from Richard Waring that Michael Grade had come in to run the BBC and put a stop to all projects until further notice. Whether this was true, or was Richard's way of telling me the sit-com would not go ahead, I will never know. Later on I turned it into a novel, *The Anxious Heart*, but news that the sit-com was off was a terrible blow at the time.

As winter began to bite and the strike escalated, I felt a sense of despair. And then something bizarre happened. I had always taken Poppy and Daisy for the injection that would stop them coming into heat, a process of which I now disapprove but which seemed sensible then. One day I was walking them in woodland near the house when a bulldog appeared and, despite my best efforts, paid Poppy some unwelcome attention, while Daisy howled disapproval from the sidelines.

Distraught, I put the dog in the car and drove to the vet. He was frankly disbelieving that it could have happened, but to calm my fears gave her an injection which would 'put things right'. Over the next few weeks I witnessed a pregnant dog growing larger before my eyes, but the vet was adamant: it couldn't be. Eventually, with her poor tummy trailing the ground, I told Jack he would have to come with me to the vet. This time the vet agreed there was 'something there'. If we brought her in the next day he would operate and have a look.

But early next morning the 'something there' materialised in the shape of a puppy. Then another puppy, and another, and another. When the count got to nine I went upstairs and had hysterics. Amid the laughter and tears there was a real fear, both for Poppy and for how we could possibly cope. Dorrie stayed to act as midwife, calling up the stairs at intervals to tell me cheerfully 'that's another one'. In all, there were thirteen.

We held a crisis meeting to decide on bottle feeding, and Jack procured a huge wooden box big enough for mum and babies. But I could see that Poppy wasn't well. After an hour, she was no better and was beginning to moan, so we lifted her into the car and sped to the vet. He delivered a stillborn fourteenth pup, and gave me a lecture. There was no way we could raise 13 pups. No bitch could cope with that number. One by one they would die, and it would be a cruel death. In addition he had grave fears for Poppy.

'What shall I do?' I asked. His solution was brutal. I must pick out the four strongest puppies, those with the best chance of survival. He would put the others to sleep. Choosing was an impossible task, and I couldn't do it. I picked out the first four my hand touched, among them the runt of the litter, a tiny little thing, black with a white chest. I know that what the vet advocated was for the best, but it pains me still. No dog I have had since has been allowed to have a litter, and I have done my very best to help the Dogs' Trust stem the tide of unwanted pups.

Having the four puppies, though, was pure bliss. They grew stronger every day, and Poppy too began to pick up, although she was painfully thin. Eventually we found homes for two of the pups, but I hated to see them go. Jack was determined the other two should go too, but one of them was the little runt, and watching her cuddle up to her remaining sister, I couldn't bear to see them parted. Jack kept sending people to inquire about taking one of them. I kept making excuses. One day I lied outright. 'Sorry, they're all gone,' I said brightly, hoping a pup wouldn't waddle into the hall and betray me.

They became a source of argument, Jack stating quite reasonably that we could hardly feed the mouths we had, let alone two more. I named the pups Aster and Lupin, carrying on the flower tradition; but the boys refused to call out 'Lupin!', and so Lupi she became.

On the day that the pups were first allowed out, I took all four dogs to the woodland area where we usually walked. They ran ahead of me, intrigued to feel grass beneath their feet. On the slope above me miners were sawing down saplings to make a fire. Their concessionary coal had run out, and men who had never lived without a fire could not bear an empty grate. I watched the dogs gambolling together, saw the decimation of the woodland that was taking place, and felt utter despair.

It now seemed almost inevitable that we would lose our house. Having four dogs in a terraced house was difficult enough; if we had to move to a flat it would be impossible. They would have to go, and it would break my heart. 'Please, please,' I said aloud, 'let me find a way to feed these dogs.'

I don't know why I used those words. The pups were only a fragment of the problem. Nor do I know whom I was addressing. I was asking for a miracle, and nothing in my life had led me to believe such things existed.

21
CHAPTER

MIRACLES

As I GOT back into the house, the phone was ringing. The dogs ran ahead of me, and milled around my feet as I picked it up. It was a man called Derek Rowell, a cousin of the boys' mother. He asked if he could come and see us, and I said of course. My heart sank as I put down the phone. He was a nice man, but he sounded quite solemn. In the mood I was in, I could see only more trouble.

In fact, he brought news of a small windfall for each of the boys, money from a family will. Each would receive £2000. It was the first nice thing to happen for ages, and an enormous lift. John and Philip each lent me £1000, and, for the moment at least, the house was saved.

Looking back on this period, I marvel at how we managed to make everything seem normal. I had held on to my support systems, the car and help in the house, because without them I couldn't work, and I knew that work was the road out of the abyss. So outwardly everything appeared OK. But the reality of living close to the brink, as we did for years, is truly frightening, whether seen up ahead or looking back. When you are actually fighting for your financial life, you are almost in the eye of the storm. You simply get on with it.

My plea in the woods had produced one miracle. Another soon followed. A phone call told me that my novel had been short-listed for the Constable Trophy. A few weeks later I learned I had won it.

But if life had improved for my family, the strife in the coalfield had worsened. Ian MacGregor, the boss of the National Coal Board, was a hate figure second only to Margaret Thatcher, but many miners were uneasy, some even incensed, by the fact that their leader, Arthur Scargill, had denied them a ballot about the strike. One man almost cried to me in the street, 'I'd have voted for a bloody strike if I'd been given the chance. But I wasn't, and it isn't right.'

Many of the pits in the Durham coalfield carried on working, and there came a shattering moment when I realised that the BBC didn't always tell the truth. I heard an announcer say, 'The Durham coalfield is at a standstill,' while outside my window miners were struggling to get into the pit, and other miners were struggling to keep them out. I have never since entirely trusted a news broadcast.

The drama going on around me impelled me to pick up my pen again, to carry on where my prize-winning novel, *Land of Lost Content*, had left off, and to use the same characters and the same pit village in a sequel set amid the strike. And I asked that the first book, when it was published, should carry a dedication, taken from the Miners' Memorial in Durham Cathedral, to those miners, and their way of life, that had inspired me. 'Remember before God the Durham Miners who have given their lives in the pits of this county and those who work in darkness and danger in those pits today'. It is followed by a biblical quotation: 'They are forgotten of the foot that passes by'.

The strike dragged on for a year. There was no more reassuring tramp of feet as the shifts changed. Instead there was conflict, and sometimes danger if you got caught between opposing forces. The streets seemed full of Panda cars and sinister navy blue uniforms. And at night men in balaclavas slid from back lanes on their way to exact retribution from anyone considered a scab.

As weeks turned into months, the misery intensified. Everyone was affected. Even if you had money for shopping, you felt uncomfortable buying anything that could be termed a luxury when around you other women didn't have money for bread. Local shopkeepers did their best, but as time went on the strain showed in their faces, too. They allowed regular customers to buy on tick at first, but as the debts became astronomical they had to say no. Most people understood; only a few were resentful, vowing vengeance when the strike was over and they could take their custom elsewhere.

But it was at Christmas that the deprivation was most keenly felt. 'I can't get anything for my bairns,' a mother told me bitterly. I said I had read in the paper that toys were coming in from mining families in Europe, but her face twisted. 'Oh, they've come, all right, but they won't go to the likes of us. They'll go to the union men – their bairns'll have a Christmas.' Another young father showed me a broken toy trumpet. 'That's what I got out of it,' he said. 'Try making a stocking with that.'

As in any stressful situation, someone found a way to make a dishonest living out of it. The vast stockpiles of coal at the pit-heads were supposed to be guarded, but men who knew every inch of the terrain could easily outwit the watchers.

One day there was a knock at our back door. It was a man selling coal, obviously stolen, from a pedal bike. I was as desperate for a fire as anyone else, but not desperate enough to handle stolen property, so I said no. He turned away and trudged off, and I was suddenly seized with guilt. Bereft of an income for months now, he probably needed his ill-gotten gains to feed his family. 'Never mind,' I called after him, 'the strike must be over soon.' He turned round, a look of horror on his face. 'I hope not, Missus. I've got a canny little business here.' Although the whole situation was far from funny, I was still laughing as I sat down to write that scene into the new novel.

Eventually, those miners still working had to be bussed through the picket lines in buses covered with steel plating, known as battle buses. Brother didn't speak to a brother who had dared to scab, father didn't speak to son. Tragically, many of the men policing the strike were themselves sons and brothers of miners, and their position was especially cruel. One young policeman told me: 'I bloody agree with them, but they still tried to push me under a lorry. When is this going to stop?'

One day I stood in the bank watching grey-faced men queuing to cancel standing orders for mortgages and cars. That night I went to Central TV to take part in an evening magazine-programme. Another item was to feature Arthur Scargill and a man who was challenging him for leadership of the union. Scargill was in the make-up room, combing his hair into a careful bouffant. He was naked to the waist. When the hair was done, he stretched both arms backwards and a giant of a man stepped forward holding an immaculately ironed shirt which he threaded on to Scargill's arms. It was a vision of master and servant that had no relevance to the sad scene I had seen in the bank that morning.

Later a researcher told me that Scargill had refused to be seated with his challenger for the leadership slot. He wanted to make an entrance, and so he did. I formed a dislike for him that night which has never wavered. The strike was a clash between two massive egos, his and Margaret Thatcher's, and in my opinion neither of them cared a damn about the men and women who were crushed in between.

The strike ended in March 1985. The day the men went back to the pits, a girl I knew slightly spoke to me in the supermarket. 'They've gone back, then?' I nodded. 'By,' she said, 'it's been a year of winter.' So it had – and I had the title for my second novel.

An award ceremony for the Trophy was held at Constable's London office. This time I had a safety pin already in place. I was taking no chances. But I still felt terrified of a literary scene of which I had no experience.

A chic, dark-haired woman who reminded me of Leslie Caron came up to me and introduced herself: 'I'm Prudence Fay, your editor.' I had not envisaged needing an editor as I knew little about publishing, but Prudence and I were to form a long and happy relationship. Prudence was a stickler for detail, but wonderfully understanding of the way my mind worked. Her notes in the margin were few, but to the point. She deplored the lack of description in my work, and on one occasion commented: 'You may be able to see this kitchen. I can't.' Admonished, I duly wrote in tables, dressers, pots and pans, the lot, so she could see the kitchen as I did. She taught me more about writing than I knew when I started.

There was some publicity after the award ceremony. I was pictured with Nelson's Column in the background and a glass of champagne in my hand. I had a broad smile on my face, but actually I was bemused. Wonderful things were happening, and I could see light at the end of the tunnel, but money for the book would be slow in coming. Could I keep us afloat till the ship came in? We had had two miracles already. A third was unlikely.

It came three days later. A voice on the telephone asked if I'd like to be BBC's *Breakfast Time* agony aunt. 'We'd need to talk to you, of course,' it said, 'but we've been told you're very good.' 'Where does the programme come from?' I asked 'Lime Grove, in London.' I couldn't work in London. I said a fervent 'No, thank you,' and put the phone down.

The following day I mentioned the call to my agent. Her howl of anguish must have been heard at sea. 'You said no? *No!*' Ten minutes later I had been acquainted with the facts of life. A: the BBC paid oodles of money. B: get your face on the television, and book sales went through the roof. C: If I didn't take it, I was a cretin, and not fit to be on her books.

Mention of money did it. I telephoned and asked whether the offer was still open. Five days later I was on my way to a screen test. In the mean time, I had switched on breakfast TV to see the utterly lovely Selina Scott draped over the Lime Grove sofa. She seemed all legs. If I sat on the sofa, would my legs be prominent? They were not my best feature.

I took what little cash I had and bought a pair of black suede boots. I also bought a remnant of black cotton splashed with poppies. This I fashioned into a kimono jacket. No seams, no darts, just a simple T shape. Worn over a black dress it looked, to my eyes, suitably exotic, and I felt reasonably confident – until the cameras loomed. I had enough make-up on my face to paint the Forth Bridge, and wires inside my frock. In addition to this, I seemed to be talking at the speed of an express train. But talk I did, at length. I was convinced I'd blown it, but the word was that I would do. I would get a fee of £120, plus a £90 overnight allowance and travel expenses. The overnight allowance could be spent how I chose, but I must be in London at five in the morning, when my day on air would begin.

I started in February 1985, complete with boots. My first fan letter said, 'You have a nice face, and you talk a lot of sense, but you haven't got the legs for the boots.' They went into the back of the wardrobe, and never resurfaced. I was one of a panel of three 'experts' who were to deal with viewers' emotional problems. Sometimes we all appeared together, sometimes we appeared separately, depending on our specialist knowledge. The spot lasted about five minutes, and we dealt with viewers' letters, much as I had done with listeners' letters at Metro.

I found a hotel in Shepherds Bush for £25 a night. If I got a basement room, and I frequently did, it came complete with cockroaches. I would sit cross-legged on the bed all night with the light on, longing for five o'clock, when a car would arrive to carry me to the warm, cockroach-free studio. I loved London at five in the morning: empty, clean, quiet, and unbelievably beautiful. But best of all was 10.30 a.m., when I boarded the train at King's Cross and could slump in my seat and go to sleep.

In the Lime Grove canteen, everyone would comment on my north-east accent, and ask about the miners' strike. I tried to explain the complexity of it, but in vain. Their view, even that of the newsmen and -women among them, was simple and unyielding. It was miners versus police. Good against evil. Mrs Thatcher was a Devil, Scargill was a saint, Ian MacGregor a buffoon. Case closed. I remembered that broadcast that had said the coalfield was at a standstill, and decided that I would be even more discriminating about what I believed in future. Behind every news broadcast is an ordinary human being who sometimes gets it wrong.

Frank Bough and Selina Scott were both helpful to me. Frank was the ultimate professional, always cheerful, but demanding. If you hadn't done your homework, heaven help you. Selina was ready to cover for you if you boobed, and was always polite, but she was something of an enigma. She was charismatic beyond belief, and normally articulate men would suddenly grow tongue-tied in her presence. One day, in the green room before the show, an MP told me confidently that her charm escaped him. She was just another pretty face, and he wasn't subscribing to the legend. Five minutes later he went on to sit beside her, she turned her gaze on him and smiled, and he turned, much to my delight, into a gibbering wreck.

My weekly appearances required quite a wardrobe, a wardrobe I didn't have. I was entitled to a car to take me anywhere after the show. Each week I asked to go John Lewis in Oxford Street. Someone had told me you could get remnants there, and I had found Aladdin's cave. Not since the days of Mrs Jefferson's patches had I had such fun. The ends of fabric were in huge tub-like containers, and I rummaged to my heart's content. Silk, velvet, wool, lace – I would choose a piece, and take it home to manufacture something for the next week. I still have some of those artefacts: a huge jade-green chiffon scarf that I swathed to great effect, red-and-white collar and cuffs, even a whole floral suit, as I got bolder. My dressmaking hadn't improved, but the camera doesn't do detail.

I was enjoying the money and the resultant relief of stress, but appearing on television terrified me. My heart used to thump so wildly that I would look down, expecting to see a palpable, pulsating lump on the left side of my chest. *Breakfast Time* had a huge semi-circular sofa. Frank and Selina sat in the centre and the guest of the moment occupied one end. While the cameras concentrated on that end, the next guest was fed on the other end to await attention. When one item finished, the cameras swung to the other end of the sofa, and the next item began. The programme was prepared during the night by people who went off when the day staff came in at five a.m. One morning I was entering Lime Grove as that night's editor was going home. 'You're on with the families of the Moors Murders victims,' she said. 'But keep it light.' I nodded, and walked on wondering how the hell you could lighten the subject of the Moors Murders.

Another day I was just finishing my spiel when a man crawled between the cameras, a look of terror on his face. He made signs with his hands which meant I should keep on talking. I did my best, but actually I'd already exhausted the subject. Eventually I heard myself saying something vague about the weather, and the contempt on Frank Bough's face was a joy to behold. Later I learned that the incoming guest had fainted, and I had had to hold the fort until someone else was put in place.

Frank was hard to work with, but I learned a lot from his dedication. He gave his all to the BBC. His replacement, when he was away, was Nick Ross, one of the nicest men I've ever worked with. He is a natural broadcaster, and a man with a strong sense of fair play. When *Land of Lost Content* was due to be published, the *Breakfast Time* editor decreed that it could not be mentioned. I worked on the programme, and must not be allowed to plug my book on it. In fact, the idea of my plugging anything was crazy: in those days I hardly dared open my mouth, so there was no argument from me. Nick, however, didn't think it was fair, especially as ITV was interviewing the winner of the Trophy's second prize. 'It's your first novel, it's won an award, it should be mentioned, and I'm going to do it at the end of the programme.'

I begged him not to. He might lose his job. More important, I might lose mine. Sure enough, as the programme drew to a close, he produced a copy of the book and told the world I had written it. A lovely Labour MP, Frank White, was sitting next to me. He gave me a dig in the ribs and hissed, 'Give the price and the publisher. Go on, tell them where to get it.' Alas, I was overcome with fear and embarrassment, and could merely gulp. I'm wiser now.

It was at *Breakfast Time* that my interest in what happens to abused children began. Like everyone else, I remembered Maria Colwell who had been starved and beaten to death by her stepfather in the 1970s. A scandal had erupted when it was revealed how all the agencies that should have helped her had let her down.

Now, in my first year at *Breakfast Time*, the report of an enquiry into the death of Jasmine Beckford was to be published, and I was asked to comment. She too had been starved and battered to death by a stepfather, and once more the people charged with her welfare had failed to protect her. The Chair of the enquiry emerged to announce that 'lessons had been learned', and Selina asked me what I felt about his remarks. 'Depressed,' was my answer. If I had known how often I was to hear that phrase, 'lessons have been learned', I would have felt even worse. The programme had used a huge blow-up of Jasmine, and afterwards it was stored in props. I walked through props every time I went to the studio, and her face seemed to reproach me. Depressed and homesick as I was, it seemed to make a bond between us. I have never forgotten her.

Nor have I forgotten Heidi Kosega, who starved to death in a locked room in Hillingdon, in west London. A private enquiry into her death found that the senior inspector from the National Society for the Prevention of Cruelty to Children who had been allocated to her case had failed to investigate a complaint of child abuse made by a neighbour. He tried to cover that up with a fictitious account of a visit to see the child. A representative of the NSPCC came on to the programme, and while we were off camera he told me that the child's stomach contents had contained wallpaper that she had clawed from the walls and eaten in an effort to assuage her hunger. When he told me this I felt so faint I could hardly answer Frank when he asked me to comment.

Since then the sickening tide of children we have failed has swelled: Kimberley Carlile, Tyra Henry, Rikki Neave, and a thousand others right up to tragic Victoria Climbie, who died from hypothermia in a tiny flat in Tottenham, north London, after suffering months of horrific abuse and neglect at the hands of her aunt, Marie Thérèse Kouao, and her boyfriend, Carl Manning, both of whom were laer jailed for life. A public enquiry into her death heard that the agencies involved in her protection had at least 12 chances to have saved her.

Much was made at the time of the fact that Victoria's parents had fobbed her off on her aunt and allowed her to come to Britain. The perception was that they couldn't have cared less. But when I interviewed the parents after the enquiry, I found that Victoria had been, in their eyes, the best and brightest of their children, and that sending her to England had been seen as a sacrifice for them but a golden opportunity for her. That England so failed her shames me.

22
CHAPTER

HOMESICKNESS

I KEPT TELLING myself the agonising homesickness I felt each time I went away would pass, but if anything it got worse. I would sit in the train, trying not to let anyone see I was crying. I had a Sony Walkman, and I played the Victoria de los Angeles version of 'Songs of the Auvergne' over and over again as the countryside rolled by. Today I have only to hear 'Balero' to feel a profound melancholy. Similarly, Newcastle station chills me because that was where I used to board the train. Nowadays I leave from Durham, a smaller and friendlier station, and I am completely at ease on the train; but then it was three and a half hours of agony, with London waiting at the end, ready to gobble me up.

At least my trips there, though, were paying off. I repaid John and Philip, and then began to tackle the rest of the debt.

The first fan letter I received after *Land of Lost Content* was published came from a man called Arthur Appleton, himself no mean writer. Sunderland-born, he wrote to tell me that it was the first time he had seen Sunderland described as anything but a dump, and he applauded me for it. I sat with his letter in my hand. Who would call Sunderland – that place of wide streets and gracious parks – a dump? I hadn't gone out of my way to heap praise on my birthplace. I had simply described it as I saw it.

By now the manuscript of the second novel was finished, and I leafed through to see if I had gone over the top in my description. But no, I had been fair about the town, and I hoped I had truthfully reported the strike. Everything I had written was documented; the letters in the fictional evening paper were authentic letters that appeared in the *Sunderland Echo*. Prudence had checked that it was legal for us to use them. I delivered the script to Constable, complete with the title *A Year of Winter*, and waited for publication.

The cover was a photograph of a dead pigeon nailed to a door that had 'SCAB' sprayed across it. I had seen doors like that. I couldn't bear to have a pigeon killed for the photograph so I searched the poulterers, but all they had were frozen birds. Eventually we used a pigeon that had been culled by its owner, and someone lent us a back door on condition that we quickly had the word painted out again. The cover would later win an award, but I received a stern letter from a gentleman who told me pigeons had been invaluable to the war effort, and he hoped I hadn't killed a pigeon merely to make a photograph.

When the book came out, I expected I might get some comeback over my portrayal of Scargill. The first time I walked into the pub, a miner I knew, a trade-union activist, was standing at the bar. 'Can I get you a drink?' he asked. I expressed surprise: 'I thought you might be angry with me.' 'Why?' he answered. 'You only told the truth.'

Life at *Breakfast Time* was a revelation. Each time I appeared, I met famous faces: Richard Branson, in and out between one daring exploit and another; Vera Lynn, not so much the girl next door as the *grande dame* with a retinue; the war-time legend Walter Cronkite, who held my hand for so long that I never wanted to wash it again.

One early morning, I had the most magical experience of all. I went into the green room at five a.m. to sit and read my mail. It was empty, except for a small man sitting quietly in the corner. I noticed he had silk socks on. I love silk socks on a male ankle – a real turn-on. We started to talk. He was Sir Jock Colville, secretary to Winston Churchill and later Clement Attlee, and was there to plug his memoirs. He told me tales of what had gone on in Downing Street, of Churchill's stoicism when the electorate had thrown him out at the end of the war, and of Attlee's patience with his wife, whose exploits were apt to interrupt Cabinet meetings. It was good to have my high opinion of those two men confirmed, and painful when we were both summoned, he to go on air, me to make-up.

But *Breakfast Time* also completely changed my hitherto reverent opinion of politicians. When you have seen a Shadow Home Secretary throw a croissant across the room because he wanted a hot breakfast, or a Government Minister choosing the exact shade of bronze he wants to be, you realise what little people some of them are.

That summer, Mark and Philip graduated. Philip came home, but Mark, still playing his drums, went on tour with a production of *Godspell* whose cast included Jacqui Dankworth. I was working flat out, as invitations came to take part in other programmes. Invitations came for charities, too, and I was happy to open this and close that, or agree to be patron of the other. I had been phenomenally lucky; I wanted to pay something back.

Certain things stand out in my memory. For instance, going to
the BBC in London to record *Conversation Piece* with Sue
McGregor, where the air was positively blue with respect. But the
great lady herself was friendly and reassuring, so that it was easy to
pour out things I might have kept to myself in different
circumstances.

We now had a new woman presenter on *Breakfast Time*, Debbie
Greenwood who had been Miss Great Britain. She was to play
Cinderella in *Breakfast Time*'s pantomime, and I was to be the Fairy
Godmother. Frank Bough played Father Time, Selina wandered in
and out looking beautiful, and the Principal Boy was our glamorous
newsreader, Sue Carpenter, who seemed to have the longest legs in
the world. The *Breakfast Time* gardening expert was one Alan
Titchmarsh. He played a garden gnome with a green face.
Impossible, then, to predict how he would set female hearts aflutter
a few years later. The rest of the cast was any celebrity who happened
to be in or around *Breakfast Time* that Christmas. Jeffrey Archer was
an archer with a bow; Dennis Healey was glimpsed playing the
piano; and the whole thing was a riotous success.

We were filming a bedchamber scene which required the green
gnome to be in bed with Debbie Greenwood while I, the Fairy
Godmother, stood by. It was all perfectly proper, but Alan began to
get uneasy. 'I don't like this,' he muttered out of the side of his
mouth. 'I shouldn't be in bed with Cinderella. It's not seemly.'
Around us they were shouting instructions; Frank was getting
tetchy; I had a train to catch. I sought desperately for something to
reassure him. That's when I remembered the old Hayes Convention,
the Hollywood rule that said a man and woman couldn't be seen in
bed together unless one of them had one foot on the floor. 'Stick
your leg out,' I hissed. A green leg ending in a dainty elfin boot

appeared from beneath the coverlet, and propriety was satisfied.

I loved making that pantomime, especially when they allowed my wand to send a trail of stars across the screen each time I moved it. But the best moment came when I was sitting in a café, and I overheard two women discussing it. They had loved every moment of it – the clothes, the set, the storyline. At that moment I realised what a boon television could be to people whose lives might be running slowly at the time.

We had a wonderful Christmas. The clouds were not only lifting, they were scattering across the sky; for between Christmas and New Year I was contacted by someone working for Eddie Shah. He was launching a new newspaper, called *Today*. Would I like to be its agony aunt? I went down to meet Eddie Shah and Brian MacArthur, the editor. I liked Brian MacArthur on sight and wanted to work for him. He had the gift of making you feel you had his full attention, and his whole manner was kindly. A week or two later the paper was on the streets, and I had a page and a by-line.

I went frequently to London, now. This meant I could see Mark more often, for he was living in London, on a houseboat moored in Chelsea. I was obsessed with feeding him properly, and would carry cooked joints leaking juice to press on him when he met me at King's Cross. I still had that lurch of the heart at the sight of a uniform at the barrier, but now there was a son striding towards me down the platform, and that made all the difference.

I was worried about his hand-to-mouth existence, busking in a tube when he couldn't get gigs. I would rehearse the speech about getting a proper job all the way down on the train, but when I got there his happy face would persuade me to leave it for another month or so.

In April 1986, I arrived at Lime Grove to be told my slot was cancelled. The Yanks had bombed Libya, and news was the only thing on the agenda. I sat in the corner of the green room, dealing with my letters, while John Simpson and the other experts came and went, discussing the crisis and what to do about it. I liked that feeling of being on the fringes while history was happening.

The rest of 1986 flew past. Gillian had remarried and moved away, but I was overjoyed when she gave birth to a daughter. Philip had a job he liked, John came home as often as he could, and the other two boys were well, and working in the south. I finished the third novel that would make a trilogy with *Land of Lost Content* and *A Year of Winter*, and called it *Blue Remembered Hills*. The A. E. Housman poem seemed to express everything I felt about the past:

Into my heart an air that kills from some far country blows.
Where are those blue, remembered hills,
What spires, what farms are those?
That is the land of lost content. I see it shining plain.
The happy highways where I went and cannot come again.

The trilogy mirrored my life without Alex. But what I had written on that little funeral posy fifteen years before had been proved true. I did love him better after death, more with every day – but now I could cope with his death, and love again

That year I was one of the judges for the Constable Trophy, and to my utter amazement the actress Jane Asher got in touch with me to say she would love to bring *Land of Lost Content* to the screen. We met several times. She was charming, but also thoroughly nice. Alas, the money to make the film couldn't be found, but it is my ambition to see her play one of my heroines one day.

That September I made my first appearance on *Any Questions*. My name had been put forward in a competition to find ordinary people to take part in the programme. My heart sank when I learned that my fellow panellists that night were to be Kenneth Clarke, then a government minister, David Owen, and Roy Hattersley. Hattersley was cold, and rather contemptuous of a woman he'd never heard of; David Owen was completely taken up with himself; and Kenneth Clarke was kind and helpful when he learned that it was my first appearance and I was scared.

He warned me to go to the loo before I went on, and showed me where it was. He warned me, too, to listen to the radio playing on the table during dinner. 'Something might happen before we go on, and if you're not up to date you could put your foot in it.' He also warned me not to catch the chairman's eye until I had my answer ready. 'If you do, he'll think you're ready to speak.'

As the programme began, I felt my mouth go dry. I was an avid listener to the programme, but shouting out fine words in my sitting-room was easy. This was terrifying. When John Timpson eased me into my first answer, I heard myself say something inane about Newcastle station, but as the programme went on I improved. The lighthearted question that is always featured was: 'Do you expect to get to Heaven?' I said yes, because God loves sinners, and that got a laugh. So far, so good. The final question was tailor-made for me. 'What can be done about the divide between the prosperous south and the poverty-stricken north?' All the facts were there in my head – I had been preparing all my life to answer that question – but all of a sudden I couldn't engage my brain. I cared so passionately that it made me tongue-tied. This taught me a salutary lesson. The next time I saw a politician groping desperately for words, I knew he might not be as daft as he looked.

Roy Hattersley and I came back to London in the same car. He slumped in his seat and was silent throughout. When we reached Westminster, I asked him if the sight of the floodlit House moved him. His answer was honest. After twenty-two years, he tended to take it for granted. Now that I had pointed it out, however, it did look rather nice.

I appeared on *Any Questions* several times, and was always treated with affection by the audience – except when I made the programme on my own home ground, in Gateshead, a few miles up the road from Sunderland. We trooped on to the platform, Tony Benn and Nicholas Winterton, someone else I can't remember, and me; and as we sat down I noticed two women in the front row. I can lip read a little, certainly enough to make out what one said to the other: 'What's she doing up there? She only comes from round here.' Truly a prophet has no honour in his own country!

Of all the politicians I met on an *Any Questions*, I thought Michael Heseltine and David Blunkett the most honest, and Kenneth Clarke the nicest – all three were the same behind the scenes as on air. Some others were very different men at the dinner table compared with the face they later presented in public. And seeing a crowd respond to Tony Benn was rather like watching people flock to Jesus. At the end of the programme they surged forward, desperate to touch him or engage his attention. One woman was desperate to get her blind son to him, and I found myself reaching out to pull him forward. It felt thoroughly biblical.

I always got appreciative fan mail after a programme. 'You said just what I would have said,' was a typical remark, and I liked that. John Timpson retired, and Jonathan Dimbleby took his place, making it a very different programme. My last appearance occurred at a time when there was unease about long- and short-range nuclear weapons in Europe. The day before the programme, I found myself at a literary lunch seated next to one of Mrs Thatcher's military advisers. He told me there was sure to be a question on the weapons, and briefed me thoroughly. The next night I waited for my chance to shine, but Jonathan obviously thought a northern housewife would know nothing about the subject. I got out my opening sentence; he thanked me and moved on – although I was probably the most thoroughly briefed panellist there that night.

Aunt Marian had developed cataracts, and needed an operation. She couldn't have a general anaesthetic, and would consent to it being done under a local anaesthetic only if I was there to hold her hand. I went into the theatre, capped and gowned, and waited as the surgeon, hands delicate as butterfly wings, replaced the faulty lens. But the stress got to me, and at one stage she asked me to stop squeezing her hand as I was cutting off the blood supply. When we left the theatre, she was asking when her lunch would be coming and I was tottering out to the car to ask Jack to get me a brandy at the nearest pub. The icing on the cake was the moment when she returned home and saw everything with fresh eyes. What had been sludgy brown was now gleaming colour; and she fingered her recent birthday presents, emitting squeaks of joy at their brilliance.

Letters continued to pour in to me at both *Breakfast Time* and *Today*, and by now I thought I must have seen twenty versions of every possible human problem. As usual, I was wrong. I opened a letter from a man who used the old line of writing on behalf of a friend, but in subsequent letters he acknowledged that the 'friend' was really himself. His 'friend', he said, was a retired senior policeman. This man knew of many cases in which men had been sent to prison without reason, having been fitted up. If the paper could arrange for him to escape prosecution by going to Spain, and compensate him for the loss of his pension, he would supply the details.

I wrote back to him, asking his permission to show his letter to my editor, and he agreed, dropping any pretence of there being a friend. The editor agreed to see him if I could get him to London. So John Smith (we will call him that) and I exchanged letters, setting up the meeting. At the last minute I had to do *Breakfast Time* and couldn't make the meeting, but afterwards I was told his demands were excessive, and that he had been very cagey with information. In the circumstances, there was nothing we could do.

'John Smith' wrote to me again once or twice; and one night I saw some old footage on a documentary which showed he had been a superintendent in charge of several murder cases. The postscript to the story came a few years later. I was at home, sorting old letters, when the phone rang. A young man's voice said, 'My father has died. His name was John Smith.' The name didn't register at once, so I muttered something sympathetic and asked what I could do for him. His reply was blunt: 'I want to know what you meant to my father.' At that moment, I remembered the name, and by one of those coincidences that can happen in real life but would seem far-fetched in fiction, I saw that one of his letters was lying on my lap.

'What do you mean?' I said, playing for time while I worked out what to say. Now he was openly hostile. 'I've read your letter to him: "Ring me. Come to London." Don't pretend you didn't write it.' I had written to 'John Smith' on my private headed notepaper, being cryptic at his request, in case his wife should see it. It could look like some kind of assignation. Nothing for it but to tell him who I was, and what I did. 'Your father had some issues of conscience,' I added. 'I can't break his confidence and say more, I'm afraid.' And straight

Above: Ooh, Lily! What a thing to say!

Below left: My favourite presenters, Fern and Phil.

Below right: Richard, Judy and I at the party to celebrate This Morning's tenth birthday.

Above left: Me as Geri Halliwell. I hope no one asks me to sing!

Above middle: Your wish is my command.

Above right: Dressed as Truly Scrumptious for the premiere of Chitty Chitty Bang Bang.

Below left: I really felt powerful presiding over the Rovers Return.

Below right: Posing in my Sunderland shirt for *A Brush with Fame*.

Letters, letters everywhere...

Above: Sharing a joke with the Princess.

Above left: These children in Uganda have little by our standards, but their happiness is infectious.

Left: I can't quite believe I'm an Honorary Doctor of Letters.

Below: A happy day with some of the Bubble children.

Above: Daisy, Titch, Aster, Lupi, Poppy and myself.

Left: Centre-forward Mitch.

Below: Tess, Primmie and Max hoping for biscuits.

Above: The men in my life on the day I married Bryan.

Below: Mark and I. This picture was taken to promote the donation of organs, which we both believe in.

Above: After five sons and four grandsons I have granddaughters at last.

Below: Almost the full complement of family on 'Family Day'. We see one another individually throughout the year, but try to all get together at least once a year.

away I knew that he knew what was on his father's conscience, because all he said was, 'I see. I'm sorry to have bothered you.' And he rang off. If he had not known the truth, could he have resisted trying to find out more?

That night, I sat down and began a new novel, *Remember the Moment*, in which a woman switches on her answering-machine to hear a young man say, mystifyingly, 'I want to know what you meant to my father.'

23
CHAPTER

THE SHADOW OF AIDS

IN THE AUTUMN of 1986, the BBC decided to turn *Breakfast Time* into a hard news programme. Everything classed as features would go, and that would include me. However, a programme called *Open Air*, to be made in Manchester, was to start in the mid-morning space, and a chosen few would transfer to that.

I went to meet the editor of *Open Air*, a man called Peter Weil. He was lovely, less intimidating than *Breakfast Time*'s David Lloyd but just as full of ideas. I liked him on sight. We were told not to talk about who would be on the new programme, nor what programme plans were in place. Especially, we were not to discuss the fact that Selina Scott was considering moving to *Open Air*.

I obeyed the instructions to the letter, until a colleague on *Today*, with whom I was friendly, rang me. 'Congratulations,' he began. 'It's just been announced that you're going to *Open Air*. You'll enjoy working with Selina, won't you?' Imagining that it had been officially announced – or else how would he know about it? – I agreed. Of course I'd enjoy working with Selina. The next day, there it was in the paper: 'Selina Scott to go to *Open Air*. Denise Robertson will enjoy working with her'.

I was seeing Peter Weil that day, and found him incandescent. Why had I disobeyed his explicit order? I had been the victim of a fishing expedition, and like a fool I'd fallen for it. Luckily for me, Peter soon saw that I was victim rather than gossip, and forgave me – but I learned a valuable lesson. When it comes to getting a story, a journalist, even your best friend, will sell you down the river without a pang. In the event, Selina decided against moving to *Open Air*, so that journalist wasn't as clever as he thought he was.

There were several presenters on *Open Air*. Patti Caldwell was good to work with, but my favourite was Eamonn Holmes. He could hold a television audience in the palm of his hand. Indeed, Peter Weil told me he had recruited Eamonn from Belfast, because 'when he is on, all Ulster comes to a standstill.' But the show had barely begun when the Government AIDS-awareness campaign sprang into action, and I was invited to take part in it. I had heard of AIDS, the mysterious disease that had come to light in America in 1981, where it had decimated the homosexual communities of San Francisco, Los Angeles and New York. An almost hysterical reaction needed calming down. At the same time, the message that there was no cure must be got across. Others would spread that message; my task was to reassure people who were not at risk but might well take fright.

We did a television phone-in, and I struggled to put my limited knowledge to good use. A fireman's wife said her husband was frequently called to accident scenes. If he came in contact with spilled blood, would he contract AIDS? Should she tell him to give up his job? Others wanted to know if they should shun cafés in case they caught the infection from cups or cutlery. They all feared for their children, as though AIDS were a cloud about to envelop everyone.

At night, we walked back to the Portland Hotel, discussing what we had just done, and pondering its worth. Later I would become patron of an AIDS charity, and see for myself the unbelievable devotion and loyalty of lovers when one of them was infected. Then, death followed fairly swiftly. I learned not to ask for people by name when I telephoned the charity, because, in all probability, they would have died since we last spoke. Eventually I saw new treatments give people longer life-spans, and the safety message go home to the homosexual community. Heterosexuals have been slower to catch on. But the spirit of those first AIDS sufferers was an inspiration.

One of the prime movers at Body Positive North West, whose patron I had become, was Ray. He was argumentative, bossy, kind, and always optimistic. His funeral, every detail of which he had planned himself, was unforgettable. A stretch-limo with twinkling stars in the roof and a cocktail bar took me to the church, where we had a full Latin mass conducted by a priest drafted in because, he said, he was one of the few priests in Britain who could remember the mass in Latin. That done, we went on to the crematorium for a less formal service which included 'tributes' from his friends – wry, a trifle bitchy, but ultimately loving. We exited to the thunderous strains of Freddie Mercury's 'Barcelona' and adjourned to the pub.

At the end of the year I went to my first Carole Stone party. Carole, for many years producer of *Any Questions*, is the most inspirational of women. Today she is a noted hostess, and the good and the great mingle at the salons she occasionally holds. That first party was a huge and glittering affair, held in the Reform Club and remarkable because you were as likely to meet an archbishop as a bin-man. Politicians, actors – anyone she had met in the course of a hectic year was invited. Her Christmas parties have now become legendary, and I have only missed one in all that time.

My postbag at *Today* had always held a large number of letters from young men. Indeed, the paper's readership was a young and highly educated one. I began to notice a common motif among the letters: the men were scared of the women they met socially or at work. 'I never know how to play it,' one wrote. 'They don't seem to need men any more, or even like them. If you don't offer to pay, you're a cheapskate; if you do, then you're being patronising. Whatever you say is wrong, or they say it's insulting. Men can't win.'

I was pondering these letters on a train journey, when I began to take notice of the couple alongside me. They were both in their early twenties, obviously in good jobs, and he was besotted with her. She was playing with him as cruelly as a cat plays with a mouse. Not the teasing of earlier days – this was something different. She was slapping him down, and, what's more, she meant it. By the time we got to Doncaster, I wanted him to slap her. By the time we reached King's Cross, I wanted to do it myself. The next week I wrote a feature about the relationship between men and women. I was sympathetic to the men, and I braced myself for an avalanche of letters from women.

They came, but they weren't what I expected. They agreed with me that the situation was difficult, but they were at as much of a loss as the men. 'I can't resist the urge to intellectually emasculate every man I meet,' wrote one ruefully. I understand this. For generations women were told to look pretty and keep their mouths shut. The last thing they should display was intelligence or spirit. Their new freedoms are intoxicating, and sometimes go to their heads. In time we will all settle down and enjoy this new-found equality. At least, I hope so.

One day in spring 1987, I opened a letter from a grandmother. Her grandchildren had been taken into care because her son had been accused of sexually abusing them. 'No one will listen,' she said. 'And we are not the only ones.' The address on the letter was Cleveland. I began to look at what was going on there, and found that something was definitely amiss. As yet, little or nothing had appeared in the national press. I asked permission to write a piece for *Today*, but the features editor was doubtful. 'I don't know,' she said. 'I can't believe they'd take children away for no reason. We don't want to get things wrong.'

Eventually I was allowed to do an article demanding that whatever was going on should be revealed without delay. The following August, a public enquiry revealed the awful truth: that innocent people had been vilified, and homes broken up without cause. In January 1987, the incidence of referrals for child abuse began to escalate rapidly, reaching a peak in May, June, and July. The referrals were being made by two consultant paediatricians at a Middlesbrough hospital, and were based on an unproven medical diagnosis termed the anal dilatation test. Once these allegations had been made, social workers were removing the children from their families on Place of Safety Orders, often in midnight or dawn raids on the family home. Children were taken from their beds and whisked away.

The initial crisis came when there were no more foster homes or residential-home places to accommodate the number of children involved, and a special ward had to be set up at the hospital to take them in. Increasingly, diagnosis that used the anal dilation test was being challenged by the police surgeon, who questioned the validity of such a test, and the police gradually withdrew their co-operation in the cases referred by the consultant paediatricians. Relationships between the police, social workers, and the paediatricians broke down as the medical dispute escalated.

But all the while children, torn from their families, were being subjected to continual vaginal and anal examinations, tests that the courts would later rule to be completely unnecessary as parent after parent was acquitted. Of 121 cases in which sexual abuse of children was alleged, the courts subsequently dismissed the proceedings involving 96 of the children – that is, more than eighty per cent were found to be false accusations.

In the early months of the crisis, the allegations involved working-class families, who were confused, bewildered, and angry at being accused of sexually abusing their children. But they were powerless against middle-class professionals with the authority, power, and legal sanctions to support their actions. Gradually, however, the allegations began to involve middle-class families, who were highly educated, employed in professional occupations, and with access to legal and political advice and to the media.

During all this, I was having lunch with my bank manager. 'Of course it would never happen to you and me,' he said. 'We're articulate. They'd never get away with it.' When I told him how many professional parents had been accused and lost their children, the colour drained from his face. Afterwards a powerful book indicting the accusers would be written by Stuart Bell, MP for the area. It was called *When Salem Came to the Boro*. That incident made me aware of how wrongful accusation can ruin lives and hurt children. The problem still exists today, but in our urge to protect the abused we must be aware that taking a child from its family for no good reason *is* abuse in itself.

Despite the bright dreams with which he had started *Today*, Eddie Shah sold out to Rupert Murdoch. Brian MacArthur went to another paper, and what had been a very happy period in my life was over. The new editor could not have been more different. I never saw or met him, whereas Brian's office door had always been open. But I received a series of messages from him, delivered by middlemen (usually female) who looked frankly terrified. He wanted the column 'sexed up'. He didn't want letters from 'losers'. *Today* was a paper for the upwardly mobile, and the letters should reflect that.

I sent back a message that I thought an upwardly mobile readership wasn't daft, and would soon recognise an agony column that didn't reflect all human life. He persisted; I resisted, determined not to tamper with letters written to me in good faith. One day I opened up the paper, and found the lead letter in my column was one I had never seen. It purported to be from a girl who had been waiting in a bus queue when a Porsche drew up and a man offered her a lift. They drove to a lay-by and had sex. Now she was hoping the car would come by again. 'My' answer was to the effect that haunting the bus stop should do the trick. This advice to have sex with a stranger – from a patron of an AIDS charity!

My agent sent a sharp letter, saying nothing should appear under my by-line unless it was written by me. A week later, I was out and Claire Rayner was in. She sent me a note saying she hoped I didn't blame her 'for all this horridness'. I replied quite truthfully that the only 'horrid' thing would have been for me to continue working there. I was happy at *Open Air*, I had just written a radio play for the BBC, my next novel was due for publication, my debts were slimming daily. I did wonder how Claire would react to appeals to sex things up. She wasn't there long, so I can only assume she liked it as little as I did.

Some months later I had a call from a *Today* executive. She greeted me warmly, and then said she'd heard I was beginning a new novel. There was a tinkle of laughter. 'Apparently there's a newspaper editor in it. . .' I felt a grin spreading across my face. 'Your boss isn't nearly important enough to be in one of my novels,' I said firmly. It was true: I had quite forgotten he existed.

Although Jack never grumbled, I knew he missed his garden. The rambling rose in the back yard continued to shower us with blossom and scent each summer, but there was nothing that needed doing for it, springing as it did from a pocket-hanky-sized piece of soil. If we tried to move, would we get a mortgage? For months I considered it, and combed the property columns of the local paper. Even if the old house had been for sale, I wouldn't have wanted to go back to that place of unhappy memory. And pleasant houses with gardens were in short supply in Seaham. Sometimes houses would be offered for sale with the description 'Tomlin-built' as a mark of excellence. I knew this pleased Jack when I drew it to his attention – but could we afford a custom-built house like those?

One night, a house sprang out of the paper at me. It was the house next door to the one we had lost, the very house in which I had lunched on the day I first met the boys. Could we afford it? Should we even try? I took myself off to the bank. The under-manager I saw was sympathetic, but I was brutally truthful. We had just crawled out from under a mountain of debt. Should we wait?

He leaned back in his chair and put his fingertips together. 'Is this your dream house?' he said at last. I shook my head. 'Not mine. But I think it might be my husband's.' Ten minutes later I was out in the street, a promise of a mortgage in my pocket, my heart exulting and panic noises in my head.

We moved in three months later, and I will never ever forget the look on Jack's face as he walked through to the garden. He was back where he belonged.

24
CHAPTER

THIS MORNING

THE FIRST CHRISTMAS back in Springfield Crescent was memorable. The sad look had left Jack's face, he was sleeping well, the boys were all happy – I couldn't have asked for more. I told Aunty Marian she must 'dress up' for lunch. She arrived, chauffeured by Philip, with large Christmas-tree decorations dangling from her ears, secured there with elastic bands, asking as she came over the step: 'Is this dressed-up enough?' Not bad for a lady of not far off ninety.

We had bought Jack one of the new fingertip-touch lighters, and I clicked it near my ear to demonstrate. The next moment my hair was in flames as my hair lacquer ignited. It was John who sprang into action and beat out the flames amid much laughter at my expense.

As we moved into spring, I had a quite shattering revelation. I was feeding the birds that thronged the garden. The sight of me arriving with nuts would send them into paroxysms of chatter. You could almost hear, 'She's coming!' shouted from tree to tree. I was spooning nuts into containers, wondering anxiously if I had enough, when I suddenly realised that, if I hadn't, I could go out and buy more. The days of ekeing out the dog food and turning over coppers in my purse in case I was short at the check-out were well and truly over. In a little more than three years, my life had turned around.

It was a good job we could afford to feed an extra mouth, for a very vocal one was on the way. I arrived home from work one day and went into the garden, the four dogs careering round me, as dogs do when you come home. Suddenly they froze, teeth bared, hackles rising. There was an alien presence in their garden – a small, ginger, cross-corgi pup, a few months old and teetering on back legs that seemed half paralysed. I brought it into the house and gave it some water, but it looked distinctly unwell. Jack was adamant that the police dog-pound was where it should go, and quick.

The last thing I wanted was a fifth dog, and I loathed corgis, but the police pound was no place for a sick animal. Policemen had been known to ring me and beg me to house a 'nice' dog they didn't want to put in the pound while they traced its owner. So I took the pup to the vet.

There was nothing the matter with it, he said, except that it had received a comprehensive kicking around its hindquarters. As it had obviously been hurled over my high garden wall, I could believe this. I decided to keep the dog for a day or two, to recover, before handing it over, and Jack reluctantly agreed to this. Within three days I had fallen for the reprobate, who was lovely to me but bit strange men on sight – including a photographer who came to record *This Morning*, filming me at home.

In all, he bit five people who he thought were invading his territory, and I decided that the sixth would have to be the finish; but suddenly he decided the world was not a fearful place, and he needn't be aggressive any more. He became the world's most lovable dog. As he could easily scoot under the bellies of the other dogs, we named him Titch, but his new docility didn't stop Jack telling me every day that he should go to the pound. 'Have you rung them yet?' was the mantra – until we went to Aberdeen to visit Jack's cousin. John rang us there to say Titch's owner had turned up and wanted him back. Aghast, I relayed this news, expecting Jack's face to light up. Instead he glowered: 'Over my dead body he goes back to him.'

We were still trying to cope with Titch when another dog, a terrier, crossed my path. Quite literally, because he ran under the wheels of my car. He was uninjured, but half starved and dirty, and obviously a stray so we took him home, fed him and cleaned him up. Amazingly, he smiled, a real ear-to-ear grin. I had to go to London for a meeting with my agent, and while there I told her, 'I'm desperate to find a dog a home.' When I got back we were discussing what to do with him, and agreeing he had to go, when the phone rang. 'You don't know me,' a voice said, 'but I hear you have a smiling dog.' It was Tony Warren, creator of *Coronation Street* and a considerable author, who had the same agent as me. 'If you can get him to Manchester, I'll take him,' he said.

Mark went down on the train with the dog, and I heaved a sigh of relief. A few weeks later I received a copy of Tony's new novel, inscribed, 'To the adoption agent'. It was the beginning of a friendship that has lasted to this day. There could not be a truer friend. You seldom hear from him, but if you are in trouble he calls you frequently, and doesn't ring off until he's made you laugh.

I had been happy at *Open Air* working for Peter Weil, but now news came that he was off to produce the Terry Wogan show. After that,

Open Air was never the same, and I decided I was done with television. I had a new book to plan, and Penguin was to publish my first three novels in one fat paperback called *Land of Lost Content*. In addition, it wanted paperback rights to my subsequent novels. That was all the work I needed, I thought, along with the occasional piece for newspapers and magazines, or Radio Four.

The call came one summer's day. ITV were planning a new daytime magazine and it would like me as its agony aunt. The show would be broadcast live five days a week from Liverpool, and would be called *This Morning*. I thanked them politely, and said no. The next day the man from ITV rang again. His editor, Dianne Nelmes, was most anxious I should be on the show. As a BBC trainee in Newcastle, she had listened to me at night while she did her ironing. Her ambition had always been to have me work for her. Would I at least come down for an audition?

In retrospect, I think that story was one of Dianne's inspired inventions, but I swallowed it hook, line and sinker, and went. It was a lovely day, the sun sparkled off the water in the Albert Dock, and Liverpool, that city of wonderful architecture, was at its best. I was hooked. I agreed to do it for one year. I have now been there nineteen.

This Morning was Dianne Nelmes's creation, something quite revolutionary: a blend of information, entertainment and human interest. To present it, she had found a married couple, Judy Finnigan and Richard Madeley, who would become just Richard and Judy to the nation. They glowed at each other, sometimes bitched – much to the nation's delight – and presided over Dianne's carefully blended concoction. She was a stickler for perfection, once ordering belly-dancing to be cut short because it wasn't 100 per cent tasteful. Early on in the proceedings, I broke down during a sad item, and emerged from the studio thinking my P45 would be waiting. Instead, I met Dianne advancing round the dock, tissues at the ready, waiting to comfort me. 'I'm really sorry,' I said. 'Don't worry about it, darling,' she replied. And then, mindful of standards – 'just don't make a habit of it.'

I did try not to, but my emotions showed easily in those days. One day I got a call from a grandmother who was not being allowed to see her grandchild. I had just had a new grandchild, Peter's son, and I found tears of sympathy filling my eyes. The next day I was on page three of the *Sun* – without taking off a shred of clothing. 'Denise cries in front of millions', it said.

At that stage, no one could have guessed that Richard and Judy would turn out to be the phenomenon they later became. *This Morning* was an amazing vehicle, giving hitherto unknown opportunities to ad lib and improvise but I think their real attraction was that, probably for the first time, people were seeing, on screen, a married couple be just that – married. There was no artifice or pretence about their relationship. If she was put out with him, she said so. If he disagreed with her, he did just that. There was no papering over the cracks with glib smiles. They demonstrated on screen how ordinary men and women co-exist, but in many ways theirs is not an ordinary marriage. They have an enormous affinity one for the other which I once likened to the bond between twins. It means they think and feel along the same lines. Watch how seldom they speak over one another. And they have a rock-solid marriage. The one thing producers didn't have to put up with was presenter rivalry. When he was good, she beamed. He never ceased telling the world what a clever wife he had. At parties, if they were separated I would start counting. By the time I got to eight each head would swivel, looking for the other. That unity showed on screen and made them, in fact, the forerunners of reality television.

There were several other experts on the show – Nicola Charles on law, Anne Ashworth on personal finances, Susan Brookes on cookery, Charles Metcalf on wine, Leslie Ebbets on fashion, and Dr Chris Steele on family medicine. Only Chris remains with the show today, and there have been dozens of others in the interim, but each of the experts has played their part in building the programme's reputation.

In March 1989, Penguin held a launch party for the trilogy in Lumley Castle. Prudence Fay was there to give me moral support, and it thrilled me that the launch was taking place in the north-east.

That month I judged the first Sid Chaplin Award for new writers. Sid Chaplin was a fellow north-easterner, and one of my favourite novelists. When inspiration failed me I would turn to his *Day of the Sardine*, and the easy flow of words and the vividness of his characters would spark off my own creativity. I was dumbfounded to be asked to be the first judge, but deeply honoured. I chose a short story, 'Me Bogey', by Mark James. He had been illiterate, and had worked as a navvy until a further-education course taught him to read and write. His work was rough and ready, but leaped from page. A worthy winner.

The judging over, I went to Jersey with Jack, our first holiday in fourteen years apart from a week in Cornwall, to research my next novel, *The Stars Burn On*. It began and ended on Tunstall Hill, a haunt of my childhood. Choosing that setting would have repercussions later on.

25
CHAPTER

THE STARS BURN ON

THE EARLY DAYS of *This Morning* were a joy, as the public adopted the programme as its own, and I came to love Liverpool almost as dearly as I love Sunderland. Liverpudlians will never give you directions, they will stop what they are doing and take you there, even if it means being late for work or having to go miles out of their way. Their sense of humour is tremendous, and no one can party like they do.

I made many friends there, chief among them Geraldine Woods, who began as our phone-room co-ordinator, and wound up as Programme Manager before moving on and upwards. Attractive, elegant and quick-witted, she was a good friend. When I got fed up and threatened to leave – a not uncommon occurrence – she would take me to the Pump Room, the local pub, and ply me with hard drink until I changed my mind. Happily, she is still my friend today.

Dianne Nelmes's imaginative approach to television had given us a striking studio set. Everything took place in front of a huge plate-glass window that gave a wonderful view of the Liver Building and the famous Liver birds. The public moved back and forth on the walkway, and beyond them was the gleaming water of the Albert Dock, with Fred the weatherman's famous map bobbing in the waves. The map was a huge attraction, especially when Fred made his daily leap from England to Ireland to report on the weather there. It was also an attraction for mischief-makers. Frogmen tried to sneak up on Fred and pull him into the water; and once there was a streaker. With great presence of mind, Fred covered the streaker's dangly bits with his clipboard, but his indignation at this violation of his precious map was so apparent that all eyes were on his outraged face, anyway.

One year, everyone on the programme changed places, for charity. Judy became Richard and vice versa, and I became Fred for the day. There was one small problem: I'm afraid of water. Access to the map was across a plank slung from the side of the dock to the map itself. When you were on it creaked and swayed, and threatened to slip at one of its unsecured ends. I was terrified! Only the thought that it was for charity got me across, encouraged and supported all the way by our floor manager, Andy Marsh. Once on, I seriously contemplated staying there for ever, between the Welsh mountains and Stonehenge, rather than make the trip back. As for the leap to Ireland, I looked at the dark, greasy water and declared firmly to camera: 'There is no weather in Ireland today.'

A few weeks later, on the final programme of the season, there was to be a mass wave from the map, with every presenter present. 'You can do it,' Andy urged. 'You've done it before.' But I couldn't do it. This time there was no charity to motivate me to conquer my fear. I've found that I can usually do things, for a compelling reason, that would be utterly impossible without one.

In summer we took full advantage of the dock setting. Platforms would be moored in the water for special occasions; and it was on one of these that Gene Pitney appeared, singing his heart out while no sound issued from the tape. This clip has been requested again and again when we do a retrospective. There was always a crowd around the dock to cheer us on, but even in winter fans would cluster round the studio door, sometimes for hours on end, simply to say hello to Richard and Judy, or the other presenters.

But *This Morning* was not just about entertainment. I did a series of programmes about two teenagers, Darren and Joanna, who had come out of care under a scheme called Barnardo's Leaving Care, and were both attempting to make lives for themselves. I liked them both, and grieved for the hard time each had had through childhood and adolescence. Darren had been particularly traumatised by separation from his brother after they were both taken into care. Again and again it cropped up as we talked. He ended up in a Young Offender Institution, and it was there that a kindly officer grasped his need, and arranged for the brothers to make contact once more.

This casual separation of siblings is something that continues to appall me today. Social workers will say that children have different personalities, and need different homes. I say that you need your roots, or as much of them as possible. My battle with the Family Courts would come much later, but the seeds of my rebellion were sown in a two-room flat in Leeds while a boy called Darren strummed his guitar and poured out his heart.

Another regular engagement was Relate's 'Family of the Year', a competition to choose a family that represented the best in Britain. The family could be of any size and shape: what mattered was that they cherished one another. Princess Diana was guest of honour, and before each occasion a representative from the Palace would come to tell us that we mustn't spit, swear, or move a muscle out of place. Then Princess Diana would breeze in, and throw formality out of the window. The first time I was presented to her was a shock. She was much taller than I expected, and her features up close were too strong to be conventionally beautiful. But she oozed charisma, and even in the early shy days she was anxious to meet people and get to know them.

That first time, I was in awe of her. She was the first royal I had met, and the attitude of the flunkies had frightened the life out of me. She was on the platform ready to make her speech, and the head of Relate was at the rostrum. One of the children, a boy of about four, suddenly climbed on the platform and began to take off his clothes, piece by piece. I started to hyperventilate, and a soft titter came from the audience as he got down to vest and pants. I was desperately trying to lure him off the platform when I realised that the royal guest was shaking with laughter. She didn't mind at all.

Much has been said of her love of the camera. But I saw her with no cameras around, and her behaviour was no different then. If there was a child around, that child was the focus of her attention. Even when she was deep in conversation, her hand would go out and fondle a child's head. She did it almost unconsciously. I was aware, too, that much of what I read about her in newspapers was rubbish. On one occasion the morning paper said she was starving herself to death. I saw her clear her plate at lunchtime.

One year, one of the families was fostering a large number of children. Social Services were willing for them all to participate, but two in particular were to be kept away from cameras. They had been abused, even forced to drink from the lavatory if they were thirsty. Their parents must not know their whereabouts. I gave a solemn promise that this would be so.

When the Princess made the announcement, it was the fostering family that won. She moved back, and the photographers rushed forward. She came to stand beside me, and we were watching what was going on when I realised that the two abused children were wandering into camera range. I let out a groan, but my feet felt nailed to the floor. The Princess asked what was wrong. 'It's them,' I said incoherently. 'Those two – they mustn't be photographed.' For a moment she looked at me, then she pulled at her quite tight skirt till it cleared her knees and in two or three strides had reached the children and shepherded them out of camera range. It was split-second thinking on her part, and total uselessness on mine; and I couldn't help wondering if any other royal would have reacted in that way.

She didn't like making speeches, but she did it bravely. When she finished, and turned her back on the audience to resume her seat, she would pull a rueful face at me as if to say 'Thank God that's over.' Manipulative she may have become, towards the end of her life, but that she had a loving heart I have no doubt. Unhappiness changes all of us, and if she changed it was not entirely of her own volition. I have fond memories of those 'Family of the Year' occasions, not least because the then fund-raiser for Relate, Peter McCabe, is the best in the business, a man dedicated to charity, and now with the smoking charity Quit.

I have less happy memories of another royal encounter. Cameron Mackintosh had given the first performance of *Les Miserables* in Manchester to Body Positive. Princess Margaret was the special guest, and she was a stickler for protocol. When a young woman, unaware that the Princess had entered the room, carried on talking, the Princess froze in her tracks. No one dared move to hush the talker, and the tension rose. Behind me, a young man was whispering, 'Oh, my God,' over and over, his voice rising with each incantation, until at last the girl realised something was wrong and turned to receive a glacial royal stare.

But the Princess knew *Les Mis* well. Sitting two seats away from her, I saw her weep quietly almost throughout, but she knew exactly when intervals would come and the lights go up. Before then, her eyes were dried, the hanky tucked away, and the royal presence restored.

I was now also taking part in other television programmes. There is a lightness about popping on to a sofa somewhere as a guest which you do not feel when you are dealing with viewers' problems. I did ITV's breakfast programme *Sky*; also *Through the Keyhole*, quiz shows, and once a duel with a new and relatively unknown comic creation, Mrs Merton. She was sharp-nosed, curious, spiteful, and weird, and it was hard to believe that underneath she was the very nice Caroline Aherne. You had to keep your wits about you as the rapier thrusts came, but we were filming in a crazy café that was actually a piece of modern art, complete with fly-blown cakes and rancid milk. Whenever she asked me one of her searching questions, I would press her to a rotten cake or offer her sugar from an encrusted basin, moves that disconcerted her. I think the result of the encounter was a score draw.

The occasions on which I verbally duelled with Lily Savage were a pure joy. Paul O'Grady is that rare exception, someone who is confident enough to walk in anywhere and deal with anything. From him there is no request to 'keep off that' or to 'bring in this'. Whatever you throw at him, he will cope with it. His Lily Savage is one of the great comic inventions of the twentieth century – a world away from the quiet man with the Liverpool accent who never has his nose out of a book. His account of my hen-night would become so notorious that some journalists believed it was true.

Work was going well, and our lives were happier than they had been for a long time. We could afford to go to the theatre once more, and I wallowed in *Les Mis* and *Phantom*, *Aspects of Love*, *Cats* – it was reminiscent of the years when Alex had taken me to see the Hollywood musicals, and I loved it.

I was now working on a new book, the story of six young graduates who celebrate New Year on Tunstall Hill, and then go off to make their fortunes. Part of it was set in Jersey, and we had enjoyed a week there to research that section, but when the book was almost finished I told Jack that there was a less entrancing piece of research to do. The book begins as dawn rises on New Year's Day. I needed to see what a winter's dawn there was really like. He drew the line at climbing the hill on New Year's Day itself, but we went on 6 January, taking the dogs, a flask of coffee, dog biscuits, and pen and paper. The one thing I forgot was something to sit on, so we sought for rocky outcrops to save us from the frosted grass, and sat down in inky darkness.

Daybreak, when it came, was a revelation. There was no golden orb rising in the east, just a gradual lightening of the dark sky as roof tops and spires of Sunderland swam gradually into view. It was beautiful – a great experience to sit there as the dogs snuffled excitedly in the bracken, and the city I had always loved came clear.

I called the novel *The Stars Burn On*, a line that comes from a poem by W. H. Auden:

The stars burn on overhead, unconscious of final ends,
As I walk home to bed, asking what judgement waits my person,
All my friends and these United States.

It fitted the storyline, as the central character did follow the fortunes of her friends and did go to work in America, but the title came in for a storm of criticism. 'Mushy', 'sickly', 'typical romantic-novel title', were some of the kinder remarks. I couldn't help wondering why it was all right for W. H. Auden to use it, and all wrong for me. I think there is an inbuilt notion that women writers, especially if they come from the north, will be writing in clogs and shawls. If you are, in addition, an agony aunt, you are truly lumbered. They liked the book, but they detested the title.

Throughout my writing career, the BBC had been a huge support. *Pebble Mill* was the popular magazine-programme of the day, with Alan Titchmarsh as the main presenter. They had always plugged my novels, asking me back twice for *The Second Wife*, a rare occurrence for a novelist. Now, though, as *This Morning* regularly wiped the BBC's morning programme off the ratings, I became *persona non grata* there. They were not about to give free publicity to a presenter of their rival. *This Morning* wouldn't mention my books either, for reasons of compliance, so I lost a valuable source of publicity. Fortunately the books sold, anyway.

Philip and John both married in 1990. John had left the Navy after nine years, and it had been good to have him back at home for a while, but I knew they were both going off to be happy and found their own families, and I was glad for them. As they left, Mark decided to come back from London. I was not going to have an empty nest again, after all.

26
CHAPTER

THE VIEWERS

Aunt Marian had always been an avid follower of sport on television. Bob Wilson, Arsenal's goalkeeper and now a sports presenter, was her favourite TV personality, and when I went to BBC *Breakfast Time*, where he was Sports Reporter, I got her a signed photograph that she carried around like a teenager. But her passion was snooker. She watched snooker matches on her small black-and-white set and could tell the colour of every ball potted. Now that I was flush, I decided to give her a treat. Jack and I bought a colour television, and arrived with it on her doorstep. It was installed, and she oohed and aahed over the spectacle.

The following morning she rang me at eight a.m. 'Get it out,' she said. And when I said, 'Tomorrow?' I was met with a firm 'Now.' The excuse was that the size of the screen and the brilliance of the colour hurt her eyes. Privately, we decided that she had realised overnight that the cost of a colour TV licence far exceeded the charge for black-and-white. Generous to a fault with other people, she was parsimonious with herself. Monochrome had sufficed for twenty years; it would do for another ten.

A few months later she complained of feeling poorly. She loved her food, and was an excellent cook. For years she had kept us supplied with pies and cakes; now I told her to put her feet up, and we would supply her lunches. We established a routine. I would ring her when the meal was ready; she would put a saucepan on the stove to boil, with a plate on top. By the time I'd made the twenty-minute journey, she would have a nice hot plate for the food.

But over the next few days, I could see her failing. She had achieved her 90th birthday, a great milestone, and now she suddenly seemed timorous, and unlike herself. One day I rang her as usual, and Jack and I set out with her meal. We found her in the kitchen, the pan bubbling away on the stove, a half-smile on her face as she lay slumped against a kitchen unit. She had achieved her aim of staying in her home to the end. The familiar robin came in through the French window, and I gave him the cheese she had already laid out. Then I dialled 999. Paramedics tried to revive her, but I knew she was gone, in the way she would have chosen; and I was glad.

Her will, according to the solicitor, was the longest he had ever had to probate. Every treasured possession was allotted to someone. The rest of the house contents she left to me, 'because you are the only person I know who is as untidy as I am'. When I came to empty her house, I was fascinated by the contents of her dressing-table. There was rouge, lipstick, powder – cosmetics I had never seen her use. Then I realised they were all old makes, brands that had been out of production for years. When I checked, I found that they belonged to the period when her husband had gone blind. His was the only eye she had wanted to please. Once he could no longer see her, cosmetics ceased to matter. I had loved her like a mother, and I think I became the daughter she never had. I hope so.

That spring I was invited to take part in the Telethon. Claire Rayner, Philip Hodson, Katie Boyle and I, agony aunts or uncles all, were to sing 'Anything you can do, I can do better' from *Annie Get your Gun*. I took an instant liking to Katie Boyle. She and I clung together as the powerful personalities of Rayner and Hodson took over. It has led to a lasting friendship. Katie is beautiful, wilful, mildly eccentric, and mad about dogs. What more could you ask? Occasionally we lunch together in London. Katie is an advanced driver, and revels in negotiating London's traffic. I couldn't understand how she always found a parking space, but she explained: 'Greville finds it for me.' As her former husband Greville Baylis had been dead for years, my eyebrows shot skywards. 'I simply ask him,' she said, 'and a place opens up.' Crazy, certainly, but after you have seen it happen once or twice you begin to wonder.

That summer of 1990, the programme decided I should go to Ladies' Day at Ascot. What's more, they would commission a hat for the event, and viewers would see the hat being designed and made. I was to supply my own outfit, so I turned to Ken Smith, a designer with a boutique in London's Charlotte Place. He recommended chiffon over crêpe, a wonderful concoction of rose-printed chiffon over a plain pink crêpe dress, at a cost of £1000. The young designer who made the hat gave it a brim with an eagle's wingspan, and swathed it in the rose-print chiffon. I looked like a pink meringue, utterly Ascot, and reeking of money.

Until it began to rain. It was the wettest Ladies' Day on record – or, if it wasn't, it should have been. Rain hit the pavement and ricocheted upwards, soaking chiffon and crêpe until they sagged around my ankles. Willie Carson kept up magnificently as I interviewed him under a steady stream of water cascading from my wide-brimmed hat. The expedition in every sense of the word was a wash-out.

I had a charity engagement back north that evening, and had a seat booked on a flight out of Heathrow. I arrived at the airport with seconds to spare, conscious of an odd sensation around my waist and knees. As I sank into my seat, I realised what was happening. The sodden crêpe was shrinking as it dried, rising above my knees constricting my waist. I got off at Newcastle airport, vainly trying to cover my confusion with rose-printed chiffon, the brim of my designer hat in waves around my face. So much for glamour!

But every piece of fun wasn't a failure. In my time at *This Morning* I have dressed up as the Spice Girl Geri Halliwell. She was in the studio the second time I did it and I'm not sure she was amused. I've played Bet Lynch in the Rover's Return; donned Edwardian costume to visit the set of *The Forsyte Saga* where I received, behind his bowler, a kiss from the unbelievably dishy Damien Lewis; been Maria Callas in a spoof of *Stars in their Eyes*; and taken part in a dozen mini-dramas.

Playing a High Court judge led to complications. I presided over a court in which Jerry Springer and Ruth Langsford played opposing counsel. I, complete with wig and gown, was authoritarian and severe, rapping my gavel and looking at everyone with gimlet eyes. This caused gentlemen of a certain age, most with public-school accents, to sidle up to me in pubs and ask when there would be a repeat performance. If all else fails, a future as a dominatrix awaits me.

But life at *This Morning* is not always fun. Often it is grim reality. I am often asked how much notice I have of questions in the phone-in. The answer is about four minutes, as I walk from the phone-room to the studio. When people ring in, they speak to a telephonist specially chosen for his or her manner and knowledge. All callers are offered helpline numbers; some are selected to go on air. No one is dismissed without help. This means that we often deal with problems that play no part in the programme whatsoever. If people's need is great, they are transferred to trained counsellors who talk through their problems, sometimes over a period of weeks or months.

We have helped victims of sexual abuse achieve justice; needy people escape eviction; and victims of crime achieve redress. In all this we are aided by voluntary bodies such as Careline, Relate, Marriage Care, Shelter and many others. And, of course, the Salvation Army. Once a woman, the victim of domestic abuse, rang in. She had been locked in by her partner when he went to work. She was pregnant and hungry. While we worked out what to do next, I said, 'Phone the Sally Army. They'll go round with a loaf and a pint of milk, and push it through the letter box.' And they did. When it comes to practical help, they can't be beaten.

It sounds extraordinary that women can be locked in, in today's Britain, but it happens. When the programme was still coming out of Liverpool, a woman rang in one day to say that she was an abused wife – and now she feared that her child was being sexually abused. Richard, Judy and I spoke as one: 'Get out now!' The answer was swift: 'I can't. He locks me in.' For a moment we were all bereft of speech, then we sprang into action. 'Stay on the line,' I said. 'Help is on its way.' By the time I got back to the phone-room, the telephone lines were red-hot. One woman even offered to set out in her car from the other side of the country and remove the caller to a place of safety.

In the end, the police intervened, and the last I heard she and her daughter were safe and well. But that call set the nation buzzing. I seldom mention my work at home, and that day was no exception.

Jack went out for a drink, and when he came back he said, 'What's this about a woman locked in the house?' He had been stopped everywhere he went by people, mainly men, anxious to know the outcome. It was the same when I went out the following day. Three weeks later I attended my publisher's sales conference. Before we started, one of the sales reps leant forward: 'Did that woman get out of the house?' he asked. 'We all want to know.' The Chairman was less impressed. 'So that's why we don't sell more books,' he said. 'You're all watching television.'

Another caller was Liz (not her real name). Her husband had moved his girlfriend into the marital bed. She was being forced to share her teenage son's bedroom, and she was afraid the boy was going to resort to violence against his father, the girlfriend, or both. Again the phone lines throbbed. Barristers rang in to offer their services free; other callers offered accommodation. Best of all, her long-lost sister rang. 'I recognised my sister's voice,' she said. 'We've lost touch, but tell her I'm coming to get her.' Later that day, I heard that the girlfriend had had to make a swift exit as the neighbours reacted to the call.

I wasn't often lost for words, but one call did for me. A child had been shot in what was apparently a gangland killing. His mother rang in to beg people to make sure it did not happen to another parent. Her call came after I had left the phone-room, so when she was put through I was unprepared. I recognised her story at once. Her child's picture was all over the papers, and I fought hard not to panic, knowing I had to find some words of comfort, and knowing too that no words of mine could be enough.

Not all calls are serious, however. A subject that always went down well was Christmas problems. One year, the phone-in co-ordinator passed me a call sheet. 'There's a woman here saying she doesn't want her husband to go to his office Christmas party.' 'Put it in,' I said. 'I'll make her see that's not fair.' When she came on the line, I was ready. 'Why don't you want him to go?' I asked smugly. Her answer was swift. 'Because he doesn't come back home for three days.' Exit agony aunt, red-faced.

And sometimes I am asked to attempt the impossible. On one occasion I was telephoned late in the day by the then editor. 'Get in here,' he said. 'We're doing penis extension tomorrow, and I need you to put a respectable face on it!' As one of the contributors was a talkative lady famous for having had more lovers than anyone else in the world, this was the television equivalent of climbing the north face of the Eiger. I just closed my eyes and kept climbing.

I am proud of the fact that I have read and answered the many thousands of letters sent to me. There are so many now that I need assistance, and for the past few years I've been more than ably helped by Helen Logan, who has a Master's degree in counselling and psychotherapy, and cares as much as I do for the audience. It has been a really happy working partnership, and I hope it will continue for a long time. The letters cover everything from rape to how to deal with baby's first tooth. I hope we have helped people. Many of them let us know that we have.

I am immensely grateful to Granada for the way it has funded what amounts to a public service. No one is ever turned away by the programme. Help is there for everyone, and that is rare in today's cost-conscious media. The result of this policy, however, has been an audience bonded to *This Morning* in a way hitherto unknown.

27
CHAPTER

THE BUBBLE

IN 1991, A colleague at *This Morning*, a director called Richard Bradley, told me about a charity called Bugbusters. His brother Nick, a civil engineer, was working in Newcastle General Hospital, and was appalled that the nurses were having to fund-raise for a special project by rattling tins in pubs when they came off shift. 'You live up there,' Richard said to me. 'You could do something.' I was already involved with several charities, so a long-term involvement was not an option. On the other hand, nurses rattling tins in pubs was not an option, either. I decided to go along and take a look at what was going on.

The unit in question was for children from all over the British Isles who suffer from severe combined immune deficiency. Put simply, that means that they are born with no immune system and therefore cannot fight off infection. They will die in the first year of their lives unless they are put into a sterile space where no infection can reach them. Eventually they receive a bone-marrow transplant. If it works, they have immunity and live healthy lives. If it fails, they die. The only other unit in Britain is in Great Ormond Street

Hospital. The fund-raising was to pay for specialised equipment and extra comforts for the children, and to pay for fathers to visit. The mother is in the sterile space with them, sometimes for a year or more.

I was shown into a side-ward where a beautiful baby boy was sitting up in a cot. A woman, presumably his mother, was crouching on a chair at the cot's side. The baby smiled at me, I smiled back, and advanced on the cot. As I drew near, the mother let out a shriek and pointed to a red line on the floor. Later I would learn that inside the line the air was sterile, kept pure by a system called lamina down-flow, a curtain of cold air that separated the baby's air-space from mine. That was why his mother was crouched so uncomfortably. She needed to be inside the line.

On that cot her baby would eat, sleep, stand up, or walk, be bathed and tended. But until the bone-marrow transplant restored his immune system, he could not step out of the cot. To do so would mean death. If his mother had allowed me to press forward, bringing with me my germs, it could have had fatal consequences.

I decided to organise some fund-raising. The hospital had only two lamina down-flow systems. If three babies were in need, the doctors had to make a terrible decision. The paediatrician in charge, Dr (now Professor) Andrew Cant, was a man sensitive to the needs of patients and their families. To impose such decision-making on him seemed barbaric. We needed money, and we needed it fast – but first we needed a change of name. Bugbusters made me think of head lice. Bubble, based on the concept of the baby living in a bubble of sterile air, seemed much more suitable.

So the Bubble Foundation was born. But as I began my efforts, the baby, Kenny, died. His mother went back to Scotland, and I was gutted. Two years later, she would come back with another baby, again a SCID baby. I held my breath in fear, but she seemed confident that she would take this baby home. One night I confessed my fears to Professor Cant. He shook his head. 'Sometimes you have to trust a mother's instinct. Again and again I've seen it proved right.' And so it was. She went back to Scotland with a healthy baby boy who had been cured in the bubble. Sadly, the happy ending had a sting in the tail. Two years later, the nurses rang to tell me the mother had died. But at least her baby lived and thrived.

We fund-raised like mad in 1991, and then a Government grant enabled a new bubble unit to be built. Eventually there would be six bubbles and no baby would be turned away, although they sometimes have to wait a while in an ordinary children's ward. The memory of Adam, whose mother, a nurse, patiently waited for a bubble to be available only for it to become vacant too late, haunts me still.

I am constantly amazed at the courage and resilience of the parents. The mother may be penned up in the bubble, a confined space even in the new unit. Her husband could well be 200 miles away – or across the sea, if they have come from Ireland, as many families do. But the bond remains, and even strengthens, as they watch their babies struggle for life. One child, a beautiful little girl, was in the bubble for two and a half years. Her mother was an extremely intelligent woman, who might well have gone mad with nothing to do except watch the cot and, as the baby grew, try to contain its energy. But she stayed focused until the day she was told she could kiss her baby for the first time.

Kisses, even face-touching, are forbidden because the mouth is the only place that cannot be made sterile. Everything else about the mother has been made safe, except that, so she must turn away when her baby reaches for her. Mothers tell me this is the hardest bit of all, but that first kiss is a special moment even for nurses who have seen the same scenario a dozen times.

The Newcastle Unit has made amazing progress in the past few years. Its success rate in treating babies, older children, and teenagers with immune deficiency is now 90 per cent, but its real triumph lies in the innovative steps it has taken to treat patients once thought to be beyond medical intervention. One boy was admitted to the unit when he was sixteen. His quality of life was nil, and he was resigned to an early death. Although a transplant cannot undo all previous damage, it can stop further deterioration and restore some quality of life. Today that boy is back home planning a future he never thought he would see.

The unit has pioneered the use of cord blood to provide complete immunity to immune-deficient children, and has also pioneered transplants in cases of juvenile ideopathic arthritis. The results of this particular procedure are little short of miraculous. In the past, transplants in very young children frequently failed because of lung infection and inflammation. The unit has devised new forms of treatment for both conditions, which has contributed in no small measure to the raised success rates.

Lupus is a distressing condition, resistant to treatment in its severest form. The unit has also performed the world's first transplant for a child with lupus with amazing results, and is concentrating its research and development on conditions hitherto thought untreatable. It also intends to find out why immune deficiency exists at all in some children.

Professor Cant now holds clinics in Manchester, Dublin, and Edinburgh, and is a leading figure in children's immunology in

Europe. The Bubble Foundation numbers Denise Welch, Paul O'Grady, Brian McFadyen, Dr Tom Stuttaford of *The Times* and Granada's Dianne Nelmes among its patrons. I am proud to be its President, and to my great delight Eamonn Holmes has also just agreed to become a patron.

The years have not been without their tears. To learn of a baby's death still hurts. But there has been laughter, too, and astonishment at the generosity of ordinary people. Sometimes, however, there is a price to pay. One day two of the nurses and I went to a police training college in Preston to accept a cheque, money they had raised during their course. They handed over the cheque, I thanked them, and we adjourned for drinks. I was on my way home from doing *This Morning* in Liverpool, and had a car and driver waiting, but there was time for one drink. I sat with the nurses and downed a white wine, but just as I was about to leave a young policeman appeared with another glass. It seemed churlish to refuse, so I thanked him and drank it. As I drained it another PC appeared, glass in hand. I drank that, and the one that followed and the next one.

The fact that I was being set up dawned on me through an alcoholic haze. I tossed the next glass back in one gulp, and rose to my feet too quickly for the next libation to appear. Smiling graciously all round, I weaved my way to the door and out into the arms of the astonished driver. The journey home was a nightmare because, so my sons informed me as they plied me with coffee, of 'the swirling pits'. But I had the generous cheque, so it was worth it.

All money donated warms the heart, coming as it often does from people who have little but give their all. Stories of generosity abound, but some stick in the memory. A teacher at a facility for young offenders lost a baby in the bubble. The inmates were touched, and offered to surrender their pocket money if the warders would submit to Mohican haircuts. A deal was struck, and a sum – small in real terms but huge in meaning – was raised. Then, 'They want a footballer to accept it,' I was told. I turned to Peter Reid, then manager of my beloved Sunderland Football Club. 'It's not a big cheque,' I said, 'but those kids deserve encouragement.' I expected a second-team player. In the end, Peter Reid came himself, stayed for hours, chatted to every boy, and did a job worthy of Sunderland AFC, whose own foundation does unbelievably beneficial work for children in the surrounding area.

My devotion to Sunderland Football Club is unbounded. I have a season ticket and go as often as I can, but I value it for what it means to the city. There were times when the town, and later the city, was in decline, when the football club was about all that I could boast of. Now, as the city regenerates and flourishes, the club has its difficulties, but the old glory days will return. Such is the nature of football.

The Bubble has become the most important of my charities. As I write, there are nine babies being cared for in hospitals, waiting for a vacant bubble, so the need is great. But all the charities with which I'm associated are dear to my heart. I accepted the presidency of a hospice, St Benedict's, in Sunderland, because I remembered those terrible days when Alex needed palliative care and none was forthcoming. The hospice movement has brought comfort to thousands of patients and their families and I am proud to play a small part.

In *The Stars Burn On*, I had one of the characters touch the turf of Tunstall Hill and say she would die for it if she had to. One day I received a phone call saying the hill was under threat from developers, and a protection society was being formed. Would I head it? I politely turned them down, my hands being full. The caller, Sheila Liddle, was not to be deterred. 'I read your books,' she said, 'and in *The Stars Burn On* you said you would die for that hill if you had to.' Whatever 'hoist with your own petard' means, I was. So I joined up, the hill was saved, and remains today the haunt of children, just as it was for me years ago.

My joy in dogs, and horror at how cruelly they are treated, led me to co-found an animal rescue charity, Pawz for Thought. It cares for animals of all kinds, and has some of the most dedicated volunteers, led by Lynne Ebdale, whom I have ever encountered.

Today I am President of the National Council for the Divorced and Separated (NCDS), and the National Association of Writers Groups. The latter sprang out of my suggestion that writers across the country should band together to form a voice for new writing opportunities; but NCDS is a somewhat unlikely vehicle for someone who believes, as I do, that a happy marriage is the nearest thing we get to heaven on earth. It's because I value marriage so highly that I also believe in divorce. I cannot believe it right that two people should be tied together in disharmony. Better by far to separate and try again.

In all, I'm patron of some thirty charities across a wide spectrum, some of them medical, all of them important because they make life better for others. But I am merely a figurehead. It is the people who labour day and night to make them work who really matter.

28
CHAPTER

A RETURN TO SADNESS

IN SPRING OF 1992, I went to the House of Commons to interview Titch, Mitch and Critch, the naughty triplets of politics. Titch was the Liberal MP Charles Kennedy, Mitch was Labour's Austin Mitchell, and Critch was the Conservative, Julian Critchley. Kennedy and Mitchell I interviewed at the House, but I had to see Julian Critchley at his home as he'd hurt his foot. He was unfailingly polite and helpful, a bit on the scatty side but definitely likeable. Kennedy was cold and appeared uninterested. An announcement about the election was imminent, and he was like a cat on hot bricks. Austin Mitchell was by far the most interesting.

There was, though, something faintly sad about him. As the election announcement came through, I asked him what advice he would give to a would-be MP. His answer was forthright: 'Don't do it.' I went on my way, wondering what had disillusioned such a bright and committed man. The director cut the piece nicely, and on the day it was screened Jon Snow happened to be in the studio. He went out of his way to come and tell me he had enjoyed it, something he had no need to do. As I respected his work I was highly honoured. It made up for Kennedy's aloofness.

I was now about to embark on what is my favourite among my novels, *The Beloved People*. I had tried to alternate between writing about the past and taking a look at the contemporary world around me. This time I could indulge my love of research and go back in time. I had come across the text of the last speech made by the ailing King George V, in which he referred to 'my beloved people'. Who were those people?

I took five families, rich and poor, and began to chart their progress from 1922 onwards. One of the families was Jewish, for I had always been impressed by the part the Jews had played in the life of the north-east. In that first home Alex and I had shared we had lived next door to orthodox Jews. The wife wore a wig in public, for her hair must not be seen by any man other than her husband; and when their baby was born he built a hut of branches in the garden and blew a ram's horn. Occasionally they had a party, and the sound of dancing on bare boards could be heard though the wall. I loved it.

So I sat in the library and studied Jewish folklore, customs – even Yiddish, but it was important that the characters shouldn't be caricatures shouting 'Oy veh!' all the time. A year or two earlier, speaking at a charitable event, I had met a man called Walter Sharman. He had taken me on a tour of his synagogue and explained attendance there, which involves the separation of men and women. He agreed to read all the passages involving Jews and give his fee to charity. And so I began to write.

The central character is a beautiful but wilful society lady named Diana, married to a husband who does not understand her. I had not intended it, but when the book came out journalist after journalist asked me if I had modelled her on the Princess of Wales. The book went on to become a trilogy with volumes covering the families during World War II and the post-war period.

At one stage I needed to know what women did about birth control in the 1920s, so I asked the ever-helpful library to obtain the original Marie Stopes book for me. Eventually, a postcard arrived from the library to say that *Married Love* was awaiting me. But the book didn't spell out what I wanted to know. So the library ordered her *Wise Parenthood*. Jack and I were in the garden when the postman delivered the postcard saying it was ready for collection. He looked at us and back at the card, shook his head, and moved on, obviously marking us down as either super-naive or decidedly kinky. After all that, the book didn't help me – again, it was too coy.

I felt a real sense of achievement when the trilogy was finished, and the reviews were good. The *Sunday Telegraph* called it 'an intelligent, evocative saga, with a fine eye for authenticity', and the *Independent* said the final volume was 'triumphant'. But I did get a shock when a woman got in touch with me to say she and her mother wanted to spend their holiday in Belgate, the imaginary village in the trilogy, but she couldn't find it on the map!

Television was going well, too. I had done a series called *Close to the Edge* that looked at problems such as drug-taking or race. The most moving featured coming to terms with tragedy, for which I talked with the parents of the two children killed in the Warrington bomb outrage, Jonathan Ball and Tim Parry. The parents' testimony was very moving, and the programme was repeated the following Boxing Day.

But the most eventful episode involved two women prisoners

allowed out on licence from prison. They came to me with two women prison officers, with whom they were on good terms. One of the prisoners was black and muscular and scary. The other was a little mouse of a girl whom I was quite sure I could take home with me and reform in minutes. How wrong I was! During the filming, she asked me to show her to the loo, and I obliged. She never came back.

But it was the attitude of the other girl that was surprising. She was outraged at her fellow prisoner's running off. Her absconding had ruined things for others, who would now not be trusted to go out. Furthermore it would get the 'misses', the prison officers, into trouble, and that was unforgivable. And then she added a rider: 'She's gone off with my coat, and all. Good job I didn't fucking pay for it!' She was doing time for shoplifting! I spent twenty-four hours dreading the headline 'Agony aunt aids jailbreak', until the absconder was recaptured in a park.

This Morning was doing well, regularly wiping out the opposition. I now had six beautiful grandchildren, and Caroline, Gillian's daughter by her second marriage, was a regular visitor.

I took up aerobics, then, with a wonderful teacher, Angela Newton, who geared everything to my unfit state, and gradually drew me on. She still comes to me today, and has quite transformed my life with her expertise. One way and another I could feel myself relaxing. Money worries were behind me; everyone I loved was safe and happy. Life was looking up.

My only worry was Jack's cough – he had smoked since his teens, and couldn't give it up. I had had occasional cigarettes myself when we first married, but I'd given up in an attempt to encourage him to do the same. Now I redoubled my efforts, getting him patches and chewing gum, and exhorting him day and night. Eventually he told me he had smoked his last cigarette, and I heaved a sigh of relief. We went out for a meal, and I lavished praise on him. 'What a hero!' was the mildest thing I said.

When it was time to leave, I went to talk to some friends I'd seen earlier, and when I left them I went outside and round to the window beside the table where I'd left Jack, rather than cross the restaurant again. He was still sitting at the table – enjoying a crafty fag. I rapped on the window, and the look on his face as he was caught red-handed was priceless. We drove home in stony silence. Once in the house, I went upstairs and began to pack a case. 'What are you doing?' he asked.' 'I'm leaving,' I said. 'If you don't care enough to stop jeopardising your health, there's no point in my staying.' That did it. He went back to the patches, and this time they worked.

I needed a setting for the next novel, and Jack suggested Nice. This gave me a pang. Of all those photographs that had tormented me at the start of our marriage, one stood out. It was of Jack and Joyce in Nice, caught by a street photographer as they walked, hand in hand, in the early evening. They were looking at one another with total adoration. After her death, he had taken the two older boys back to Nice. It obviously meant a lot to him.

My old doubts resurfaced, but I banished them. We had had twenty storm-tossed years together; we deserved a holiday; and Nice was as good a place as any. As it happened, I fell in love with its old-world charm, adored the flea market that replaced the flower market on a Monday, and could sit happily each evening on the terrace of the magnificent Hotel Negresco while hawkers offered 'jasmeen' from baskets down below.

We had not been back home for long when I realised that

Poppy wasn't well. She had always been 'my dog', her head on my knee when I sat. Now I fought the truth, that she had leukaemia and was suffering, because I couldn't bear to lose her. Then one day, as she was lying on the sofa beside me, I heard her whimper. The next day the vet came to the house. She lay in my arms while he administered an injection, quite trusting, in the way dogs do, that if I was there no harm would befall her. Daisy and Aster and Lupin, Poppy's daughters, were out walking, and before they returned we buried Poppy beneath the pear-tree in the garden. I have regretted ever since that I did not let her go sooner.

A few weeks later, Jack looked up from the breakfast table. 'I can't read,' he said. 'The lines are jumbled up.' We went straight to an optician, who sent us to a doctor. Three days later we saw a neurologist. Jack had had a mild stroke. Over the coming weeks his condition improved, and I began to relax again. He even appeared with me on *This Morning* to celebrate Chris Steele's wedding anniversary. All the presenters were there with their partners, but, when R&J addressed them, Jack was strangely silent. Now I know that he was slipping away from me, and I was failing to acknowledge it.

I needed to go back to Nice, to finalise details for the novel. Jack loved driving on the Continent, taking to the Grande Corniche above Nice with gusto. He was never happy without a car. I used to joke that he would drive to the loo if it were possible. But parking in Nice, I knew from the previous visit, was impossible, every road being lined with cars. Each night we had had to park a mile away from the hotel and walk back. This time I wasn't sure he was up to walking in the heat, so I had to find an hotel that had a car park.

I sat in Thomas Cook for an hour while the travel agent

scanned brochures. At last we found one, on our favourite Promenade des Anglais, facing the sea. We arrived there, tired but looking forward to picking up the hire car I had ordered to be left in the car park. The trouble was, the hotel didn't have one: the car park mentioned in the brochure was an underground public car park nearby, which was always full. We spent a miserable week trudging back and forth, and when it was time to come home I was relieved. I took it up with the travel agent and with Trading Standards, who were outraged. One thing stopped prosecution: in the small print at the front of the brochure was an insert disclaiming responsibility for any untruths or errors in the text.

A month or two later we went to stay with Gillian in Bolton for a few days. We were in a garden centre when Jack's left arm and leg failed him. He insisted on coming home with me, and the doctor confirmed that he had had another stroke. This time I decided we needed a second opinion. We made an appointment with a consultant in Cleveland, who did sophisticated tests and promised to let us know. The first line of his letter when it arrived said it all. 'Due to your previous smoking habit. . .' Jack's carotid artery was furred up, and there was nothing to be done.

But he seemed to recover well. His driving licence had been suspended, but after examination by an independent doctor it was renewed for three years. He was euphoric, and I was relieved – Jack without wheels was a lost soul, and it was lovely to see his unalloyed pleasure in the fact that he no longer had to be driven by me!

I was on my way back from *This Morning* in Liverpool when the call came, saying Jack had collapsed. Mark was caring for him, and had ordered an ambulance, but would I hurry home? The car took me straight to the hospital. Philip was waiting for me, unwilling to go in until I got there. Jack was conscious, but not speaking. His eyes flashed fear at me, and I said very firmly, 'You're going to be all right.' I like to think he relaxed then.

Over the next few days he drifted in and out of consciousness, and I went back and forth from the hospital. I had promised to do a Valentine's Day piece for Tyne Tees and didn't want to let them down, but it was difficult to talk to young lovers, knowing my love was lying in hospital unaware. One day they rang and told me to be quick. I found a nurse beside him holding his hand. She put a chair beside the bed, and I sat with him for the rest of the day. The boys came one by one, but at last everyone went home.

It was night now. Nurses came and went, easing his breathing when it was needed, until everything was quiet and we were alone. I held his hand and told him I loved him. Perhaps he heard. I thought about our marriage. It had been a long struggle – to survive, to give the boys their chance, to keep a roof over our heads, to whittle down a mountain of debt. Now the good times had come, and I would have to enjoy them alone.

We had come together out of need. There had scarcely been time to be man and wife for being partners and parents, but there had been a kind of love, too. For a long time a pulse beat in his neck, the only sign of life. I sat and watched, all the time remembering. At last it ceased, and as it did a picture flashed into my mind, of Joyce and Jack together on that evening street in Nice. I touched his cheek, and hoped they were together once more.

A nurse confirmed that he was dead. 'He must have been a very handsome man,' she said. He had died the day before Joyce's birthday. On the day of the funeral, the police mounted patrols at the roundabouts from the church to the crematorium, so as to speed us through. I don't know who arranged it, but the sight of the young constables bowing their heads as the cortège passed by was very moving. When we had enjoyed listening to the music from *Les Miserables* together, again and again, over the past two years, there was one song Jack particularly loved. It is sung by Jean Valjean as he tries to save the boy his daughter loves. More than once I had seen the gleam of a tear in Jack's eye as he heard it, and I knew it reminded him of his sons. Now I asked for it to be played at the crematorium. It was 'Bring Him Home'.

29
CHAPTER

ALONE AGAIN

I WENT BACK to work a week after the funeral. Everyone tried to persuade me to take time off, but I knew the danger of sitting with nothing to do except brood. The first day back at *This Morning* there were anxious faces around. Dianne Nelmes stood behind the cameras, and I knew she would make a professional last-minute judgement as to whether or not I could cope. Keith Chegwin and I were to do a joint item about starting again, he after personal problems and I after bereavement. Richard and Judy were calm and matter-of-fact, which was exactly what I needed. The item went through without a hitch, and I was back in harness.

The letters flowed in from the moment R&J had announced that Jack was ill. Geraldine was, as usual, a tower of strength, and Cath and Anne, her deputies, helped me answer them. At home, letters overflowed every surface until, in the end, we kept them in wash-baskets. Every letter, both at home and at the programme, was full of comfort. One pensioner sent me a £5 note, 'to have a night out and cheer up'. Another viewer sent me a rose bush. I planted it in a tub, and it went with me when I moved house. It showers blossoms still. And there was another letter – from the travel agent offering £75 compensation for the disastrous holiday in Nice. I never replied.

When I was working, I felt OK. Bill McLennan, the driver who took me back and forth to Liverpool, was kind and solicitous. But when I reached home, I had the same urge I had felt when Alex died, to rush inside and bolt the door. One day I found the step covered in roses. They came from the doctor I had met when Alex died, and whom I had known sporadically over the intervening years. The note that accompanied them said, 'Thinking of you. When you want to talk, let me know.'

But I had no wish to talk. Mark, who was still living at home, was endlessly considerate, but he was working as a musician, which meant that he had late gigs most nights. I was back to the old regime of the light on all night, the World Service on the radio, and a chest of drawers against the bedroom door. But this time I had the dogs, and they were a comfort.

Another problem was the unfinished building work. Jack had drawn up plans for an extension to our house, and two dormer windows. The extension was built and one of the windows. I decided I couldn't face having the house hacked about, and living with a gaping hole in the roof and wall. I wouldn't have it done. But David, Jack's eldest son and a building engineer, pointed out that I had no choice. 'The planners won't stand for you leaving it like that, unbalanced. They may give you time, Denise, but they'll want it done eventually.'

It was still winter, and alone I roamed the house, looking out on the frozen garden. We had a wonderful bird population now, thanks to regular feeding. A woodpecker came each day, chaffinches, tits, doves, sparrows. . . I hired a film crew and took six hours of film of the winter garden and the birds who came to feed. Edited down, it was a wonderful record of an ordinary garden, with eight minutes'-worth of the woodpecker flaunting his scarlet undercarriage. Making the film took me through March and April until the nights were lighter.

I still didn't go out, except to work or occasionally to dine with friends in their homes. One reason for this was that my driving had become erratic. Several times I had crashed into the brick gateposts entering or leaving the drive. One day John and I stood looking at the damage. 'I think I'll have those gateposts demolished,' I said. Drily he answered, 'I think you've just about done that.'

When it was time for the building work to recommence I was ready. There would be a hole in the wall and scaffolding leading to it, ideal entrance for an intruder. I had six bolts put on the landing side of that bedroom door, and kept them bolted till the hole was filled.

And then an invitation came to a reception at the civic centre in Sunderland. 'Go!' Mark urged. I knew he was getting worried about me, so I agreed. He drove me there and stopped at the entrance. I didn't get out of the car. 'Go on,' he said. 'You can do it.' I had my new mobile phone, so as to call him back when it was done. I got out of the car, waved him goodbye, and walked on. I was almost inside the door when I felt I couldn't make it. I turned on my heel, but a woman who had been standing in a group just inside, a woman I had never seen before, hurried after me and took my arm. 'Come on,' she said, 'I know who you are and I know how you feel.' Her first husband had been killed in an accident years before, she said. She drew me in, her friends absorbed me, and I was over a hurdle.

Now I could go out, but I still didn't want to, especially at weekends.

Gradually there seemed no point in getting dressed, unless I was going to work.

Work itself was going well. I had a new column in a national newspaper, the *Daily Express*, and I liked its editor, Richard Addis. I could write about anything I liked, and occasionally do a whole page on a topical event. I had always freelanced for national newspapers. There is a heady feel about writing about something that is actually happening, especially when you have to do it in an hour. I remember when Prince Edward left the Marines managing 1000 words in forty minutes, saying, in effect, that I thought he was brave to do it. But, sadly, unless what you write fits the paper's ethos, it won't get printed.

As the summer progressed, we noticed a lump on Aster's head. It didn't seem to bother her, but it bothered me, and Lupi, her twin and constant shadow, seemed strangely uneasy. Mark and I took Aster to the vet, and he diagnosed a tumour. They wanted to remove it and hoped for the best. She came through the operation well, and I hoped against hope; but the lump grew again, and the time came when she had to be put to sleep. She died in my arms, and Mark and I buried her next to her mother, under the pear-tree.

Aster had always been irrepressible because she had known no fear. Admonish her, and her tail would wag with pleasure. Chase her after some misdemeanour, and it became a game. She had been born at my feet, and had never known a harsh word. Rescue dogs, however long you love them, never forget what it is like to be abused. Ten years after I had rescued Titch, I brandished a stick at someone in a play fight, and turned to see Titch flattened to the floor in fear. Even if it was in my hand – I, who had never hurt him – he knew what a stick was for.

The house was a quieter place without Aster, and I mourned her, but Lupi spent hours searching for her. When we took them out, Daisy and Titch would leap from the car when we reached our destination and rush off to explore. Lupi would get out, and then wait for Aster to follow; and no amount of coaxing would get her away from the car she was sure must contain her sister. It went on for a few weeks, and it was heartbreaking, especially as I knew exactly how she felt. When someone you love vanishes from your life, you live each minute expecting them to walk back in.

I'd left my publishers Constable and Penguin, some time before, but I had not been happy with my new publishers. However, I was contracted to do another novel for them. I started it half-heartedly, writing about someone who learns, as long-buried secrets are revealed, that her belief that she is part of a united family is an illusion. But there was a grimmer piece of writing ahead of me.

As I was driven back and forth from Liverpool by Bill, he and I would listen to Radio 4. I have a passion for Radio 4, especially the news broadcasts. But in 1995, every news bulletin seemed to carry details of the trial of Rosemary West for the multiple murders she and her husband Fred had committed. Fred West had hanged himself in prison, so Rosemary stood in the dock alone. The details revealed at the trial were gruesome, and I decided not to listen to, or read, anything about the trial. When it came on air, I would close my ears and look out at the landscape, often at the bleakness of the moors where those other murderers, Brady and Hindley, had buried their victims.

Rosemary West was due to be sentenced in November, and a newspaper meanwhile made me an offer: if I would write a piece on the case, they would give money to charity. It was too good an offer to refuse. They sent me a pile of cuttings, and I settled down to read.

It was a sickening tale of evil, and I found it hard to write with objectivity. I was particularly upset by the part Rosemary West had played. Whoever says women are, by nature, kinder than men, is wrong. We are as ruthless, as strong, and, when we go bad, as evil as any man.

But some writing had a more joyous outcome. In my column for the *Express*, I wrote a piece about the cricket umpire Dickie Bird's appearance on *Desert Island Discs*. Some months later I got a letter from the great man himself. He had appreciated the piece, and would like to include it in his autobiography. In fact, he used it in the ending, much to my delight. Dickie Bird is a character, and there are too few of them in the world.

So, between work and charities, I filled my life. But still I didn't want to socialise. Occasionally I would go out to lunch or dinner with the doctor who had filled the step with roses, but these were duty affairs. He was kind, and I admired him, so I made the effort. The rest of the time, outside of work, I was a slob. One weekend Mark grew desperate. 'We'll go out,' he said. 'Somewhere in the car.' Outings with Jack had always meant going somewhere to eat or drink. Now I couldn't bear to go back to the places we had gone to together. Mark drove me away from Seaham, to a quiet pub. I knew he was making a big effort to get me out again, and I appreciated it. But he had a life of his own. He couldn't bolster me up forever.

They say that if a butterfly flutters its wings in Brazil it sets off a chain reaction that travels around the world. Although I didn't know it, somewhere some butterfly's wings were to have a profound effect on my life.

30
CHAPTER

AN UNEXPECTED SONG

THROUGHOUT ALL THE ups and downs of my life, my sister Joyce's daughter Gillian had been a constant, loving support to me. Her own life had not been altogether smooth. Her second husband had died suddenly, ending a very happy marriage, but now she was happily married to Jim. She rang me to say she would be travelling down from Scotland to Bolton the following weekend. 'Let's meet for lunch,' she said. We arranged to lunch at the Seaburn Hotel on Sunderland's sea-front; but then, on the Friday night, she rang me again to say she had just been told it was the weekend of the Sunderland Air Show. This enormous affair attracts a million visitors, and takes place above the sea-front. 'We won't get near the Seaburn,' Gillian said. 'Better meet somewhere else.'

We picked a pub in the nearby village of East Boldon, and on arriving were shown to a table tucked away in a corner. This wouldn't do for Gillian. A good table was vacant in a window, and she commandeered it. It was a pleasant meeting, and I was sorry when it was time for Gillian to go. So the next weekend, when Mark suggested taking me out for that drink, we went back to the pub, the Grey Horse. It was friendly, and just far enough away from Seaham to have no memories of Jack.

We were enjoying a glass of wine when a man approached. It was Mike Barden, whom I had known more than thirty years earlier. We found we had an acquaintance in common, Terri Moore, a friend of mine whom he had once taught with. 'I'd like to see Terri again,' he said, on hearing that she was battling with breast cancer, and I promised to arrange a meal.

A few weeks later, we all met in a local restaurant. While he and Terri reminisced about their teaching days, I talked to Mike's wife, Aileen. 'You must come to lunch with us,' she said. 'And I'll ask Bryan Thubron, too. You knew him years ago. He's a widower now, and often lunches with us.'

I had indeed known Bryan years ago. First, when he had been a rather handsome boy just back from his public school, and very lovable. I was still at school then, and quite smitten with him. But as he got into his twenties, I thought he changed, and became rather arrogant. I also remembered that he had almost killed me in his car, racing a friend along a straight road and having to brake sharply as the other driver zoomed in front. We were on our way to a party at his cousin's house, and I was wearing a boned sun-dress. The shock of the emergency stop threw me forward, and the straps of my sun-dress snapped clean off. I followed him into the party holding up my dress, and the first person we encountered was Bryan's mother. She took in the picture with a glance that would have frozen molten lava. You don't forget an encounter like that.

I'd last met him in a men's outfitters in Sunderland, when I was with Aunt Eve, choosing a birthday present for my father. He came up to chat, and I took pleasure in snubbing him. Outside in the street, my aunt chided me: 'Why did you treat that handsome boy like that?' 'Because he deserved it,' was my reply.

So now I thanked Aileen, but said I'd rather come to lunch without Bryan. I reckoned without her persistence. Over the next week we spoke on the phone, and eventually it just seemed simpler to let it happen. I was, after all, now well equipped to deal with him, however arrogant he might have become in the past forty years.

Philip gave me a lift over; Mark would come to pick me up as soon as I phoned him. I arrived at the house to be greeted by a beautiful pale-golden retriever. This was Bunty, Bryan's dog, and by all accounts the apple of his eye. If he had a dog he couldn't be all bad. The day began to improve.

Bryan, obviously nervous, was almost unchanged. He was still a huge man, six feet four and broad-shouldered, but his black hair was silver now, and he was not at all arrogant. As we sat at the lunch table, I found it surprisingly easy to talk to him. Afterwards, Mike told me he had felt as though Bryan and I were alone at the table and he and Aileen were merely spectators. I hope that wasn't true, for they were perfect hosts, and were obviously enjoying bringing old acquaintances together. It was so pleasant that 'lunch' stretched into the evening.

When it was time to go, Bryan wouldn't hear of my phoning for a lift. 'I'll drop you off on my way,' he said. It was January, and the ground outside was slippery. As we made our farewells and walked up the path, he reached for my hand to make sure I didn't fall. I felt suddenly young and uncertain, about to get into a car with a man who was having a strange effect on me.

In the car we talked easily, as though our last meeting had been days ago instead of forty years. Somehow the conversation got round to snowdrops. 'I could show you a field of snowdrops,' he said. 'It's called the Duchess's seat, and it's near my home.' In the old days, when he pulled up at my door we would have kissed goodbye. I was not running the risk of old habits resuming. As the car stopped, I was out of the door in a flash and in front of the bonnet, waving. Mark was crossing the hall as I came in. 'Good time?' he asked. 'Nice lunch,' was my answer, 'but I met someone from the past I don't much care for.' I went upstairs to work, anxious to get life back to normal as quickly as possible.

A couple of weeks later I arranged a reunion, so that Aileen could meet some of the people we'd known years ago, whom she had not yet met. I didn't ask Bryan Thubron. He lived miles away in Yorkshire, and, anyway, I didn't want to see him again. I had reckoned without Mike Barden. 'You'll have to ask Bryan, too,' he said. 'He always comes over for bridge on Wednesdays. He'll be here, anyway.' So I invited him. Arriving at the restaurant, I saw he was getting out of his car, obviously just arrived from Yorkshire. Mike was unrepentant. 'I got the days mixed up,' he said.

Again Bryan drove me home, and the invitation to see the snowdrops was repeated. I told him I had an aerobics lesson on the day he suggested. 'I know you're fit,' he said drily, 'because the other night you got out of my car like Nijinsky.'

He rang a few days later. 'They're out now,' he said. 'But you'll have to hurry.' We met in the car park of the Scotch Corner Hotel, and I followed his car through the snowy countryside. The snowdrops were indeed beautiful, stretching as far as the eye could see from the stone seat where the Dowager Duchess of Northumberland had liked to sit. Bryan's house was built in what had been her Italian garden. His garden walls were huge stone arches, lined on one side with poplars, on the other with fruit trees, apple, pear, plum and cherry.

We went there after a meal in a country pub and a visit to a garden centre. I bought him a hydrangea as a thank-you gift and we found a pot to put it in. Then he lit a log fire in a huge grate, and we sat down to listen to music, stopping every now and then to remember something from the old days. I told him I had once met his wife: she had put Mark into my arms after he was born, and I had noticed the name on her badge, Staff Nurse Thubron. 'I used to know someone called Thubron,' I had said, still sleepy from the effects of the anaesthetic. 'Yes,' she'd replied. 'I married him last year.' Now that baby was a man, and she was dead. Her picture sat on a side table, beautiful, and bearing a distinct resemblance to Catherine Zeta Jones. Wherever I went, it seemed, beautiful women preceded me.

I cried then, remembering old ghosts. Bryan didn't react, just added a log to the fire and put on another LP. I went on weeping until there was no more need for tears.

When it was time to go home, he drove ahead of me as far as the A1, and then pulled over to let me pass. As I drove on, a tape was playing on the car stereo – Julia McKenzie. Again and again, I played one track, 'An Unexpected Song': 'I don't know what's going on, can't work it out at all, your smile has really thrown me . . .' It was true. I wasn't handling this at all well.

There followed a spring and summer straight out of romantic fiction. We spent every moment we could together, usually at Bryan's house at Stanwick. As if it approved of our being together, the garden went into overdrive, bringing forth an abundance of fruit, which lay in piles on the grass. I, who had not a domesticated bone in my body, peeled and blanched and froze as if my life depended on it, determined not to waste this rich harvest.

There is a notion that love is the province of the young. As for sex among the older, forget it. But we were falling in love, or rather I was – and I suspected, from the first time we kissed, that Bryan felt it, too. The time together was glorious – walking Bunty through the pea-field, watching her antics as tiny grouse chicks blew like fluff balls across the path; seeing pheasants roost in the trees, and, when he switched on the garden lights, sit up and brace themselves for a new day, although it was really midnight; meals out together, or shared across his dining table.

But at night, as I drove home alone, and those words echoed and re-echoed – 'I don't know what's going on, can't work it out at all, why ever did you choose me?' – the doubts resurfaced. I couldn't face another relationship with its inbuilt risk of loss. I had done it twice, and twice was enough. I had a life, children, a thriving career. What need did I have of love? And even if I did, how could I explain to the boys? Only Mark knew I was seeing Bryan, and I couldn't be sure how even he was taking it. We now shared a home: what would my entering another relationship do to him?

In July, as the warmth of Bryan's circle closed around me, particularly his cousins, Toby and Mary Lee, he showed me a ring, an oblong emerald surrounded by diamonds. I had once joked about emeralds as we sat in a Yorkshire pub. A woman coming near had looked at my hand and said, 'I thought it was you. I recognised the ring.' It was a ring I had bought in the palmy days before Jack died: three diamonds. Bryan had pulled a face, and said, 'If I ever gave you a ring, it would have to be a recognisable one, then,' and I had laughed and said, 'Make it an emerald.' Now there was an emerald nestling in a box, and scaring the living daylights out of me. I put it away and tried to work out what to do. I confided in Mark and Gillian, but still I couldn't tell the boys. They had loved Jack deeply: how would they feel if it seemed I had replaced him?

It was John who sorted it. 'You married Dad after Mark's dad died, and we've all been happy. I don't see why you shouldn't do it again.'

That night there was a party at the local cricket club, and I was to join Bryan there, I slipped on the ring in the car park and walked inside. 'Look,' I said, holding out my hand. And I saw him beam. We were engaged. News spread round the room. Toby, a most lovable man, came up to me, shaking his head. 'Mike Barden told me this would happen, and I tried to tell him he was mad.'

If our friends were pleased, the press were only partly enthusiastic. There were suggestions that I was marrying too soon, hints that perhaps I had never loved at all. One journalist who had commiserated in print with my sadness about Jack rang me to say, 'You certainly had me fooled.' It didn't shake me. I knew what I had felt, and still felt, both for Alex and Jack. But there was room in my heart for new love, and now I had it.

If I had needed confirmation, the audience for *This Morning* provided it. There were offers to make my wedding cake, embroider cushions, take my wedding photos – best of all, the lady who had sent me the rose bush when Jack died now sent me bulbs: 'I expect you'll move house. These are for your new garden.' I entered into marriage plans on a tidal wave of love, not least from Alex's family in Shetland.

My column at the *Express* was now beginning to oppress me. I found myself listening to every news bulletin, desperate to keep my finger on the pulse. And bit by bit I was becoming bitchier. One day I was writing an article sympathising with Paula Yates, but I began it by saying: 'I like Paula Yates about as much as I like dog mess.' When I read that line in print, I was appalled at myself. Surely I wouldn't have said a thing like that? But I had. I wrote my last column for the *Express* a week or two before the wedding, and it was a relief not to have to worry any more whether Mary Kenny, whose column appeared the day before mine, would have scooped my lead.

There had been one huge bonus to that column, however. As well as writing about Dickie Bird, I had written a lyrical piece about Cliff

Morgan, the former rugby player and a wonderful broadcaster. Suddenly an invitation came from the Wombwell Cricket Lovers' Society to speak at a dinner they were giving for Cliff Morgan, in the presence of Dickie Bird. Bryan was ecstatic at the prospect of meeting Dickie, so I said yes. Bryan enjoyed it; I less so. Cliff Morgan spoke before me, an effortless stream of art and anecdote. My heart sank with every word. How do you follow a class act? I was glad when it was all over. When Bryan admired Cliff's tie, Cliff generously handed it over to him. If Bryan needed convincing he had made a good move in proposing to me, that did it.

We arranged to be married in the Minster in the centre of Sunderland, a church that meant a lot to me. As for the honeymoon, I had finishing touches to put to my almost completed novel which was partly set in Paris. Paris it would be, for a working honeymoon. As it turned out, I would not write another novel for years.

A few weeks before the ceremony, *Hello!* magazine announced that they wanted to film the wedding. We didn't want them to. A week later I was at a function, and I mentioned the *Hello!* offer while I was chatting. Suddenly, a man sidled up to me. 'We can't get doctors to come and work in Sunderland. Doctors' wives read *Hello!*. A nice wedding picture might make a difference.' That night Bryan and I discussed it, and decided to do it, dividing the fee among various charities. Allocating the money was great fun. Finding out I still had to pay tax on it, even though I had given it away, wasn't fun at all.

I wore a hyacinth-blue suit, and my granddaughters, Jennifer and Sarah, were bridesmaids, along with Gillian's daughter Caroline, and Toby Lee's granddaughter, Gemma. The first time I married, I had obsessed about the length and weight of the veil, and how my dress would look from the back. The second time I had been conscious only of the burden I was taking on, and the need not to let the children down. This time I couldn't have cared less about my appearance, although the wonderful Lee Din, *This Morning's* make-up artist, arranged flowers like a chignon at the nape of my neck to match the flowers I carried. I was conscious only of the words of the service, the promises to love and cherish, and the fact that the packed church was full of people who wished me well. And my daughters-in-law Janet and Susan presented me with two new grandchildren around the time of the wedding – perfect presents.

One picture has stayed in my mind: of Philip sprinting across the grass, camcorder in hand, to catch my arrival at the church. He was glad for me, after all. Mark gave the father-of-the-bride speech, looking back to that night when I had been so casual in the hall. He said: 'The moment she told me she didn't much care for him, I phoned the vicar.'

Mark drove us to the airport, and as we said goodbye he whispered in my ear, 'You have married one of the best human beings in the world.' As the plane took off, I marvelled at how small things can have huge effects. Somewhere, someone planned an air show on a certain day, and it changed the course of my life.

31
CHAPTER

DIANA

HELLO! PRINTED FOUR pages of photos. *OK!* magazine printed one, too, though how they got it I don't know. The caption said: 'Denise marries for the fourth time'. I've been looking for the fourth man ever since. Paris in the spring is always wonderful. We were there on 1 May, the day when the whole of Paris is given over to *les muguets des bois*, lily of the valley, for it is the Fête du Travail, Labour Day. Everywhere we went was fragrant with its scent, and more than once a man would press a bunch upon me and call me '*jolie madame*' . It's only a custom, but it's heady stuff at any age!

I had learned my lesson twenty years before, when I moved into the house Jack had shared with his first wife. I would not make that mistake again, nor would I ask Bryan to move into a home I had once shared. He was anxious to come back to his birthplace, so we looked at houses near to Sunderland. His preference was for something off the beaten track, but I knew my capacity for being nervous.

I set my heart on a Georgian house, built in 1790, in East

Boldon on the busy Newcastle/Sunderland road, but with a large, secluded garden behind. It was also close to pub, cricket ground and an auction rooms, which would allow me to indulge my passion for antique china. The trouble was that most of the garden was taken up by a huge heated swimming-pool. Bryan hated the proximity of the traffic, and the garden filled him with despair. We went on looking, but came back again and again to what I now saw as my house. There was something about it that made me feel welcome, and at last Bryan gave in, on condition that the swimming-pool went.

I was quite agreeable to this. I would be bringing three dogs with me, and Daisy and Lupi were both elderly. Daisy had a type of dementia, but seemed quite happy. However, we'd no sooner moved in than she wandered on to the cover of the pool, and had to be rescued. Eventually a JCB came over the wall, the pool went, and Bryan set to work. He created a paradise for me, a place of flowers and trees with a water feature meandering through it. My dogs and his Bunty soon learned to co-exist, although Titch did his best to be cock-of-the-walk. As Bunty was three times his size he didn't succeed.

Sadly, Lupi and Daisy both died the year after we moved in, and Bunty and Titch were left, sometimes confederates, sometimes rivals. In fact, Bunty bullied him a little, so when she died, sadly before her time, of cancer, I decided to leave him in sole occupancy, at least for a while. To my amazement he began to fret, searching the house for Bunty, and going off his food. Something had to be done. We went to a local rescue centre, seeing cage upon cage of delightful dogs just longing to be taken home. And then I spotted the only dog that wasn't showing any enthusiasm. Tiny, black-and-tan, she had turned her face to the wall of her cage, and no amount of coaxing would make her take notice.

I asked if we could get her out of the cage, but the attendant wasn't hopeful. 'A few people have looked at her, but her leg's put them off. I think it's been broken.' She did indeed have difficulty standing, but as we handled her she came to life a little, wagging her tail. Mark collected her later that day and we took her to the vet. 'It's not broken,' was her verdict, 'but it's been dislocated. Her knee-cap is out of place. I think she's been swung round on it like a football rattle. And she has mites – you'll have to bathe her with this. And feed her up.'

She was certainly thin. As we gave her the anti-mite bath, it was like handling a plastic bag full of pencils. But as we fed her, she improved markedly. Today, although her hind leg is out of kilter, she can run like the wind. We called her Tess, and she is the sweetest of dogs. Still scared, though – a sneeze will send her scurrying to the opposite end of the house.

So now we had two small dogs, but no golden retriever. Bryan had had a retriever bitch for as long as he could remember, so I applied to the Retriever Rescue Society. In the mean time, however, Max, a rescue dog, came into our lives. 'I don't want a dog,' Bryan said, when told it wasn't a bitch, but one look at Max changed his mind. Now we were back to three dogs, although we almost lost Max. He took off after a scent in the fields above the sea, Bryan running behind him, and went clean over a thirty-foot cliff. Bryan climbed down, expecting to retrieve a dead body. Instead, he found a startled dog wagging his tail, but with a damaged leg. Twenty-three weeks, six plaster casts, and a steel-rod implant later, Max was as good as new.

Titch, aged seventeen, died that summer in the garden after a long walk and his favourite meal of ox-tail gravy and biscuits. I miss him still. He had been a tempestuous little animal, but his end was peaceful. We agreed that two dogs was more than enough for us now, and got on with enjoying our new home.

I had put the finishing touches to my novel *Illusion* when I returned from Paris, and then the urge to write deserted me. I made half-hearted attempts, but the truth was that, at that moment, real life was much more interesting than fiction. Bryan was introducing me to the world of cricket, and it was to become a big part of my life. The boys had played, and Peter, in particular, had been very good, but cricket for Bryan was a passion. He has a huge library of books on the subject; cricket memorabilia are everywhere in the house, and he is always watching results of some match somewhere in the world

We had been married for three or four months when I woke one Sunday morning and I heard the announcer on the bedside radio say, 'Crowds are already moving towards Kensington Palace . . .' I raised myself on one elbow and, still half asleep, thought, 'The Queen Mother has died.' But the Queen Mother didn't live in Kensington Palace. It was Diana, Princess of Wales, who was dead in a Paris underpass. We were going to church in Yorkshire that morning, and I got ready in a daze. I had known and liked her so much. How could someone so alive, so young, possibly be dead? At a function a few months earlier she had caught sight of me as she was leaving, and crossed to speak to me, telling me that someone we both knew from one of her charities was on the other side of the room. We had talked for a few moments, and then she was swept away by the organisers, mouthing, 'See you again,' as she went. And now she was gone.

No one at the church could talk of anything else, and I felt angry as the vicar said that, although the Princess was no longer a member of the royal family, he intended to pray for her, anyway. She had been struck off the list of royals included in Church of England prayers pretty much as she had been deprived of HRH. I had thought it petty, then. Now, in church on the day of her death, it seemed obscene.

The summons to London was waiting when we returned home. The whole programme would be turned over to the tidal wave of emotion that was already engulfing the nation. I was upset, and I expected that feeling to be shared; but I was surprised at the depth of emotion displayed at all levels of society. To this day, I'm not sure what happened. That there was genuine grief I have no doubt, but somehow I feel people were weeping for themselves, too, glad that they had an excuse to cry.

London had filled up with foreign journalists, and I was told my usual hotel was full. I was to stay at the Savoy. The suite was magnificent, but I wandered from room to room like a lost soul. When morning came, I was out in the Savoy's horseshoe-shaped entrance waiting for my car, unable to settle to anything. That day we talked of our personal memories of Diana, turned frequently to ITN for news updates, and took phone calls from viewers. By the time the programme ended we were all exhausted, but it was obvious that the furore was not going to die down. A decision was made to repeat the format the next day.

I had brought only one set of performance clothes, so a car took me to the centre of London to buy something else. As we threaded our way from the studio, we could see the tide of people converging on Kensington Palace. They carried flowers, many of them were weeping, and they came from all classes, creeds and colours. I left the car, and started to talk to people. Many of them, particularly the men, were angry, and angry about one thing: 'Why did they take away her bloody HRH?' That came from city gents with briefcases and from red-eyed countrywomen, obviously drawn into London by the urge to mourn.

When eventually I went into a shop largely staffed by young black women, they were huddled in a group. I could have filled my arms with dresses and walked out, and I don't think they would have noticed. By the next day, animosity was growing. When I got back home, there were rumblings of displeasure even at the Queen. All I could think of were the two young princes, and the void that would be left in their lives.

I watched the funeral from start to finish, and then I watched the replays in the news bulletins. When Bryan asked me why, I couldn't give him an answer. It was as if I was reluctant to let her go. Now, ten years on, I still can't explain the hold she had, and still has, on our hearts. Nine months later, the BBC asked me to take part in a tribute programme on the first anniversary of her death. I tried to analyse my feelings then, but it was difficult. She remains an enigma.

No sooner was that programme made than I was crossing the Atlantic on my first trip to America. I have always had a soft spot for America: no one who was a child in the war could fail to feel affinity for it. When I was told my destination was Chicago, however, I was disappointed. All that I knew about Chicago was that it was windy and full of gangsters. The purpose of my trip was to make five short films about Jerry Springer, whose American talk-shows were world famous – or perhaps notorious would be a better word, since participants often had to be separated by heavies standing by for that very purpose.

Geraldine Woods, my close friend and the programme manager, was coming with me, which added to the fun. Geraldine is the best of company at any time. On a jaunt like this she was priceless. We flew via Dublin on an Aer Lingus flight, lolling back in upgraded luxury. The air-hostesses plied us with everything, including miniature liqueurs. They came thick and fast, too many to down at one sitting. 'Can't waste them,' Geraldine said, so I stashed them in my bra and exited the plane clinking.

Chicago, situated on the south-western tip of Lake Michigan, was a revelation, a wonderful mix of old and new. Most of the old city was destroyed by fire in 1871. The few original buildings that remain are almost objects of reverence, and the new is designed to blend in with them. I rather liked that mix – and the skyscrapers were amazing. You could take a carriage-ride along busy streets, the huge gas-guzzlers giving way to the horses, or walk in complete safety along gracious boulevards, or skirt the edge of Lake Michigan. To cap it all, there was not a breath of wind around.

I ate Bill Clinton's favourite meal – crab fritters – in his favourite restaurant, and explored the magnificent dockyard. But best of all was meeting Jerry Springer. He is a most interesting man. Born in England to parents who had fled the Holocaust, he is at once immensely friendly and intensely private. I don't feel I really got to know him, but what I did meet with I liked.

The shows were something else. There were rows of baying people chanting for blood. When I 'vox popped' one of the audiences who had just seen a show that was so raunchy it couldn't be screened, people were loud in their disappointment. 'Ah came all the way from Ohio to see a fight,' one woman said, 'and Ah ain't seen nothing.' As my hair was still standing on end from what we had just witnessed, I couldn't find a single word in reply.

The show in question was 'Sex with Animals', more often known as 'I Married My Horse'. People may have seen an excerpt from it – the man who did 'marry' his horse – but no audience has ever seen the show in its entirety. As I settled into my seat, the woman next to me told me she was from an animal-welfare society. 'When this one is over, I'm going to have them all arrested,' she told me. One by one, people came on accompanied by their animals. The man with the horse, women and men with dogs – I kept waiting for my mother to send a thunderbolt from heaven and strike me dead, and the impulse to duck out of camera range was almost overwhelming. Furthermore, I was under strict instructions to jump to my feet and chant 'Jerree, Jerree!' with the others, just in case the camera caught me sitting po-faced in my seat.

What was noticeable was that animals and owners got on remarkably well; in fact, the animals had to be restrained from showing affection. At the end of the show, I turned to the animal-welfare lady. 'Well?' I asked. She pulled a doubtful face. 'I don't know. The animals seemed very happy.'

Some of the owners were obvious disguised, especially one woman whose voice had also been electronically altered. 'You may have disguised *her*,' I challenged the producer, 'but I'd know that dog again anywhere.' The producer smiled, and pushed open a door. There was the black Labrador being hosed down to its true golden colour.

I saw two further shows. One featured transvestites, and introduced me to Stephanie; the other involved a young woman who held the record for sex with the greatest number of men in the shortest possible time. Strong stuff. But I knew that Springer had a more serious side to him. Shows in which he had tackled the Ku Klux Klan or talked to prisoners on chain-gangs were legendary. When the time came to interview him in depth, I sensed he was wary. However friendly we had been the previous week, he was now on his guard. But he answered questions without hesitation.

I asked him why he didn't concentrate on the more serious subjects, instead using people who seemed to have few, if any inhibitions. His answer made a kind of sense. He wanted to give voice to people who would otherwise never be heard. 'You and I get listened to,' he said. 'No one will hear them unless I give them a platform.' Whether or not that platform was in their best interests is another matter. When I asked whether or not some of the stories were invented by the show, he simply pointed me in the direction of the office taking calls from all over America. Listening to the people ringing in, I could see he had no need to invent a thing. Whether or not these people had invented or exaggerated their stories so as to get their fifteen minutes of fame, I couldn't say.

I was also shown round the wardrobe – clothes not for the participants, but for the audience. 'We like them to look their best,' the wardrobe lady said. That's attention to detail!

At the end of the week I still had my doubts about the shows but I knew I liked Jerry very much indeed. He is a complex individual and I've very much enjoyed his occasional stints as a presenter on *This Morning*. That week was rounded off by a visit to a nightclub where Jerry, who has an excellent voice, sang and played to a rapturous audience. The next day, my last, I interviewed the priest who heads the 'Stop Jerry Springer' movement. He was very fair, I thought, but forthright in his condemnation. I didn't dare to mention 'Sex with Animals' – he was worried enough without that. But he didn't want the shows banned. He wanted people to exercise judgement and turn away from them of their own accord. I doubt that they ever will.

We flew home tired but happy, still laughing, and conscious of some good stuff in the can. For me it was especially memorable. I had cherished a dream of America my whole life, and I had not been disappointed.

32
CHAPTER

ALL HUMAN LIFE

OVER THE 19 years of *This Morning*'s existence, I have watched it grow into an institution. Children born in its first year are now at work or university. Students who skipped lectures to sit at the feet of Richard and Judy are now almost middle-aged. We have seen our viewers through sickness and health, first love, marriage, and divorce; have thrilled them in school holidays, entertained them in retirement. But it is at times of crisis that *This Morning* comes into its own.

The morning after any national drama – the Gulf War and the war in Iraq, the death of Diana, Dunblane, and, most recently, the London bombs – we are there, fielding phone calls, calming fears, providing information, and liaising with government and voluntary organisations to provide a service. I respond to this situation with what Geraldine Woods calls my Blitz mentality – and perhaps it *was* born in the air-raid shelter. Wherever it came from, it sends adrenalin coursing through me.

In times of war, feeling runs high. Try to calm the situation, and you will be accused of playing it down; but the mother who has rung in to ask if it's safe to send her child to school does not want to hear you say the situation is dire. This is when *This Morning's* phone-room comes into its own. Its telephonists are chosen for their tact and intelligence, and also for their patience. No one is turned away without helplines being given, or their dilemma being drawn to the attention of someone who can help.

The death of Princess Diana was difficult, extending as it did over several days, but the event that most took its toll on me was Dunblane. That small Scottish town was racked with grief and horror when a killer who had lived in their midst shot dead 16 small children and a teacher in three minutes of carnage in a primary school. A whole class was wiped out, bringing back, for me, memories of Aberfan. The first day we calmed the fears of mothers, all of them saying that they had had faith in the security of their children's school; now they could never feel safe again. And so many of the callers said that the deaths of innocent children had destroyed their faith in God that, on the second day, a Bishop and I attempted to deal with their crisis of faith.

My own faith has never been a cut-and-dried affair, but I did believe in the power of good over evil. For a little while, seeing the picture of children wiped out by a madman's whim, it seemed evil had triumphed. I had now learned not to cry on camera, but by the time I was free to go home I felt drained.

By chance I was due to go to an infants' school in Northumberland to plant a tree as part of a nature-conservancy programme. I was led into the school through the cloakroom, past the pegs low down so that tiny hands could reach, each with its nameplate – Chloe, Richard, Sam, Jennifer. In the hall the children awaited me, the very same age-group that had been eliminated in Dunblane sitting cross-legged in front. I looked at them, and burst into tears.

The aim of *This Morning* is to entertain and inform, but human-interest stories are one of its mainstays. Latterly the audience came to love Charlie, the young man who, with Dr Chris's help, shed 30 of his 44 stone, and intends to run the New York marathon. I spent six months filming with Graham, the homeless man whose progress we charted as he moved from cardboard box to hostel and back on to the streets again. Not every story has a happy ending, but I grew fond of Donna Anthony, the young woman cleared of murdering her two babies, though not before she had served six years in prison. We filmed her struggle to adjust to life outside, and to try to recover the life taken from her by a trial that was no more than a witch-hunt. Indeed, we followed the stories of several of the mothers wrongly convicted of murder – Angela Cannings, Sally Clark, Trupti Patel, all of them failed by a system that should have protected them.

Interviewing people in the public eye is not easy. In all probability, they will have been spooked by media attention, will have read all the unkind things written about them, and be on their guard. If the 'game' has lasted for a while, they will probably have become blasé, and will give you what they think you want rather than the truth.

An exception to this rule was Louise Woodward, the young British nanny convicted in America of murdering her charge. She had been in the spotlight, much of it unfavourable, for several years, but I found her to be straightforward, even stubborn. I had long thought her an innocent victim of injustice. Either the baby's injuries were inflicted elsewhere, as she contended or, over-burdened by housework as well as child-care, she had slipped up. Neither of those probable explanations constituted murder to me.

The interview went well. She set out her case squarely, and gave a good account of herself right up to the end. She was endlessly sad about the death of their baby, but reluctant to show compassion for its parents, two people she felt had lied about her, and gone out of their way to get her jailed. At the end of the interview, her innocence was confirmed, in my view, and, I hope, in that of the watching audience.

James Hewitt was an altogether different character, but I liked him. Perfect manners and the air of being wounded by life are a sure way to my heart. I asked him if he had really loved Diana. He thought for a moment. 'Yes,' he said, 'I did.' But his most genuine emotion came when he talked of his army career. 'I've brought disrepute on my regiment,' he said. 'That's what I regret most of all.'

On occasion, my work has taken me to other countries. Nine months after 9/11, I went to New York to make a film about what happened on that day, and to see how the £600,000 donated by *This Morning*'s viewers had been spent. Even after that lapse of time, it was gut-wrenching to see the devastation. What I had not seen on news footage was that all the great buildings around about were shrouded in a fine metal mesh, presumably to stop further crumbling. On the day we arrived, human remains had been found on the roof of a nearby skyscraper. This was a common occurrence, but each time there was DNA testing to establish identification, and then a funeral.

I interviewed relatives of the dead, people who had put their small tributes on the railings of the nearby church: 'We love you, daddy'; 'We all miss you'. Weather-bedraggled, they hung there, testimony to the fact that not even a cataclysm puts an end to love. One man I interviewed was glad about one thing: his wife had worked on the floor the aeroplane hit. 'I knew it would have been quick,' he said. 'That meant a lot'. She had gone to work early that day because the boss was returning from holiday and she wanted to be prepared. If she had been less conscientious, she would still be alive; but he was not bitter. Indeed, I found no bitterness, no howls for revenge.

Bernie Kerik, Chief of Police at the time, now working for Rudi Giuliani, in whose offices I interviewed him, told me that he arrived at the scene just in time to witness people leaping from the upper floors to escape the flames. 'I see it every time I close my eyes,' he said. The cameraman told me that there had been much speculation about whether or not workers would be willing to return to the huge skyscrapers when the area was at last declared free from danger. He had been sent to cover the entrance to the subway that morning. 'And then out they rolled,' he said, 'looking apprehensive but determined to make a start.'

This Morning's money went to help with the education of the children orphaned by the tragedy. In all, 63 children were born after 9/11 to the wives of men, firemen and policemen mostly, who had died as the towers collapsed. The lovely nun who explained all this to me – smart as a carrot nine times scraped in ordinary clothes, earrings in place – told me that the Bishop had instructed her to pray for money. 'Pray!' she said. 'I told him he was asking the impossible, and then out of the blue came your money!' Yet again a miracle, but born out of the generosity of *This Morning* viewers.

On the whole I welcome foreign travel, but the night before I went to Uganda I had real doubts. World Vision had asked me to go there to look at the work they were doing with AIDS. I had just sponsored a child in that country, Mercy Adembabazi, so the trip would enable me to meet her and her family. I was enthusiastic – until I was asked to sign a paper saying I wouldn't expect the charity to ransom me if I were kidnapped. All of a sudden pictures of blindfold hostages sitting slumped against a wall sprang into my mind. But I was too far in to pull out, so I boarded the plane, warnings of never to go out after dark ringing in my ears.

Uganda was a revelation. We were to make two short films to be shown on or near World AIDS Day, and the hope was that they would persuade people to come forward and agree to sponsor a child. Sponsorship costs you about the same as buying a morning paper each day, and it can change a child's life. Not only that, sponsorship can permeate a community, so that the whole place looks up. When I met Mercy, I found that World Vision had trained her father as a carpenter. Now he could earn a living for his family.

Everywhere I looked, I saw evidence of what had been done. A headmaster showed me the tree under which he had started a school thirteen years earlier. Now he had a proper school building with desks and teachers' quarters, all provided by sponsorship money. In schools, children were being educated about AIDS. That education was sorely needed. I talked to one grandmother bringing up seventeen grandchildren. She had outlived the average life-expectancy in Uganda – forty-four years – because of the burning need to rear her grandchildren. All her children had died of AIDS. So had her husband and several of her grandchildren. Some of the others were probably infected, but she didn't want them tested. If they were positive, she couldn't afford the drugs needed to treat them, so she couldn't see the point. She would rather live in hope, until it became obvious that hope was misplaced.

I walked with her among the seventeen family graves in her garden, dispensing with the interpreter because I found I could converse with other women there by signs and facial expressions. I could nurse their grandchildren, and sign details of my own, and even laugh with them about all that we had in common.

One day we went to a World Vision clinic. One of the things that amazed me was the way in which different groups co-existed happily while retaining their sense of identity. When they danced for me, and they did this wherever we went, this was particularly apparent. In some places it was the vigorous jumping jigga-jigga; in other places a graceful almost Hawaiian dance. This was most apparent down by the Rwandan border, where many refugees had been absorbed. You could instantly pick out the ethnic groups, but they lived and mingled happily. In the particular area served by the clinic, the women wore elaborate headdresses and dresses bunched at the hip. They walked, or rather swayed along, gracefully, and were particularly beautiful. Today, though, they sat in the sun, children playing at their feet, each clutching a white slip. One by one they went in to see the doctor. Some of them came out beaming. Others came out with death upon their faces. They had been told they were HIV positive.

I became very friendly with Sam, the driver. One day I remarked on how many lorries we saw crammed with men, each clutching a huge plastic water-carrier. 'Do they really have to transport water like that?' I asked. He roared with laughter and explained that the 'water' was home-brewed beer, and strong stuff. Later, in some of the villages, I saw men congregating at night to drink copiously, but there was no violence, no riotous behaviour. They handled their drink better than lager louts in the cities of Britain.

Once we left Kampala we stayed in small 'hotels' that were really hostels. There was only a fridge full of bottled beer, which I couldn't drink. As time went on, I became desperate for a glass of wine, especially as what we were seeing during the day was often depressing, and I was homesick. One night I asked Sam if he knew where I could get a drink. He told me of the Springfield Hotel, a place he could easily drive me to. Hotel had a good ring to it, and Springfield had the sound of home. I hurried in to change, and climbed back in the Land-Cruiser. By this time, I'd lost my fear of the dark, even though baboons had approached the car at dusk one day when we were stuck on a road. We sped through the night and eventually the lights of the Springfield Hotel sprang up. I offered to buy Sam a drink, but he declined. He would wait for me outside.

I walked into a large room filled with tables at which sat men, and only men. My appearance caused consternation. My instinct said get out, but the demon drink prevailed. I bade them a courteous good evening, and advanced on the only empty table – empty except for a bottle of brown sauce. I sat for a while, and then a woman appeared through a beaded curtain. 'Wine?' I enquired. Not a flicker of comprehension. 'Wine,' I repeated desperately, miming a wine-glass with my hands. Nothing. I changed tack. 'Gin?' Still nothing. 'Gin! Gin!' Surely they had gin! All of a sudden, she beamed. 'Gilbey's!' At the back of my mind a bell rang. 'Yes!' I whooped. She vanished and returned with a glass and an unopened bottle of Gilbey's gin. No ice, no lemon, no mixer. I poured myself three fingers of neat gin, raised my glass to the by now rapt male audience, and downed it in one gulp. Then I rose to my feet, put the gin in my handbag and a 10-dollar bill on the table, and exited in as regal a manner as I could manage.

I brought many memories back from that trip – the maribou storks wheeling above Kampala like dinosaurs in the sky; the faces of baboons as they approached the car, curious and somehow friendly; the snow-white dove dashed to pieces on our windscreen because it had no fear of vehicles; the friendliness of the people; the disabled woman scampering crab-like among the traffic in Kampala, begging food for her child; the determination of tiny children who walked several miles to and from school each day. Education is the answer to Uganda's problems, and probably to those of all Africa too.

The children I met there were amazing – friendly, curious and apparently utterly happy, although, to Western eyes, they had little or nothing. In one village I was surrounded by boys and girls, some wearing wonderful headdresses made from pampas grass. They all wanted to touch my head and were all uttering what I could tell was the same phrase. 'What are they saying?' I asked the interpreter. She smiled. 'They're saying "Yellow hair."'.

But my most abiding, and happiest, memory is of two brothers, Fred and Emmanuel. Their parents had died of AIDS when Fred was seven and Emmanuel three. Now they were eleven and seven. In the intervening years, Fred had brought up his brother, finding him food each day and keeping him from harm. We found them in a kind of hut in the bush, with only two rough piles of blanket: Fred would not sleep with Emmanuel, who occasionally still wet the bed. At night they lit a fire of twigs in a corner, and waited for dawn. That day, their only meal had been white ants grubbed from the ground. When I asked why World Vision hadn't done more for them, I was told that there were 123 child-led families in that area alone. AIDS has wiped out the sexually active middle generation, and they were also the workers. Without breadwinners or quick-witted grandmothers, orphans, even if they escape infection, are almost doomed.

Emmanuel was friendly and forthcoming. Fred never smiled. Responsibility was written large on his face. Emmanuel was shivering, and I asked the interpreter what was wrong with him. 'He's probably hungry,' she said. There was a basket of sorts on the floor containing one tomato. 'Give him that,' I suggested. She spoke to Fred, and then turned to me. 'That's for tomorrow,' was the answer. I thought of my boys, always hungry, raiding the fridge or the biscuit tin. To camera I could only manage three words: 'It isn't fair.'

When the film was shown, the *This Morning* audience rose as one. Offers to sponsor poured in. I had gone to Uganda with the hope of securing twenty sponsorships. We got 569. Bryan and I had decided to sponsor Fred and Emmanuel, which meant they would be fed and clothed and go to school. When I went to Pure Bliss, the beauty salon that occasionally repairs my ravaged face, the owner, Lisa, herself a young mother, had seen the film. 'I want to help those boys,' she said. I had just made enquiries about building Fred and Emmanuel a house. 'If you've got $3000, you could build them a house,' I said jokingly. Within weeks she had raised the money. Today the two brothers live in a brick-built house in World Vision's American sector, and their future is assured. The latest letter, written on their behalf, enclosed a picture of them with the house: 'kitchen, latrine, clothing, beds, shoes, saucepans 3, kettle, jerry-can and stocks. I am happy to tell you that our life has really changed. . .'

The feedback after items such as Africa and Ground Zero is heart-warming, but viewers respond every day to what they see. I think that at *This Morning* we have the most generous audience in the world. However, live television can be scary. You have to watch your words, for that same kind audience can rap your knuckles when they you deserve it.

I had faced up to the possibility of kidnap in Africa, but you don't have to go out of the British Isles to meet trouble. Filming in Northern Ireland at the height of the Troubles could be alarming. I was having breakfast in a hotel dining-room at six a.m. when nearby bushes suddenly became young soldiers in camouflage gear. They filtered on to the road and took up their places, backs to the wall, strain showing in their faces. They looked about fourteen. 'This is when the IRA move their arms,' the waitress said casually. After that I took the many road-blocks that detained us more seriously.

In 1991, when riots broke out in some areas of Newcastle, I was sent to find out what was going on. It was a weird experience to have rocks thrown at me as I spoke to camera only a few miles from my home, but I kept on talking. I belonged there; they weren't going to drive me out. Well, I thought I was speaking to camera, except that the camera team had scarpered and locked themselves in their van. 'To protect the equipment,' they told me when I hammered on the window.

And sometimes you come back from an expedition with more than you bargained for. The Christmas before last I went filming at a dog refuge. 'No more dogs!' was Bryan's stern warning, so when I saw a tiny nose, skinned by constant peering under the door in the hope of rescue, I stayed resolute. Well, partially resolute, in that I didn't sleep that night.

The next day we got her, a Shetland sheepdog-cross who was four or five months old. We called her Primmie, short for Primrose. Prim she wasn't. In the first few months she saw off two carpets. As I wrote at the time, 'She thinks the whole world is her toilet, but she likes indoors best.' She ate the front of a sofa, a full tub of margarine, and the rubber lining of a crucial part of Bryan's garden stream, so that all the water ran away. All this without suffering any after-effects whatsoever. To date she has cost us several thousand pounds, every penny worth it. At five months old, she forswore her life of crime, and became the dearest of dogs. No story of my life would be complete without her. But I won't film at a dog sanctuary again!

This Morning has given me the opportunity to see and do things

I could never have imagined when my world was the area where I was born. If anything, what I have seen has enhanced my love of my roots, but it has also made me see that people are the same all over. My mother taught me to see the world as a place full of friendly people. 'Look at the eyes' was good advice.

Its experts have helped shape lives. Indeed, Dr Chris Steele has actually saved lives by giving people access to information. We have dealt with breast and testicular cancer, performed a vasectomy live on air, and shown procedures that have ultimately led to diseases being caught in time for recovery. A succession of health-and-fitness experts have transformed people's appearances; and other experts have tried to help them with their emotional and practical needs.

We have made people laugh and cry, while at the same time entertaining and informing them. I am proud to have been part of that. In its first year, we decided that on our Christmas programme I should send a message to anyone who could not look forward to a joyful Yuletide. It has become a tradition, and each winter I will hear from people hanging on to get that recognition that life cannot always be easy. Being *This Morning*, I deliver that message from a throne, and my leg is pulled about its being the 'Queen's speech'; but its sentiments are sincere, and the whole team are behind them.

This Morning has always been a crusading programme. I was able to give evidence to the National Commission on the sexual abuse of children and see my advice – that children should be able to tell without the roof falling in on the family – written into its report. As I write this, our campaign to shed light on Britain's family courts appears to be bearing fruit. I had always received the odd letter from parents who had had their children taken from them by Social Services, but in the past few years the letters have become a flood. I am not so naive as to take every letter I receive at face value, but some of them had a desperate ring of truth about them.

All of the writers had one thing in common: they had been gagged by an injunction. By talking to me, they were risking prosecution. This offended my idea of justice, especially when I learned that they had, until recently, not been allowed even to contact their MPs. They still cannot, today, disclose all details of their case to the man or woman elected to represent them in the House of Commons.

The case that brought things to a head concerned two people – I'll call them Mike and Mary – happily married and devoted to their three children, all under the age of five. The middle child suffered from lactose intolerance, and was difficult to feed, and when his anxious parents took him to hospital he was found to have metaphyseal fractures in one leg. This was not remarkable, since his mother's family carries the brittle-bone gene. In spite of this, the family was accused of abuse. Health visitors, policemen, the eldest child's teacher, all testified to their worth as parents. But still all three children were the subject of hostile adoption, and are now with separate families. The mother has had a fourth child, and as I write is waiting to see if this child too will be taken from her.

When she wrote to me, I looked at the evidence and decided they had a case. In desperation, I contacted George Hawkes, the crusading solicitor who worked without pay for seven years to secure Donna Anthony's release from prison. He is, in my opinion, akin to a saint. He took on Mike and Mary's case, and is campaigning for them to be allowed to keep the baby with them. Their other children they will never see again – and this in a land that professes to be humane. Fern and Philip, both devoted parents, have thrown themselves into the fight with gusto. Please God we will win. Already a Government Minister, Harriet Harman, has promised to reform the family courts, and came on to *This Morning* to discuss it. I trust her to keep her word.

But *This Morning* could not function without the team, each one irreplaceable from the editor to the floor manager to the green-room staff who know just when you need a cup of tea. The make-up room is not only the place where you are made presentable: Jane and Michelle and Shari will lull you into the belief that you, and only you, can go out there and do the job. As for wardrobe – before the last Commonwealth Games I was asked to carry, on its last lap in my area, the torch that went around Britain and was finally presented to the Queen. But I had to wear the regulation sweatshirt and shorts. 'Shorts!' I wailed to David in wardrobe. 'I'll frighten the horses.' Almost within the hour he had dropped the waist so that the shorts would cover my knees. They were still shorts, but now decent enough for me to stride up to the rostrum without blushing. *This Morning* is a family, and like a family it never lets you down.

33
CHAPTER

FATE

A S I LOOK back at my life, there is no denying that *This Morning* has been a huge part of it. I went there for one year, and have stayed for nineteen. Today the programme excites me as much as, or more than, it did in the early days. It has racked up some remarkable achievements, but for me the important one is the differences it has made to the lives of the ordinary men and women who make up its audience. And I know it has made a difference because thousands of people have written to tell me so.

And, oh, it has been fun! What other programme could have given me both the opportunity to clown occasionally and also to make a difference? It survived the departure of Judy Finnigan and Richard Madeley, and now has equally charismatic presenters in Fern Britton and Phillip Schofield. They are heaven to work with – respectful of their fellow presenters, concerned for the viewers, and, above all, hugely good-humoured. They have given me some of my happiest times on the show.

I have had other television ventures. I did a series with Dave Gorman, his *Astrological Experience*, which was such a joy to record that I hoped there would be no film in the camera and we would have to start again. Jon Culshaw's impression of me, in *Dead Ringers*, as an ardent if vocal fan of Sunderland AFC, has won me enormous street cred. For his *Alter Ego*, a plaster cast was taken of my face, from which a rubber mask was made so that Jon and I could sit, identically dressed and like peas in a pod, to interview his George Bush and Dr Who. I enjoyed it hugely but couldn't bear to turn and look at the other version of myself. In Paul O'Grady's *Shanghai Lil*, I played a drunken prostitute – a wonderful opportunity to behave badly!

At present I write a comment column for *The Journal* which is syndicated in some of Trinity Mirror's regional papers. I am free to bellyache there as much as I like. A man told me recently that his blood pressure had gone down since I started the column. 'When I see something outrageous,' he said, 'I think: "No need to get angry. Denise will get angry about it on Tuesday."' I no longer have the bitches of Fleet Street breathing down my neck, but my anger and my urge to right things remain the same. My agony column in *Chat* magazine deals with everything from puberty, through marriage and divorce, to looking for a good nursing home. And now there are a myriad helpful organisations to which I can refer people – a big change from those far off Metro days when there were only Marriage Guidance and the CAB to cover the whole spectrum of the human condition. In all this I am assisted by my daughter-in-law, Janet, and by Mark, who, when he is not playing drums, is no mean computer expert. He it is who retrieves the lost *magnum opus* when I have pressed the wrong button.

Five years ago, I launched 'Dear Denise', a website for anyone with a problem. It is non-profit-making, and I answer every message posted on it, helped by Liz Dallas Ross, whose encyclopaedic knowledge of the internet is stunning. The people who turn to 'Dear Denise' come when they are in trouble and then, when their problem is resolved, stay to help others. It has become a club in the best sense of that word, open even on Christmas Day. Last Christmas one message said simply, 'Thank God for this site.'

When I ceased to write novels, I found a new outlet for my imagination. Mark had two friends, brothers called Peter and Dean Robertson. We were not related, but I liked both the boys very much. They wrote songs that Mark would play for me, praising them to the skies. The songs were good, but record deals were not forthcoming. One day I said idly, 'They should write a musical.' A few weeks later they sat in my living-room and we mapped out *Someone Should Have Told Me*, later to be called *Fine, Fine, Fine*. It is the most intoxicating experience to sit in a darkened theatre and hear an audience laugh and cry, and know that you caused those emotions. So far it has been produced twice, and we are hard at work on another.

Perhaps that might have satisfied my desire to write, but in 2000 I was asked to write a book on bringing up children. I had been uneasy about the number of letters I was receiving from parents terrified of the responsibility of parenthood. What had seemed so natural and enjoyable for me had become a minefield for them – terrified to photograph their children in the bath for fear of false accusation, anxious about E numbers in food, scared of buzz words like 'bonding'. So *Relax, It's Only a Baby* was born, and I hope continues to give comfort. Most of us, I believe, have a parental instinct. Trust it, keep yourself informed, and you won't go far wrong.

In 2004, I wrote the biography of Sir Tom Cowie, the founder of the mighty company Arriva and the greatest philanthropist the city of Sunderland has known. Detailing his rise to great heights was a pleasure, particularly as the proceeds of the book went to benefit the University of Sunderland, the establishment that honoured me with an honorary doctorate in 1997, and on whose Development Trust I now serve. And in 2005 I returned to novel-writing with *The Bad Sister*, my first novel for nine years.

So life is full – too full, according to my long-suffering husband whose unfailing support has seen me through all kinds of trials. But there is always time to revisit the past. Each time I come home to the north-east, often in the early hours of the morning, I thrill to the sight of the Cleveland Hills, the place where we were so happy, where Mark remembers frying sausages, and I first saw the blaze of limestone that became The Scar in the best of my novels. I did transport it seventy miles north, but that is a novelist's privilege. And I still keep my contact with Shetland, where whole generations of Alex's kin are.

But the past can be a dangerous place, just as Housman wrote. His 'air that kills' is nostalgia, at once exquisite and terrifying. And 'the land of lost content . . . those happy highways where I went and cannot come again' should be glimpsed only occasionally.

I remain as fascinated by the human condition as I was at the beginning of my career. The greatest enigma of all, as far as I am concerned, is why the pendulum must always swing from 0 to 100, and never stop at the midway point where most of us would prefer it to be. And I have come to believe that fate plays a part in our lives. We can change some things by our efforts. Other things we must accept.

As I grow older, I understand my mother so much better than I ever did while she was alive. She was made by her past, as I have been made by mine. But where life made her fearful, it has made me determined. If you believe in something enough, it comes within your grasp. Now the child who was seldom photographed is sometimes photographed fifty times in a day. The girl who had no clothes grows weary of having to choose yet another outfit for work. Cockroaches in hotels have been replaced by chandeliers – but these things are not important.

I raised five children, and now I have dozens: sons, grand-children, great-grandchildren, nieces and nephews to treasure, and god-children, too, as well as the children of the Bubble, thriving as Professor Cant and his team grow ever more skilful. And if I never achieved that dream of a daughter, I have had Gillian and five daughters-in-law, all precious.

I live in the place that I love above all others, my native north-east, in a garden Bryan has created for me which is a constant source of delight. I have never lived more than five miles from the house where I was born, and I count myself lucky in that. Marriage took me out of the County of Durham, but the Lord Lieutenant, Sir Paul Nicholson, made me a Deputy Lieutenant, so the link remains. Each day I hear the sound of seabirds wheeling above me: it has become part of the fabric of my life. The face of the north-east may have changed as old industries vanished, but its people have not.

When the pits closed in the late 1990s, a young miner told me, 'I'll never work again. Neither will my child.' He was wrong. Renewal comes, for people and for places, whether or not we expect or even want it. If I had known at twenty-one the shape my life would take, I would have said I couldn't face it; but when a woman, a stranger, stopped me in the street a year or two ago and said to me, 'You've had a tragic life,' I looked at her, amazed. My life has not always been easy, but I wouldn't really have changed it. For I have loved, I do love, I am loved. And all heaven is in those words.

EPILOGUE

WHEN I BEGAN to write this book, there was not a cloud in my sky. As the chapters mounted, things got better. I was awarded the Freedom of the City of Sunderland, and then the MBE in the Queen's Birthday Honours. But as I neared the last chapter, I learned that John was gravely ill. The boy who was wont to copy Evil Knievel has grown into a fine man, and is dealing bravely with his illness. We stand with him, united as a family. It is one more battle, and I am a veteran.

Also from Denise Robertson:

The Beloved People Trilogy
The Beloved People
Strength for the Morning
Towards Jerusalem

This much-acclaimed trilogy sweeps from Durham to London and back again, capturing more than five decades of British history through the twentieth century. From the tough years of the Depression, through the war years, to the growing confidence of Britain in the prospering Fifties and Sixties, the residents of the Durham mining village of Belgate are caught up in it all, rich and poor alike – meaning life for them will never be the same again.

'An intelligent, evocative saga with a fine eye for authenticity. This is big-hearted stuff in the best style'
Sunday Telegraph

The Bad Sister

Set at the turn of the millennium and spanning the Highlands of Scotland and the bustle of London and Liverpool city life, this exciting novel captures the tensions of sibling rivalry, unfulfilled love, passion and murder in a drama of human experience and relationships.

'A gripping read'
The Independent

Wait for the Day

As World War II comes to an end, four young service women return to their former lives. Firm friends throughout the war, they are filled with an overwhelming sense of hope and the happiness peace can't fail to bring. They each have dreams, but what will the future hold for these women who survived and were irrevocably changed by war?

'Another scorcher from one of this country's best storytellers'
The Daily Mail

Available from all good bookshops, price £6.99.

The books may also be purchased direct from the publisher, with FREE postage and packing, on credit card hotline number
01933 443862.
Please allow up to 28 days for delivery.